The
Vegetarian
Family
Cookbook

ALSO BY NAVA ATLAS

Vegetarian Express

Vegetarian Celebrations

Vegetarian Soups for All Seasons

Great American Vegetarian

Pasta East to West

Vegetariana

The Vegetarian 5-Ingredient Gourmet

WRITTEN AND ILLUSTRATED BY

Nava Atlas

The Vegetarian Family Cookbook

BROADWAY BOOKS   NEW YORK

BROADWAY

PRINTED IN THE UNITED STATES OF AMERICA

BROADWAY BOOKS and its logo, a letter B bisected on the diagonal, are trademarks of Random House, Inc.

Visit our website at www.broadwaybooks.com

Book design by Pei Loi Koay
Illustrated by Nava Atlas

Library of Congress Cataloging-in-Publication Data
Atlas, Nava.
  The vegetarian family cookbook / written and illustrated by Nava Atlas.
    p. cm.
  Includes index.
  1. Vegetarian cookery.   I. Title.

TX837.A854 2004
641.5'636—dc21

2003051890

ISBN 0-7679-1396-5

10 9 8 7 6 5 4 3 2 1

For my sons,

Adam and Evan

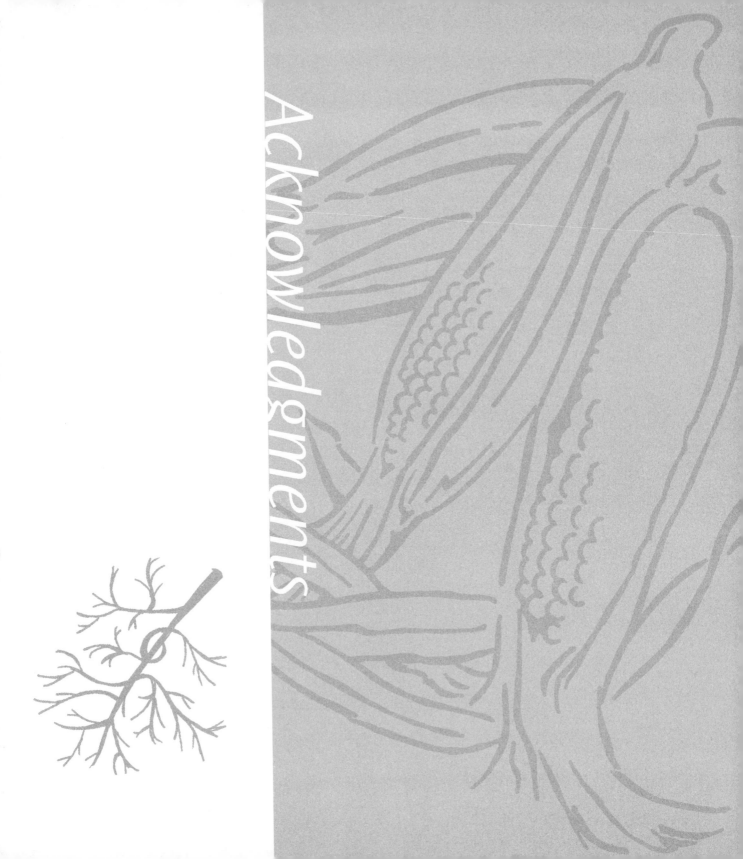

Acknowledgments

I'd like to thank everyone who contributed to this book, whether in large or small ways.

For suggestions, recipes, and help in testing, Carlie Graves, Nancy Judson, Susan Webb, Jesse King, Sue West, Ann Sorocki, Phyllis Becker, and Olive Harris.

Sylvia Diaz for research assistance on this book's appendix.

Sylvia Tawse of the Fresh Ideas Group in Boulder, Colorado, for a most compelling look at the benefits of choosing organic foods.

The Poughkeepsie Farm Project (the Community Supported Agriculture farm to which my family belongs) for keeping us supplied with great organic produce for nearly half of each year.

The friendly staff at Mother Earth's Storehouse who have made shopping for all the ingredients I needed for these recipes such a pleasure.

Oldways Preservation & Exchange Trust in Boston (oldwayspt.org) for permission to use their Traditional Healthy Vegetarian Diet Pyramid, shown on page 316.

All the kids I've fed over the years, too numerous to name, for helping me prove that children love good healthy food.

A few extra-special thanks:

Reed Mangels, Ph.D., R.D., for the foreword and "fine-tooth combing" of the nutrition information in this book.

My son Evan, for being such an able assistant in the kitchen, for doing the baking when company comes, and for being able to tell just what a recipe needs to make it better.

My son Adam, for 24/7 tech support and for helping to maintain my website, *In a Vegetarian Kitchen* (www.vegkitchen.com), which has become such an important supplement to my books.

My husband Chaim "Rocky" Tabak, for all he does for our family and for an amazing quarter of a century!

Leslie Cerier (author of *Going Wild in the Kitchen*) gets an extra thanks, not only for supplying a recipe for the Wholesome Baked Goods chapter but for being a most supportive colleague.

Barb Bloomfield, who has done the nutritional analyses for all my books, thanks for another job well done.

To the staff of Broadway Books who have been involved in this project, thanks for all the ways you have contributed and for making Broadway such a welcoming place to publish books.

Jennifer Josephy, my editor, whom I always save for last but who is definitely the greatest, for her unwavering support for my quiet but steady career over the course of many years.

Contents

Foreword by Reed Mangels, Ph.D., R.D.   **x**

Introduction   **xii**

CHAPTER ONE *Easy Breakfast Treats*   **xxviii**

CHAPTER TWO *Soothing Soups and Savory Stews*   **26**

CHAPTER THREE *Salads and Such*   **60**

CHAPTER FOUR *Pasta and Noodles*   **98**

CHAPTER FIVE *Tofu and Seitan*   **132**

CHAPTER SIX *Vegetable, Grain, and Bean Main Dishes*   **162**

CHAPTER SEVEN *Vegetable and Grain Side Dishes*   **198**

CHAPTER EIGHT *Sandwiches, Wraps, and School Lunches*   **236**

CHAPTER NINE *Healthy Snacks and Fruity Treats*   **254**

CHAPTER TEN *Wholesome Baked Goods*   **276**

*Appendix: General Nutritional Information, Books,
and Web Resources to Explore*   **316**

Index   **329**

Foreword

by Reed Mangels, Ph.D., R.D.
Nutrition Advisor, Vegetarian Resource Group

Long ago, before becoming a parent, I wrote, "Of course it takes time and thought to feed vegetarian children. Shouldn't feeding any child require time and thought? After all, the years from birth to adolescence are the years when eating habits are set, when growth rate is high, and to a large extent, when the size of stores of essential nutrients such as calcium and iron are determined."

After more than 10 years of feeding my own vegetarian children I still find truth in this statement. No, I don't spend hours at the stove, but I do try to take time to prepare meals and to think about what my children eat. That's one of the reasons why I find Nava Atlas's *The Vegetarian Family Cookbook* so valuable. Nava has children of her own and has obviously put a lot of thought and caring into her family's meals. I applaud her for sharing her ideas with other families.

Today, Americans are struggling with an epidemic of childhood obesity. This is not cute "baby fat"; this is a serious health problem that is setting up our children for an unhealthy adulthood and a lifetime of diseases like diabetes, heart disease, problems with bones and joints, and high blood pressure. There are many reasons for this crisis in children's health, but one thing is certain: what our children eat makes a difference.

One way to begin to bring this epidemic under control is with a focus on healthful eating. The foods we offer to our children as toddlers and young children are often the foods they will prefer throughout life. Certainly a preference for foods like fruits and vegetables, whole grains, nuts, and dried beans is a better gift for our children than a lifelong struggle with cravings for candy bars, potato chips, and soda. Many families are choosing vegetarian diets that can make it easier to comply with recommendations like "eat more fruits and vegetables" and "limit saturated fat and cholesterol." Other families are choosing to eat diets that, while not completely vegetarian, are based on healthy vegetarian foods.

Dietitians and other nutrition professionals often encourage eating a variety of foods. Unfortunately, this message to eat a variety of health-promoting foods has often been misunderstood or ignored. This book does much to advance the *real* health message. Not only is this book full of tasty recipes and ideas and quick tips, but it also gives ways to put it all together—for making whole meals that will work, even for a busy family. *The Vegetarian Family Cookbook* is a celebration of good food—good-tasting food, food that's good for you, food that you'll enjoy eating!

IF YOU'RE PART OF A FAMILY THAT

- includes one or more vegetarians or vegans,
- has children or teens who want to go vegetarian or vegan,
- is not necessarily vegetarian but wants to serve more meatless meals,
- wants to use more organic foods,
- needs easy ways to please picky eaters,
- is looking for easy ways to transition from vegetarian to vegan, and/or
- wants the daily fare to include more vegetables, fruits, whole grains, and soy foods,

then you've come to the right place!

This project has been many years in the making; I've been compiling recipes and ideas that my children and their friends have enjoyed from the time they were very young, and those that we have loved eating together or sharing with other families. What has stood out for me over the course of time is that children are more open to new adventures at the table than their parents give them credit for, especially if the food is kept simple and served attractively in a warm and welcoming setting. Our friends have been amazed at what their kids are willing to eat when visiting us ("What? He's eating tofu?"). Lately, playing host to hungry adolescent and preteen friends of my sons (few of whom are vegetarian), it's amusing to observe how they start to wonder what there is to eat just moments after walking in the door. No one leaves my house disappointed, whether I'm serving tofu, sushi, chili, vegan macaroni and cheese, or whole-grain baked goods.

My sons (who at the time of publication of this book are twelve and fourteen) are lifelong vegetarians, so we've had plenty of years of experience as an all-vegetarian family. We look forward to the meals we share, not only for the delicious food but for the time spent together at the table. It wasn't always this easy—when the boys were younger, each had his quirks and preferences. I often made one thing for my husband and something totally different for the boys. Luck may have something to do with my sons' good eating habits, but I'd like to think that my patience and creativity had some effect, too!

Vegetarian and vegan kids can be as finicky and variable as omnivorous children. My own strategy was to regularly introduce and revisit a wide variety of healthy fare, with no pressure to make the kids have "just one bite." I persisted in trying new ways to present and arrange vegetables, fruits, grains, and other good foods simply and enticingly, until the magical day arrived when making one meal, not several, was enough to please our family of four. Approaching the double-digit ages seemed to do wonders for the boys' appetites and sense of culinary adventure. I've observed the same in many of their friends, though I can't claim this to be universally true.

When this project was in the stretch, my younger son, Evan, then 10 years old, came home from camp one day and announced he had become a vegan. Though the boys and I had given up eggs some months before, Evan's announcement took me by surprise. My older son, Adam, followed suit a few days later. I had been privately considering going vegan for some time but wavered, not quite ready to give up goat cheese. Once the boys became vegan, I felt inspired to follow their lead. As for my husband, he happily ate what the rest of us did at the dinner table but remained on the lacto-ovo path. Recently, with one egg left in the fridge, he announced that he was a vegan, almost as suddenly as our younger son had.

Ultimately, this book benefits from having both the vegetarian and vegan perspectives. While vegetarianism has certainly been accepted as more mainstream in the last decade or two, the number of fully committed vegetarians has not exactly swelled. However, within the ranks of vegetarians, the movement toward veganism is going strong. I'm not here to advocate for one type of diet or another. Being vegan can be challenging and is a personal decision. What I offer you here is not persuasion but an abundance of options, information, and resources to make healthy, delicious meatless meals as often as possible, whether your family is vegetarian, vegan, omnivorous, or a combination.

For an earlier generation of vegetarians, a primary reason for making this lifestyle choice was for health reasons, and indeed, research has proven that people with primarily plant-based diets suffer from a fraction of the heart disease, cancer, diabetes, and other diseases of their meat-eating counterparts. For younger vegetarians, the motivation is primarily ethical and sometimes environmental. A family's shared concern for health, compassion for animals, and sustainability of resources can be a powerful bond at the table, as it is in my own family.

The Vegetarian Family Cookbook is a compilation of favorite recipes and meals my family has eaten, enjoyed, and shared. It's my sincere hope that many of these will become your family's favorites, too.

The Recipes and Menus

The recipes in this book reflect the truth about family eating habits—they come in a wide range, even within the same family. Vegetarian and vegan kids have as many dietary quirks as their nonvegetarian counterparts. And so, a plethora of possibilities will be presented here, from kid-friendly comfort food (which parents may certainly enjoy as well) to more sophisticated (yet easy-to-make) recipes for developing appetites and adult tastes. I'm not going to claim that all kids will love all the recipes presented here, but given the array of options, I'm confident that parents will find a range of foods to please budding palates.

Among the recipes are many that are flexible and adaptable. Simple dishes can be dressed up for adult preferences; conversely, more complex dishes can be broken down to simple components for young eaters. The result is that the cook doesn't feel that he or she needs to cook separate meals to suit everyone's tastes. Many of the main dish recipes (as well as some of the soups, stews, and sandwiches) are followed by menu suggestions. Throughout the book, you'll find many vegan recipes; in fact, the majority are suitable for vegans or offer a vegan option. You'll find these designations next to each recipe's title.

Included in this book are a range of recipes from super-quick and almost mindlessly easy to those that take more time and a leisurely attitude; none, though, would qualify as complicated. Some recipes, like casseroles and certain baked goods, are more suited to the slower pace of weekends than to busy weeknights.

To help you plan complete meals and make the recipes appealing to various palates, you'll find one or all of these features with many of the recipes in this book:

- **Embellish it:** Suggestions for what can be added to a simple recipe to give it bolder flavor will be given here. For example, a mild dish like Ricotta Pasta with Raisins and Peas (page 118) can be enjoyed just as is, but adults and teens may enjoy giving it a boost with curry and cilantro.

- **Make it a meal:** For dishes that can be the start or centerpiece of a meal (such as soups and salads) or for main dishes, this feature helps you create a complete menu, referencing other recipes in the book. Sometimes the suggestions include simple, recipe-free accompaniments. The menus aren't set in stone, of course, and as you become familiar with some of your own favorites, feel free to mix and match as you choose.

- **For picky eaters:** Some dishes with more challenging ingredients and combinations may be too much for finicky children but have components that can be taken apart. The picky eater can still get plenty of nourishment without having an entirely separate meal.

In addition to formal recipes, you'll find lots of simple ideas that require more inspiration than exact proportions. If you're looking for breakfasts, snacks, sandwiches, and other on-the-go-type foods, I think you'll find these easy quasi-recipes most useful.

A note about the nutritional analyses: These are given per serving, for the average yield of the recipe. For example, if a recipe serves four to six, the analysis is based on five servings. Optional ingredients and suggested embellishments are not included in the analyses. In cases when the vegan option makes a significant difference in the analysis, the statistics for both the vegetarian and the vegan options will be given.

Tips for Busy Cooks

If you have a family, whether with one child or seven, then by definition you're a busy cook. Vegetarians and vegans aren't part of some mythical, laid-back counterculture but are soccer parents, carpoolers, corporate executives, and

 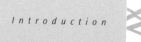

self-employed entrepreneurs. Our children are involved in just as many extracurricular activities and have just as much homework as anyone else's kids! Many people say they are too busy to cook, but no one is too busy to eat. Even among vegetarians and vegans, this is often remedied by a lot of eating out, getting takeout, and using prepared entrées. I'd like to encourage people to cook and eat at home, so here are some of my tried-and-true tips for making cooked-from-scratch meals a daily reality, even after the most exhausting days:

1   Make sure your pantry and freezer are stocked with good-quality ingredients for quick and/or "emergency" meals. My pantry standbys include canned beans, quick-cooking grains (like couscous and bulgur), white and sweet potatoes, and pastas. In addition, I keep on hand prepared sauces like marinara, barbecue, Thai peanut, and salsa. In the freezer are whole-wheat English muffins, veggie burgers, pita bread (for quick pizzas and sandwiches), and corn and wheat tortillas. My basic frozen veggies are corn, peas, green beans, and spinach (all organic). And with fresh produce always at the ready, there are myriad nearly instant meals that can be created with these basics.

2   Plan three full meals for the week ahead, allowing for two nights of leftovers. Plan your meals *before* you go grocery shopping to prevent running back and forth to the store all week for ingredients. There's nothing worse than walking into the kitchen after a long day without a clue as to what you want to make. I try to practice what I preach, but whenever there is a week that I've left unplanned, I really regret it! Just 15 or 20 minutes of meal planning per week saves lots of time and simplifies your life immeasurably.

3   On Sunday, prepare a couple of basics for the week to come. Cook some plain brown rice (or other grain); bake some potatoes, sweet potatoes, or squash. Bake quick bread or muffins, or prepare a good pasta sauce. Knowing that you have even one item that's already prepared when you enter the kitchen at 6:00 P.M. is a sweet feeling, and the rest of the meal then comes together quickly.

4   Once a week, make a big one-pot meal that can stretch to at least two nights, such as a hearty soup or stew, chili, or casserole. Double recipes if you have a larger family. Then, all you need is a salad and fresh whole-grain bread to round out the meal.

5   Develop repertoires and routines. If you are extremely busy and don't mind a little repetition, you can choose just a few menus that your family likes and rotate them throughout the month. An example of a routine would be something like that described in tip 3 (above), which suggests that you prepare certain ingredients in advance. Another would be to get your older children and teens to take turns making dinner, or at least part of it, once a week. Try designating each night of the week for a certain kind of meal. Monday could be soup and salad night (with the soup having been prepared on Sunday); Tuesday, homemade Asian; Wednesday, pasta night; one night to clean up all leftovers; and so on. This kind of predictability makes meal planning easier when you're strapped for time.

6 Keep it simple! You need not spend hours cooking or use dozens of ingredients to create tasty meals. I truly believe that it's the quality of ingredients, rather than the quantity, that matters most.

Great Reasons to Go Vegetarian

Many people who are vegetarians think of their diet as a way of life rather than merely as a way of eating. It's not necessary to be a strict vegetarian to be a natural foods enthusiast, but generally, vegetarians almost by definition are more conscientious about the foods they eat. Those who have chosen to go vegetarian appreciate knowing that their food choices can be not only tasty and healthy but compassionate and humane as well. Not to mention the enormous benefit of plant-based diets to our rapidly deteriorating environment. Common wisdom tells us that vegetarian diets

- may be overall the healthiest way to eat. Research has shown that vegetarians tend to have lower rates of obesity— a significant and timely point, now that 60 percent of American adults are overweight and 300,000 die each year of obesity-related diseases. Some of these diseases are heart disease, hypertension, kidney disease, osteoporosis, arthritis, and adult-onset (type 2) diabetes.

- give their practitioners the edge against some forms of cancer. Studies of vegetarians show that, overall, they have lower rates of cancer than the general population. Vegetarians are believed to have stronger immune systems, possibly due to higher-than-average intake of vitamin-packed vegetables, grains, and legumes. Fiber-rich vegetarian diets may reduce the risk of cancers of the digestive organs.

- may protect against heart disease. Health experts agree that eating foods high in fiber and complex carbohydrates can help reduce the risk of heart disease. In addition, plant-based proteins reduce cholesterol levels, while animal protein raises them.

- help avoid some of the most virulent forms of food-borne illnesses caused by *E. coli*, *Salmonella*, and *Listera*. Food-borne illness is particularly dangerous to children, whose immune systems may not be developed enough to withstand the dangers of contaminated meat products.

- may hold the key to a longer life. Studies, including those conducted on Seventh-Day Adventists (who advocate a vegetarian diet), have shown that vegetarians live an average of 7 to 15 years longer than their meat-eating counterparts.

Other benefits of plant-based diets are numerous and include the following:

Weight control: It's hard to get fat—or stay fat—on a balanced vegetarian diet. Grains, legumes, many types of vegetables, and soy foods are bulky and filling yet contain little or no fat. They provide a feeling of fullness that keeps the body fueled and satisfied for hours.

Economy: There's great economic value in bulk grains and legumes, supplemented with fresh produce carefully chosen in season. Even a ready-to-eat food such as tofu averages about $1.75 a pound—far less expensive than quality meats and fish.

Ecology: Many environmentally aware consumers derive gratification from eating low on the food chain—that is, getting the bulk of their diets from plant-based foods. It's not only good for the body, reducing the intake of pesticide and animal antibiotic residues, but also for the planet, since livestock deplete enormous land and water resources. Consider that

- raising livestock contributes to the loss of millions of tons of irreplaceable topsoil each year.

- it takes 25 gallons of water to produce 1 pound of wheat compared to 390 gallons of water to produce 1 pound of beef.

- livestock produce massive amounts of excrement that is left untreated, allowing the runoff to pollute soil, water, and air.

Compassion: Animal agribusiness is one of the cruelest practices imaginable. Millions of sentient creatures are subject to confinement, overcrowding, and disfigurement (as in the common practice of debeaking poultry) only to face an equally cruel demise in the slaughterhouse (which, by the way, is no picnic for its human workers, either). A primarily plant-based diet is a more humane way to enjoy the fruits of the earth. Animal agribusiness also primarily goes to feed those who already have enough to eat. The vast stores of grain used to feed animals each year could be put to better use by feeding it directly to those who need it most.

Great Reasons to Go Organic

I'm an avid supporter of organic foods; my kitchen is 90 percent organic, and if given the choice, I always opt for organic. It's gratifying to know that organics are a growing trend: In 2000, organic product sales totaled $7.8 billion.

And approximately 69 percent of shoppers bought these products at their primary supermarket. Sales of organic products are growing substantially each year.

Organic foods are grown in soils fertilized with organic rather than synthetic fertilizers and are not sprayed with inorganic chemicals (foods described as "whole" or "natural" aren't necessarily organically grown). Organically grown foods are more expensive but not so much more as to make them prohibitive. Natural food stores, food co-ops, some farm markets, and a growing number of supermarkets now offer organic choices to consumers concerned with the effects of pesticides, additives, and chemical fertilizers on both human health and the environment. The new federal guidelines and labeling (USDA Certified Organic) help ensure that consumers understand what they are buying.

That said, it's important to know that many small organic farms have actually been hurt by the new organic labeling standards; the massive amount of paperwork required by the government can be prohibitive for a small operation. Thus some small organic farms might begin to label their products "certified ecologically grown," or some similar variation on this. If you know and trust your local small farms, you can make the decision, as I do, to continue buying and supporting their products.

As often as possible, purchase fruits, vegetables, nuts, seeds, grains, legumes, and products made from them in organic form. It is challenging, no doubt, to buy 100 percent organic, but the important thing is to do the best you can and, at least, purchase the top most contaminated crops in organic form. Note that different organizations have found somewhat different results from studies of contaminated foods. What some studies look for is pesticide residues classified by the Environmental Protection Agency (EPA) as probable human carcinogens, nervous system poisons, and endocrine system disrupters. Other studies focus on foods most eaten by children and thus likely to do most harm if there are residues. Below are three different views.

The Top 10 Most Contaminated Crops (in alphabetical order) Source: Consumer Reports, March 1999	The Top 10 Foods to Buy Organic (in alphabetical order) Source: Mothers and Others for a Livable Planet
Apples	Apples
Bell peppers	Baby food
Cucumbers	Bananas
Green beans	Corn
Peaches	Dairy products
Pears	Grains (all)
Spinach	Green beans
Strawberries	Peaches
Tomatoes	Rice
Winter squashes	Strawberries

The 12 Most Pesticide-Contaminated Foods (in order of contamination)

Source: The Environmental Working Group

1. Strawberries
2. Bell peppers, green and red (tied with spinach)
3. Spinach (tied with bell peppers)
4. Cherries, U.S.
5. Peaches
6. Cantaloupe, Mexican
7. Celery
8. Apples
9. Apricots
10. Green beans
11. Grapes, Chilean
12. Cucumbers

I've seen many variants on these studies; others cite oranges, potatoes, and any leafy vegetables in the top 10 or 12. Some of the produce and other plant foods rarely seen in these kinds of top-ten lists are broccoli, cabbage, carrots, cauliflower, Brussels sprouts, legumes, and plums. Still, with so much variation in the lists of most contaminated foods, the strategy should be apparent: Buy organic versions of produce and dairy products whenever available. Simply put, it's better for you, your children, and the planet.

Choosing Organic

Here are the top 10 reasons to choose organic foods for your family:

1 **Protect future generations:** The average child receives more exposure than an adult to at least eight widely used cancer-causing pesticides in food.[*] The food choices you make now will affect your child's health in the future.

2 **Prevent soil erosion:** The Soil Conservation Service estimates that more than 3 billion tons of topsoil are eroded from U.S. croplands each year. That means soil is eroding seven times faster than it is being built up naturally. As a result, American farms are suffering from the worst soil erosion in history.

[*] "Children's diets are different from those of adults. One-year-olds, for instance, eat three times as many fresh peaches, per pound of body weight, as adults, and four times as many apples, bananas, and pears. All this means it's easier for children to ingest relatively large amounts of pesticides." ("How Safe Is Our Produce?" *Consumer Reports,* March 1999.)

3 **Protect water quality:** Water makes up two thirds of our body mass and covers three fourths of the planet. Despite water's importance, the EPA estimates pesticides—some cancer causing—contaminate the groundwater in 38 states, polluting the primary source of drinking water for more than half the country's population.

4 **Save energy:** American farms have changed drastically in the last three generations, from family-based small businesses dependent on human energy to large-scale factory farms highly dependent on fossil fuels. Modern farming uses more petroleum than any other single industry, consuming 12 percent of the country's total energy supply. More energy is now used to produce synthetic fertilizers than to till, cultivate, and harvest all the crops in the United States. Organic farming is still mainly based on labor-intensive practices such as weeding by hand and using green manures and crop covers rather than synthetic fertilizers to build up the soil. Organic produce also tends to travel fewer miles from field to table.

5 **Keep chemicals off your plate:** Many pesticides approved for use by the EPA were registered long before extensive research linking these chemicals to cancer and other diseases had been established. Now the EPA considers that 60 percent of all herbicides, 90 percent of all fungicides, and 30 percent of all insecticides are carcinogenic. A 1987 National Academy of Sciences report estimated that pesticides might cause an extra 1.4 million cancer cases among Americans over their lifetimes. The bottom line is that pesticides are poisons designed to kill living organisms and can also be harmful to humans. In addition to cancer, pesticides are implicated in birth defects, nerve damage, and genetic mutation.

6 **Protect farmworker health:** A National Cancer Institute study found that farmers exposed to herbicides had a six times greater risk than nonfarmers of contracting cancer. In California, reported pesticide poisonings among farmworkers have risen an average of 14 percent a year since 1973, and doubled between 1975 and 1985. Field-workers suffer the highest rates of occupational illness in the state. Farmworker health also is a serious problem in developing nations, where pesticide use can be poorly regulated. An estimated 1 million people are poisoned annually by pesticides.

7 **Help small farmers:** Although more and more large-scale farms are making the conversion to organic practices, most organic farms are small, independently owned family farms of less than 100 acres. It's estimated that the United States has lost more than 650,000 family farms in the past decade.

8 **Support a true economy:** Although organic foods might seem more expensive than conventional foods, conventional food prices don't reflect the hidden costs borne by taxpayers, including billions of dollars in federal subsidies. Other hidden costs include pesticide regulation and testing, hazardous waste disposal and cleanup, and environmental damage.

9 **Promote biodiversity:** Monocropping is the practice of planting large plots of land with the same crop year after year. While this approach tripled farm production between 1950 and 1970, the lack of natural diversity of plant life has left the soil lacking in natural minerals and nutrients. To replace the nutrients, chemical fertilizers are used, often in increasing amounts. Single crops are also much more susceptible to pests, making farmers more reliant on pesticides. Despite a tenfold increase in the use of pesticides between 1947 and 1974, crop losses due to insects have doubled—partly because some insects have become genetically resistant to certain pesticides.

10 **Taste better flavor:** There's a good reason why many chefs use organic foods in their recipes—they taste better! Organic farming starts with the nourishment of the soil, which eventually leads to the nourishment of the plant, and ultimately of our palates.

(Contributed by Sylvia Tawse, The Fresh Ideas Group)

Some Notes on Ingredients Used in This Book

Organic Dairy Products and Eggs

The term *organic* is most commonly applied to produce, but if you and your family use dairy products (and eggs), it's important to know how this term applies to these, as well.

Organic dairy products come from cows (and less frequently, goats) that feed on certified organic crops grown on lands that have been pesticide-, herbicide-, or fertilizer-free for three years or more. Organic dairy cows are never given antibiotics or synthetic hormones such as rBGH. Organic dairy farms generally claim to allow their cows more outdoor time and natural grazing access, compared to conventional dairy herds.

Most any dairy product comes in organic form, and it's worth seeking it out. Aside from milk and yogurt, there is cream, cottage cheese, ricotta cheese, sour cream, and all manner of hard and soft cheeses. Organic goat's milk products (primarily goat cheese and milk) offer another alternative.

Eggs labeled "organic" come from hens that are never treated with growth hormones or antibiotics. *Cage-free* and *free-range* are terms commonly found on cartons of eggs that are organic. This means that the hens are allowed at least some access to fresh air and the outdoors; unfortunately, these terms are unregulated and so it's difficult to determine if the eggs you are purchasing are truly from free-range hens or whether the hens are allowed only limited access to the proverbial barnyard. Either way though, hens that produce organic eggs are generally believed to receive more humane treatment than those kept in battery cages around the clock, as in conventional agriculture.

Rennetless Cheeses

Nonorganic hard cheeses often contain rennet, an enzyme extracted from the stomach lining of slaughtered calves. Vegetarians may be uncomfortable about using this product. Some cheeses list the ingredient as "enzymes," but if they don't specify that the enzymes come from a nonanimal source, then it's hard to make any assumptions. Organic cheeses also use enzymes, but they are most often from a vegetable, fruit, or microbial source and usually specify that this is the case. Kosher cheeses, which are not necessarily organic, also use vegetable enzymes or "vegetable rennet."

Dairy Substitutes: Soy, Rice, and Almond Products

Many people avoid dairy products because they are allergic to them or can't digest them (lactose intolerance). Vegans don't use them because they have made a conscious choice to avoid any animal-derived products. If this describes your family members, the recipes in this book provide plenty of options and substitutions.

Soy products offer the widest variety of dairy substitutions. Soy milk, yogurt, cheeses, and even coffee creamer come in numerous brands and flavors. Soy cheeses have come a long way in the last few years. Once rubbery and unpalatable, some are virtually indistinguishable from dairy cheese when incorporated into cheesy dishes. Many soy-based dairy products are fortified, so their nutritional content closely matches that of their dairy counterparts.

Once my family went vegan, I saw how easy it was to start relying, perhaps too much, on soy. So I like to vary our dairy substitutes by using rice milk products as well and, to a lesser extent, nut milk products. Unlike soy products, there aren't many brands or variations of rice milk products, Rice Dream being the primary producer. Rice milk is excellent in soups and smoothies; Rice Slices, which come in American-style, mozzarella-style, and more, are nearly indistinguishable from the dairy variety in grilled or cold sandwiches (and are a good source of calcium); and rice cream cheese comes in handy in many ways. Rice milk products can be useful for people who can tolerate neither dairy nor soy, as soy allergy is quite common as well. Rice milk products, like soy milk products, are fortified, but do not contain as many vitamins and minerals. If you are using rice milk as a primary replacement for soy or dairy milk, you may wish to choose Rice Dream Enriched, which is a good source of vitamin B_{12}, an important vitamin to supplement if one is on a primarily plant-based diet—see more on this vitamin on page 320. Note, too, that rice milk is not as rich in protein as is soy or dairy milk.

Almond milk and almond cheeses are not in as generous supply as soy or even rice equivalents, but these products taste quite good and can be used from time to time for variety.

Casein in Nondairy Products

Those who wish to adhere to a perfectly strict vegan diet or whose allergies to milk products are severe, need to know that many soy- and rice-based cheeses contain a minute amount of casein, a milk protein. It is this protein that allows the cheeses to melt and have a more cheeselike texture. Some vegans feel it is okay to use nondairy cheeses containing casein, as it represents "doing the best they can" in reducing dairy consumption overall. For stricter vegans, this is not at all acceptable. This issue is probably comparable to a lacto-vegetarian deciding whether or not to use cheeses that contain animal rennet.

Of course, people whose milk allergies are severe should certainly consult their physician before attempting to use any product that contains casein. For many of them, this would not be acceptable.

At this writing, there are few nondairy products that have a really good "melt" without casein. Follow Your Heart brand nondairy cheese is one brand currently available; for information on how to obtain it, see www.followyourheart.com. Those who are interested can make their own cheeselike substitutes at home; sources for this information are also in the Appendix.

Choosing Good Oils for Cooking

There has been much talk in recent years about the importance of reducing fat intake in a healthy diet. Nevertheless, fat is vital in small quantities and, along with protein and carbohydrates, is one of the three "large" nutrients.

One of the best ways to provide the body with the small amounts of fat it requires is with nuts and seeds, avocados, and good-quality cooking oils rich in polyunsaturated and monounsaturated oils from vegetable sources. Some common vegetable oils are those expressed from peanuts, sesame seeds, olives, corn, safflower, and rapeseed (this is marketed as canola). Many of these oils, particularly nut and seed oils, are a good source of vitamin E.

Natural foods stores offer organic versions of the common oils listed above, and if you can obtain an organic version of anything, so much the better. Try finding oils labeled "cold pressed" or "expeller pressed" as well; that means that the oils were not expressed with solvents or extreme heat, as may be the case with some oils prepared by large manufacturers.

One of the premier oils that has stood the test of time as both healthy and highly palatable is olive oil. A primarily monounsaturated oil, extra-virgin is best for salads and dressings (though I like to use it occasionally for low-heat sautéing, especially for Italian, Mexican, and Spanish dishes). Light and pure olive oils are good all-purpose oils. I specify which form of olive oil I prefer when calling for it in a recipe. I have found that children are not as amenable to the stronger flavor of extra-virgin oil, so take your family's preferences into account when using it. Safflower is another oil I like, especially for use in baking.

You might note the absence of canola oil (long touted as one of the most heart healthy) from the recipes in this book. There has been much said and written, both good and bad, about canola oil in recent years. An Internet search on the term *canola oil* will yield an equal amount of favorable and highly unfavorable articles. Proponents claim that it has the best fatty acid ratio of all oils, including the lowest levels of saturated fat. It is sometimes recommended for fulfilling vegans' need for linolenic acid (which can also be derived from ground flaxseeds or flaxseed oil). Opponents charge that rapeseed (the plant from which canola oil is derived) is a questionable food source and that nonorganic canola oil is genetically engineered food. If you feel, as many do, that the pros of canola oil outweigh the cons, consider using it in organic form.

The canola debate is not for me to decide, and for now, I choose to stay out of the fray until the discussion is settled, or at least clarified. Instead, I've opted to recommend oils that are less controversial.

Margarine versus Butter

In some of my books I've offered readers the option of using either margarine or butter. In this book, I call for only nonhydrogenated margarine. If you do use butter, at least use it in organic form. It's no secret that pesticide, hormone, and antibiotic residues are more prevalent in fatty animal products, whether in the meat itself or in high-fat dairy products like cheeses and butter.

Also at issue is the trans-fat controversy. While it has become well known that margarines, especially harder stick margarines, are high in partially hydrogenated oils (unhealthy trans-fats that clog arteries and raise cholesterol levels), the American Heart Association (AHA) has concluded that "because butter is rich in both saturated fat and cholesterol, it is potentially a highly atherogenic food (causes the arteries to be blocked). Most margarines are made from vegetable oils and provide no dietary cholesterol. The more liquid the margarine, the less hydrogenated it is and the less *trans* fatty acids it contains. Therefore, margarine is still a preferable substitute for butter and soft margarines are better than hard ones" (from AHA, "Know Your Fats," http://www.americanheart.org).

Still, there is no reason to use conventional margarines now that nonhydrogenated margarines are readily available. My favorite brand is Earth Balance, available in natural foods stores. A supermarket brand of nonhydrogenated margarine is Smart Balance. A small amount of nonhydrogenated margarine in a healthy diet is not a problem, but it's good to note that good-quality vegetable oils are a superior source of fat for vegetarians and vegans, since they can be a better source of key fatty acids.

Soy Mayonnaise

I am referring to commercially prepared tofu-based mayonnaise, and you'll see this ingredient called for in salads, dressings, and dips. Two leading brands are Nayonnaise and Veganaise. Both are excellent. Unlike conventional mayonnaise, these contain no cholesterol, and they have less fat and saturated fat overall. Of course, if you want to use regular mayonnaise, or if soy mayonnaise is unavailable to you, go ahead and use what you'd prefer. Please note, however, that the nutritional analyses of the recipes are based on the use of soy mayonnaise only.

Salt-Free All-Purpose Seasoning

The use of a multi-herb-and-spice seasoning is prevalent throughout the book. Salt-free all-purpose seasoning mix is a boon to people who don't have the patience to measure minute amounts of many seasonings. There are many brands of this popular seasoning, and you may use whatever brand you prefer or is available to you. Some examples of supermarket brands are Mrs. Dash and McCormick; natural foods store brands include Spike and Frontier, though there are many other good ones.

Other Ingredients of Note

In this book, I make greater use than ever of the following ingredients, and I provide brief explanatory sidebars in the chapters in which they most frequently appear:

Flaxseeds: page 290
Natural granulated sugar: page 283
Seitan: page 153
Tempeh: page 240
Tofu (several forms): page 134
Whole-wheat pastry flour: page 281

Each chapter throughout the book offers plenty of information on the ingredients used; you'll find these tidbits in the sidebars.

My Favorite Kitchen Tools and Supplies

I try to keep my kitchen streamlined and uncluttered and have always thought long and hard before investing in gadgets. The following items have stood the test of time for me. Here, in order of how frequently they are used, are my favorites:

1 **Wire (or coated wire) whisk:** This inexpensive tool is indispensable for making lump-free sauces and fine-textured cooked cereals and grains (such as farina and polenta). It's also perfect for making smoothly blended salad dressings and perfectly textured pancake or waffle batter.

2 **Kitchen shears:** Another inexpensive must-have, these kitchen-drawer scissors have many uses, including thinly slicing scallions, cutting long noodles cooked for soup, cutting up whole canned tomatoes when you meant to open a can of diced, opening cellophane-wrapped packages, cutting pita pizzas into wedges—trust me, these are very useful.

3 **Good-quality baking and roasting pans:** You need to spend a bit more on these than the average, but they last much longer and brown baked goods and foods more evenly. Cheap or too-dark bakeware can result in overly browned, yet underdone, baked goods. They're also harder to clean, as food sticks to them.

4 **Stir-fry pan:** Having a wok-shaped pan makes stir-frying a pleasure, and it's less cumbersome and easier to store than a large wok. It's nice-looking enough to serve food from at the table (with a trivet underneath, of course). If you're a fan of bright-colored, lightly cooked veggies or Asian-style dishes, this kind of pan will get a lot of play in your kitchen. Still, if you prefer using a full-fledged wok, there is no reason not to do so.

5 **Immersion blender:** This is a more recent favorite, and I just love it. Basically, it's shaped like a wand that comes apart in two sections. You can literally immerse it into a pot or container of ingredients and push a button for an on-the-spot purée. No transferring ingredients in and out of a food processor or blender. This is especially appreciated when it comes to making hot puréed soups.

    The immersion blender is unbelievably easy to use, even easier to clean, and costs a fraction of what a food processor does, if you have to choose but one. If you like to make smoothies, puréed soups, and velvety sauces as much as I do, you'll find this indispensable.

6 **Waffle iron:** Of course, it's easier to pop ready-made waffles into the toaster, and there are a variety of natural and even organic brands. But they can't compare to homemade waffles. Since having homemade pancakes on weekends is a family ritual, it wasn't much of a stretch for me to start making waffles (see Chapter 1). This is a compact piece of equipment that stores easily and adds an element of fun to breakfast.

7 **Pizza pan:** Another inexpensive, easy-to-store item, this is simply a 14-inch round pan with holes on the bottom. Since we no longer eat pizza-parlor pies and since I see little point in buying health food store pizzas (how hard is it to put tomato sauce, grated organic or soy cheese, and some veggies on a crust?), this pan gets regular use.

CHAPTER ONE

Easy Breakfast Treats

LET'S FACE IT: Even the best of intentions won't change the fact that many of us are tired and rushed in the morning. Also, since some people are just not that hungry first thing, the not-yet-awakened appetite is none too ambitious. It's unfortunate that the first hour of the day is rush hour, but for most of us, that's the reality.

My sons have always liked a fairly hearty breakfast, so for us, the morning meal is a given. We try to decide the night before what to have for breakfast on school days, so that if the choice is waffles or a hot cooked cereal, I know to allow a little extra time. And because time is so short in the morning, one of my strategies has been to compile a list of possibilities so we're not scrambling for ideas. Speaking of scrambling, you'll note that eggs play a small role in this chapter, with a suggestion or two in the simple breakfast ideas and breakfast sandwiches list; that's because most people who eat eggs already have a set of simple ways to fix them to their family's liking. Instead, you'll find many ideas and easy recipes based on whole grains— these complex carb foods are perfect for getting revved in the morning yet are easy on the palate. Smoothies and other fruit-augmented recipes round out the selections.

A Basic Breakfast Pantry

One way to mitigate the breakfast rut is to have an array of good-quality breakfast foods on hand. Go through some of the recipes and ideas in this chapter and jot down the basic ingredients to shop for. See if you can clear a portion of a pantry (or at least a couple of shelves) to keep together all your nonperishable breakfast items—such as hot and cold cereals, granolas, and pancake mixes.

Here is a list of what you might consider keeping in your pantry. Of course, you need not buy everything on this list, only what appeals to your family. Once you have a basic breakfast repertoire, you may enjoy adding new items from time to time or changing some items seasonally.

- **Good-quality cold breakfast cereals:** Have an assortment of organic, whole-grain varieties on hand.
- **Granolas:** These are good on their own or mixed with other cold cereals.
- **Hot cereals:** See the listing of possibilities on page 17.
- **Embellishments for hot and cold cereals:** Dried fruits, nuts, and seeds (see page 4).
- **Flour tortillas:** These are great for roll-ups and breakfast quesadillas (page 3).
- **Fresh fruits in season:** Bananas are welcome all year around, berries are good for summer, and oranges and mangoes are delicious in winter. Serve as is or use for making juices and smoothies or topping cereals.
- **Whole-grain flours for pancakes and waffles:** Whole-wheat pastry flour, spelt flour, and cornmeal are especially useful. You might also like to stock good-quality prepared pancake and waffle mixes if you can't see starting from scratch on weekday mornings.
- **Whole-grain frozen waffles:** If you're not inclined to make fresh ones in the morning, there are some excellent organic toaster waffles available.
- **Maple syrup and/or honey or other natural sweeteners:** Use sweeteners, even natural ones, sparingly in the morning!
- **Fresh whole-grain breads, rolls, bagels, and English muffins:** Mix and match for variety; keep some in the freezer.
- **Spreads for bread:** All-fruit preserves, nonhydrogenated margarine, dairy or nondairy cream cheese, peanut and other nut butters.
- **Yogurts:** Organic low-fat dairy or nondairy varieties; aside from eating on their own, yogurt is useful in homemade pancake and waffle batters (pages 6–7), and for making biscuits (page 12) and other baked goods (see Chapter 10).

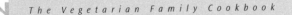

- **Organic dairy or nondairy cheeses and cottage cheese**
- **Organic cage-free eggs**
- **Soy-based faux breakfast meats:** This one is entirely optional, but if you like this type of product, you can keep "sausages" and "bacon" in your freezer to use from time to time as a side dish or in breakfast sandwiches.

Some Simple Breakfast Ideas

Breakfast Burritos: Wrap a flour tortilla around a scrambled egg or a small portion of the basic recipe for Tofu Scrambles Galore (page 140); Sprinkle with grated dairy or nondairy cheese if desired. Roll up snugly. Serve with orange slices in the winter and strawberries in the summer.

Breakfast Quesadillas: For each serving, place a 6- to 7-inch flour tortilla in a dry skillet over medium heat. Sprinkle the entire surface lightly with dairy or nondairy cheese and cover. When the cheese is melted, fold over to a half-circle. Continue to cook on both sides, uncovered, until the tortilla begins to turn golden and crisp. Cut in half to form two wedges to serve. Serve with a fruit smoothie (see page 20) or a breakfast fruit salad (see below) for a lively way to start the day.

Peanut Butter and Banana Roll-ups: For each serving, heat 1 flour tortilla in the microwave until warm and flexible, about 20 seconds. Spread the entire surface with peanut butter (or other nut butter) and place thin banana slices here and there (you'll need about ½ medium banana). Roll up snugly; cut in half crosswise to serve.

Cream Cheese and Berry Roll-ups: For each serving, heat 1 flour tortilla in the microwave until warm and flexible, about 20 seconds. Spread the entire surface with dairy or nondairy cream cheese. Place thinly sliced strawberries over most of the surface or sprinkle with small wild blueberries (or use a little of each). Roll up snugly; cut in half crosswise to serve.

Pasta for Breakfast: I'm always happy to find plain leftover noodles in the refrigerator in the morning. Angel hair or any small pasta shape (tiny shells, elbow macaroni, ditalini, and such) seem more palatable for breakfast than large, chunky shapes. I like mine with a bit of nonhydrogenated margarine and a little salt, generously topped with wheat germ and ground flaxseed. My husband likes his mixed with nonhydrogenated margarine, cinnamon, and natural granulated sugar, then topped as I do mine. I haven't yet convinced my sons to try pasta for breakfast, but maybe they'll learn eventually. This meal is nicely completed by a fruit smoothie (see page 20).

Breakfast Fruit Salad with Cottage Cheese or Yogurt: For a refreshing start to the day, consider fruit salad. To make it more feasible, make your fruit salad the night before and pack it in an airtight container. Summer is easy, with its abundant offering of melons and grapes; strawberries, blueberries, and other berries; peaches and nectarines; and more. Winter fruits are more limited, but you can still get creative with bananas, pears, mangoes, orange slices, and canned pineapple; embellish with some dried fruit if you'd like, such as apricots or pitted prunes. Top your breakfast fruit salad with a mound of cottage cheese or a scoop of low-fat vanilla yogurt or soy yogurt. If you'd like, sprinkle with chopped nuts or granola. Serve with a slice of whole-grain toast or an English muffin.

Cottage Cheese Salad: For those who are open to veggies in the morning, this is a tasty way to start the day. Simply mix some finely diced tomato, cucumber, and bell pepper into a scoop of cottage cheese. If you'd like, sprinkle with toasted sunflower seeds and fresh dill. Serve with a slice of whole-wheat toast.

Morning Parfaits: I always thought of parfaits as dessert, even if they were made with yogurt rather than ice cream, until a reader gave me a new view of this treat. Layer low-fat vanilla yogurt or soy yogurt with seasonal fruits in a tall glass or parfait dish, and top with toasted walnuts, almonds, or a sprinkling of granola. Serve with a toasted English muffin or whole-grain bagel.

Dressed-up Cold Cereal: There are all kinds of ways to make cold cereals more exciting. First of all, make sure the cold cereals you choose are whole grain and all-natural. If they're organic, so much the better. Top cold cereals with any of the following or with any combination that appeals to you:

- **Fresh fruit (berries and diced peaches in summer, sliced bananas in cold weather)**
- **Dried fruit (raisins, cranberries, chopped apricots, dates)**
- **A sprinkling of chopped nuts (toasted slivered almonds or chopped walnuts are particularly good on cereal)**
- **A sprinkling of granola**
- **Wheat germ**
- **Ground flaxseeds**
- **Toasted sesame or sunflower seeds**

Breakfast Sandwiches

Spreading something nourishing between two slices of bread is an easy and sensible way to start the day. But in the morning, most appetites dictate lighter choices than those you might crave for lunch or dinner. You don't need recipes for making breakfast sandwiches, just a cache of good ideas. Here are some to get you going, and remember, if using dairy cheeses or cream cheese, choose organic whenever possible.

- Nut butter (try almond, cashew, or soy nut butter as alternatives to peanut butter) and banana on whole-grain bread

- Any nut butter and fruit butter or all-fruit preserves on whole-grain bread or a roll (apple butter, pear butter, or orange marmalade offer a change of pace from all-fruit preserves)

- Grilled cheese (using dairy or nondairy cheese of your choice; try sliced rice cheese, which is low in fat and high in calcium) on whole-grain bread; add sliced tomato, if desired

- Cream cheese (dairy or nondairy) on good-quality cinnamon-raisin bread or Quick Cinnamon-Raisin Bread (page 282)

- Cream cheese (dairy or nondairy) and sun-dried tomatoes or cured olives on a whole-grain English muffin or bagel

- Scrambled or fried egg and a slice of organic dairy or nondairy cheese or sautéed soy Canadian bacon on a whole-grain roll

- Sautéed soy Canadian bacon and a slice of dairy or nondairy cheese on a whole-grain English muffin

- Sautéed soy Canadian bacon, tomato, and mayonnaise on a whole-grain roll for the heartier appetite

- Grated organic Cheddar or Cheddar-style soy cheese melted over thinly sliced apple, avocado, or tomato on open-faced English muffins

2 cups whole-wheat pastry flour

1½ teaspoons baking powder

1 teaspoon baking soda

2 tablespoons ground flaxseeds, optional

1½ cups low-fat yogurt or soy yogurt

1¼ to 1½ cups low-fat milk or rice milk

2 tablespoons nonhydrogenated
   margarine

Pure maple syrup, all-fruit preserves, or
   one Quick Fresh Fruit Sauce (page 8)

Dairy option	Vegan option
Calories: 270	Calories: 266
Total fat: 6 g	Total fat: 6 g
Protein: 13 g	Protein: 8 g
Fiber: 5.9 g	Fiber: 6.5 g
Carbohydrates: 44 g	Carbohydrates: 49 g
Cholesterol: 7 g	Cholesterol: 0 g
Sodium: 485 mg	Sodium: 444 mg

Basic Yogurt Pancakes

This recipe is wonderful as is, or it can be used as a starting point for variations. Buttermilk is the traditional base for pancakes, but for me, this raised several dilemmas: One, even the largest supermarkets were often out of stock, and two, even when I did find it, it was never organic. I discovered that yogurt is an excellent base for pancake batter, producing tender, golden results. Once we went vegan, I found that soy yogurt works just as well.

1   Combine the flour, baking powder, baking soda, and flaxseeds, if using, in a mixing bowl. Make a well in the center and pour in the yogurt and milk. Stir with a whisk until the batter is just smooth; it should have an easy-to-pour consistency, but not too thin. Add more milk as needed. Don't overbeat.

2   Heat a nonstick griddle or a large nonstick skillet that has been lightly coated with some of the margarine. Ladle on the batter to form 3- to 4-inch pancakes. Cook on both sides over medium heat until golden brown. Serve hot with maple syrup.

Variations

Multigrain: Substitute ½ to ¾ cup of the flour with another type of flour such as spelt, kamut, buckwheat, cornmeal, or rye, or use a combination of two different types of flour equaling ½ to ¾ cup.

Fruity pancakes: Add a cup or so of thinly sliced fruits—one kind or a combination—to the batter. Try pears, peaches, nectarines, strawberries, wild blueberries, or other berries.

Cinnamon-apple pancakes: Add 1 heaping cup very thinly sliced, peeled apple (any soft cooking variety such as Cortland, McIntosh, or Golden Delicious) and ground cinnamon to taste to the batter.

Banana-nut: Add 1 medium thinly sliced banana, ¼ to ½ cup finely chopped walnuts or pecans, and a pinch of ground nutmeg to the batter.

Turning Pancakes into Waffles

THE BASIC PANCAKE RECIPE (page 6) makes a good waffle batter if you reduce the amount of milk to 1 cup, or just a bit more if needed. You can use the multigrain variation, but the fruity variations may be too chunky and/or sticky for your waffle iron (waffles are delicious, however, topped with any of the Quick Fresh Fruit Sauces, below). Before cooking the waffles, I like to lightly spray the waffle iron with cooking oil spray (light olive oil spray is a good choice). On weekday mornings, I don't consider it a big job to prepare waffles, if I cut the Basic Yogurt Pancakes recipe in half to yield 4 large Belgian-style waffles.

Quick Fresh Fruit Sauces
for yogurt, pancakes, and waffles

These nifty combinations of finely diced fruit and all-fruit preserves create nearly instant sauces. Each combination makes enough for four to six $\frac{1}{3}$- to $\frac{1}{2}$-cup servings as a topping.

Peach or Nectarine Sauce: Combine 2 cups finely diced peaches or nectarines with 2 to 3 teaspoons all-fruit peach or apricot preserves. Stir together well.

Strawberry or Strawberry-Blueberry Sauce: Combine 1 pint thinly sliced strawberries (or 1 cup each blueberries and sliced strawberries) with 2 to 3 teaspoons strawberry jam. Stir together well.

Pear and Mango: Perfect for winter! Combine 1 cup diced, peeled pear and 1 cup diced mango with 2 to 3 teaspoons peach or apricot all-fruit preserves. Stir together well.

Purely Mango: Combine 2 cups diced mango with 2 to 3 teaspoons mango, peach, or apricot all-fruit preserves. Stir together well.

Muffin Tin Popovers

Classic recipes for popovers often call for popover pans. I don't have any, nor do I know anyone who does, and muffin tins work just fine. The fun of popovers is seeing how they "pop over" the muffin tins as they come out of the oven. They deflate quickly, leaving a moist, eggy treat to be eaten while warm. Before they went vegan, this was one of my sons' favorite weekend breakfast treats.

1 Preheat oven to 450° F. Oil two medium nonstick muffin tins.

2 Beat the eggs well, then whisk in half of the flour and half of the milk. Add the remaining flour and milk and whisk until the batter is very smooth. This may be done in a food processor or blender instead.

3 Whisk or blend in the oil and salt.

4 Divide the batter among 12 oiled, nonstick muffin cups. They should be about three quarters full.

5 Bake for 15 minutes, or until golden and puffed up. Don't open the oven door during this time! Serve immediately with margarine and/or preserves.

DAIRY AND EGGS / NONDAIRY OPTION

Makes 12

4 eggs
1½ cups whole-wheat pastry flour
1¼ cups low-fat milk, rice milk, or soy milk
1½ tablespoons safflower oil
1 teaspoon salt
Nonhydrogenated margarine
All-fruit preserves

Dairy	Nondairy option
Calories: 101	Calories: 104
Total fat: 4 g	Total fat: 4 g
Protein: 5 g	Protein: 4 g
Fiber: 1.8 g	Fiber: 1.8 g
Carbohydrates: 12 g	Carbohydrates: 14 g
Cholesterol: 72 g	Cholesterol: 71 g
Sodium: 212 mg	Sodium: 209 mg

2 ripe bananas, well mashed

1 cup whole-wheat pastry flour

Pinch *each* ground cinnamon and
    ground nutmeg

½ cup dark raisins, optional

1 cup low-fat milk, rice milk, or soy milk

2 tablespoons nonhydrogenated
    margarine

Maple syrup or all-fruit preserves,
    optional

Dairy option	Vegan option
Calories: 176	Calories: 181
Total fat: 5 g	Total fat: 5 g
Protein: 5 g	Protein: 4 g
Fiber: 4 g	Fiber: 4 g
Carbohydrates: 30 g	Carbohydrates: 34 g
Cholesterol: 2 g	Cholesterol: 0 g
Sodium: 62 mg	Sodium: 56 mg

Banana Fritters

This recipe, given to me by a wonderful Jamaican cook, makes a pleasantly offbeat breakfast treat.

1 Combine all the ingredients except the maple syrup in a mixing bowl and stir until just smoothly blended. Add a bit more milk if the mixture is too thick.

2 Heat a nonstick griddle and coat lightly with some of the margarine. Drop the batter onto the griddle in ¼ cupfuls. Cook each fritter over medium heat on both sides until golden brown. Serve hot, either on its own or with maple syrup.

Variation
Add ⅓ to ½ cup chopped walnuts or pecans to the batter.

Here are a few additional ideas for the morning meal:

- Tofu Scrambles Galore (page 140)
- Polenta (page 182)
- Tofu and Potato Hash Browns (page 142)
- Potato and Tempeh Hash (page 181)
- Beyond Brown Rice (pages 234–35)

If you like fresh baked goods in the morning, make any of these in the evening and wake up to a healthy treat:

- Quick breads and muffins (Chapter 10)
- Spoonbread (page 284)
- Fruit Cobblers of All Sorts (page 312)
- Jam Bars (page 302)

Yogurt Biscuits

Once in a while, you may find it fun to make biscuits on a leisurely Sunday morning (though I have been known to get up a little earlier to make these on weekdays). If so inclined, children enjoy rolling out the dough and helping cut the biscuits. Reheat leftover biscuits and serve with soup.

2 cups whole-wheat pastry flour

2 teaspoons baking powder

1 teaspoon baking soda

1 teaspoon salt

½ cup low-fat yogurt or soy yogurt

¼ cup low-fat milk or rice milk

¼ cup safflower oil

All-fruit preserves, apple butter, softened cream cheese, or nonhydrogenated margarine

1 Preheat the oven to 400° F. Lightly oil a baking sheet.

2 Combine the flour, baking powder, baking soda, and salt. In a small bowl, whisk together the yogurt, milk, and oil. Make a well in the center and pour in the wet mixture. Work together to form a firm dough, using floured hands once most of the flour is moistened.

3 Turn the dough out onto a well-floured board. Knead for 1 to 2 minutes, adding a small amount of additional flour if the dough is too sticky.

4 Roll the dough out until ½ inch thick and cut into 2- to 2½-inch circles with a biscuit cutter or drinking glass. Place 1 inch apart on the baking sheet. Bake for 12 to 15 minutes, or until the tops are golden.

5 Serve with desired spread.

Dairy	Vegan option
Calories: 117	Calories: 116
Total fat: 5 g	Total fat: 5 g
Protein: 3 g	Protein: 3 g
Fiber: 2.4 g	Fiber: 2.5 g
Carbohydrates: 16 g	Carbohydrates: 16 g
Cholesterol: 1 g	Cholesterol: 0 g
Sodium: 354 mg	Sodium: 349 mg

YOGURT IS A TERRIFIC ITEM for the morning meal, though certainly welcome any time of day. Made from milk or soy milk fermented with special bacterial cultures (either *Lactobacillus bulgaricus* or *Streptococcus thermophilus*), good-quality yogurts contain these live beneficial cultures. They may thus be more easily digested by some (but not all) people who are lactose sensitive, since the lactose is turned into lactic acid during fermentation. Live cultures help keep intestinal tracts healthy by encouraging the growth of beneficial organisms, while guarding against harmful bacteria. Active cultures have been shown to benefit the digestive and immune systems.

Soy yogurt is a good dairy-free substitute for this healthful food; most brands contain active cultures and are combined with some of the same fruits and flavors that make dairy yogurt so appealing. Both low-fat dairy yogurt and soy yogurt are excellent sources of high-quality protein and calcium.

When buying flavored yogurts, avoid those containing gums, gelatins, and artificial flavorings and colorings. Even some "natural" brands may be high in sugar or high-fructose corn syrup, so stick with organic plain yogurt (or vanilla organic, which is less cloyingly sweet than national brands) and embellish it yourself with fruit butters, unsweetened crushed pineapple, frozen fruit juice concentrate, all-fruit preserves, mashed bananas, or chopped dried fruit. See Your Own All-Organic Fruity Yogurt (page 268) for more ideas.

Buy yogurt well before the date stamped on the container. Yogurts keep from 2 to 3 weeks if unopened and refrigerated. Sweetened yogurts last longest, since the sugar acts as a preservative. Once opened, yogurt is best used within a week. Yogurt whose freshness is waning can be used in baking. Yogurt with a sharp, fermented odor is spoiled and should not be used.

There are numerous ways to use and enjoy organic dairy or soy yogurt: in pancakes (page 6) and smoothies (page 18); as a snack; as a fat substitute in baking (see Chapter 10); as a substitute for sour cream; and in salad dressings and dips.

Yogurt: A Versatile and Healthful Staple

4 cups rolled oats (or oatmeal for a finer
  consistency)
1 cup wheat germ or oat bran (or ½ cup
  of each)
¼ cup untoasted sesame or sunflower
  seeds
½ cup slivered or sliced raw almonds
⅓ cup honey or maple syrup
2 tablespoons safflower oil
1 cup raisins, currants, or other chopped
  dried fruit of your choice

Per ¾-cup serving
Calories: 359
Total fat: 15 g
Protein: 13 g
Fiber: 7.8 g
Carbohydrates: 48 g
Cholesterol: 0 g
Sodium: 5 mg

Classic Crunchy Granola

To my mind, store-bought granola is a pale imitation of the homemade version. This and the following granola recipes take minutes to mix, bake just a short time, and taste fresher than those bought in bulk or in boxes. If you'd like, add ¼ cup of ground flaxseed to give an added healthful boost to this or any of the granola recipes that follow.

1 Preheat the oven to 275° F. Lightly oil one or two baking sheets.

2 Combine oats, wheat germ, sesame seeds, and almonds in a large mixing bowl.

3 Combine the honey with the oil in a small container. Drizzle into the oat mixture, stirring constantly; mix thoroughly until evenly coated.

4 Spread on the baking sheets. Bake, stirring every 10 minutes or so, for 20 to 30 minutes, or until golden.

5 Allow the granola to cool on the baking sheets, then stir in the raisins. When completely cool, transfer to jars and store at room temperature. Keeps 1 to 2 months in a cool, dry place.

Cinnamon-Apple Granola

1 Preheat the oven to 275° F. Lightly oil one or two baking sheets.

2 Combine oats, wheat germ, cinnamon, nutmeg, and walnuts, if using, in a large mixing bowl.

3 Combine the honey with the oil in a small container. Drizzle into the oat mixture, stirring constantly; mix thoroughly until evenly coated.

4 Spread on the baking sheets. Bake, stirring every 10 minutes or so, for 20 to 30 minutes, or until golden.

5 Allow the granola to cool on the baking sheets, then stir in the dried fruit. When completely cool, transfer to jars and store at room temperature. Keeps 1 to 2 months in a cool, dry place.

HONEY / VEGAN OPTION

Makes about 6 cups

4 cups rolled oats (or oatmeal for a finer consistency)
1 cup wheat germ or oat bran (or ½ cup of each)
1 teaspoon ground cinnamon, or to taste
Dash of ground nutmeg
½ cup finely chopped walnuts, optional
½ cup honey or maple syrup
2 tablespoons safflower oil
1 cup finely chopped dried apples
½ cup raisins, optional

Per ¾-cup serving
Calories: 328
Total fat: 7 g
Protein: 10 g
Fiber: 7.2 g
Carbohydrates: 59 g
Cholesterol: 0 g
Sodium: 13 mg

HONEY / VEGAN OPTION

Makes about 6 cups

4 cups rolled oats (or oatmeal for a finer consistency)
1 cup wheat germ or oat bran (or ½ cup of each)
¼ cup untoasted sesame seeds
⅓ cup honey or maple syrup
2 tablespoons safflower oil
½ cup chopped pecans
1 cup dried cranberries

Per ¾-cup serving
Calories: 362
Total fat: 14 g
Protein: 11 g
Fiber: 8.3 g
Carbohydrates: 51 g
Cholesterol: 0 g
Sodium: 5 mg

Cranberry-Pecan Granola

1 Preheat the oven to 275° F. Lightly oil one or two baking sheets.

2 Combine oats, wheat germ, and sesame seeds in a large mixing bowl.

3 Combine the honey with the oil in a small container. Drizzle into the oat mixture, stirring constantly; mix thoroughly until evenly coated.

4 Spread on the baking sheets. Bake, stirring every 10 minutes or so, for 20 to 30 minutes, or until golden.

5 Allow the granola to cool on the baking sheets, then stir in the dried cranberries. When completely cool, transfer to jars and store at room temperature. Keeps 1 to 2 months in a cool, dry place.

THOUGH CREAM OF WHEAT and oatmeal are fine choices as hot cereals, there is a world of grains to explore for breakfast, from tiny whole grains to cracked, rolled, and ground grains. Explore the hot cereal section of most any natural foods store and see what appeals to you. If these grains are new to you, buy them in packaged form so you can follow specific instructions for cooking. Once you are familiar with them, you have the option of purchasing them in bulk for greater economy. Here are some of the products you may enjoy exploring:

Rolled grains: This type of grain product is made from whole grains that have been steamed, then flattened with steel rollers. Rolled grains include barley, rye, rice, kamut, and spelt. In my opinion (and in my younger son's) the latter two are particularly tasty.

Whole grains: Here's where you can get somewhat adventurous in the morning, with nutritious cooked ancient grains: quinoa, millet, amaranth, and teff. You will more likely find these shelved with whole-grain products rather than with the hot cereals.

Cracked grains: Many (but not all) cracked grains have been presteamed, so they cook fairly quickly. Try bulgur (wheat) and couscous (semolina wheat). Other grains available in cracked form are rye and barley.

Cornmeal and corn grits: Cooked cornmeal is often referred to as polenta, from the Italian tradition, but cooked cornmeal also has a long and illustrious background in American cuisine, in which it is referred to as cornmeal mush. Grits, or hominy grits, are a traditional breakfast staple of the American South. You can find grits in most any supermarket, but I prefer stoneground grits (available in natural foods stores); they're more flavorful and robust.

Oats: Many forms of cooked oats can grace the breakfast table. Rolled oats and oatmeal are perhaps the most common; oatmeal is simply a finely ground form of rolled oats; it cooks even more quickly than the relatively quick-cooking rolled oats. Oat bran is the outer covering of the whole-oat groat. It has been recognized by some nutritionists as a rich form of soluble fiber and a possible aid in reducing overall serum cholesterol levels. Steel-cut oats, sometimes called Scottish or Irish oatmeal, are sliced whole-oat groats; they make for a hearty, gritty cereal.

"Cream of" cereals: In this category we find farina, or cream of wheat, and cream of rice. These are generally made from refined grains; sometimes vitamins and iron are added back in. Their smooth, light textures make them especially appealing to youngsters. If heartier hot cereals may not appeal to your young children, "cream of" cereals may help get them into the hot cereal habit. Stir in a little wheat germ for extra flavor and nutrition, and gradually mix with a portion of heartier hot cereals. Look for organic versions in natural foods stores.

For more ideas, see Beyond Brown Rice, pages 234–35.

Embellishments for hot cereals:

Low-fat milk, rice milk, or soy milk: Once the cereal is cooked, you can add a little milk or nondairy milk to the saucepan and cook until it is absorbed to give the grain a creamier texture.

Liquid sweeteners: Honey, maple syrup, rice syrup, or barley malt can be used for sweetening.

Dried fruits: Dark or golden raisins, cranberries, cherries, and currants; chopped apricots, dates, and Turkish figs; and diced dried tropical fruits are all worth a try mixed into hot cereals.

Nuts and seeds: Toasted slivered or sliced almonds, chopped walnuts or pecans, and sesame and sunflower seeds are all good for sprinkling on hot cereals.

Wheat germ and ground flaxseeds: Both of these provide concentrated nutrition. Wheat germ is an excellent source of vitamin E and the B vitamins; ground flaxseed is the best plant source of valuable omega-3 fatty acids.

Spices: Ground cinnamon gives a lively flavor boost to sweetened hot cereals; ground nutmeg works, too, in small doses. Organic sweetened cocoa mix is a favorite topping of my husband's; maybe some of your family members would enjoy the same.

Margarine and/or cheeses: Some people like their hot cereals with a sweet theme; my sons and I have always been the margarine and/or cheese types. Any hot cooked cereal we have for breakfast we flavor with a small amount of nonhydrogenated margarine and salt. If you are going for a sweeter effect, you can, of course, also melt a bit of nonhydrogenated margarine into the hot cereal for added richness.

My sons have always liked a small amount of cheese melted into hot cereal. They now use a small amount of rice cheese for extra flavor and body. A little chunk or even just a sprinkling of any grated or crumbled organic cheese or nondairy cheese goes a long way.

Start Your Day with Smoothies

FRESH FRUIT STRIKES ME as a great food to start the day with, whether cut up in some way or liquified. Personally, I prefer my fruit liquified in the morning; smoothies are at once soothing and invigorating, luscious yet low in fat. They also offer a concentrated source of nourishment for children and teens (and indeed anyone) whose morning appetite is sluggish.

Smoothies are especially easy to make and clean up after, using an immersion blender (see page xxvii). Use the following recipes as a starting point for creating combinations of your own. Here's a basic formula: 2 cups coarsely chopped fruit; 1 cup low-fat yogurt, soy yogurt, or crumbled silken tofu; and 1 to 1½ cups liquid (fruit juice, vanilla soy milk, or rice milk). Bananas appear in many of these smoothies—they add substance and sweetness.

Sunshine Smoothie

The cheerful color and sprightly flavor of this smoothie gives the morning meal a welcome boost.

Combine all the ingredients in a food processor or blender and process until smoothly puréed. Or place in a container and process with an immersion blender. Serve at once in tall glasses.

2 ripe bananas, broken into several pieces
1 cup pineapple juice
½ cup orange juice, preferably freshly squeezed
1 cup lemon or orange low-fat yogurt or soy yogurt

Dairy	Vegan option
Calories: 281	Calories: 215
Total fat: 2 g	Total fat: 1 g
Protein: 6 g	Protein: 4 g
Fiber: 3 g	Fiber: 3.5 g
Carbohydrates: 63 g	Carbohydrates: 50 g
Cholesterol: 7 g	Cholesterol: 0 g
Sodium: 85 mg	Sodium: 39 mg

Carrot-Orange Mango Smoothie

DAIRY / VEGAN OPTION

2 servings

Get a healthy dose of vitamin C first thing in the morning in a concoction that tastes like an intensely delicious Creamsicle.

1 to 1½ cups carrot-orange juice

1 ripe mango, peeled and coarsely chopped

1 cup mango, peach, or apricot low-fat yogurt or soy yogurt

Combine all the ingredients in a food processor or blender and process until smoothly puréed. Or place in a container and process with an immersion blender. Serve at once in tall glasses.

Dairy

Calories: 241

Total fat: 2 g

Protein: 6 g

Fiber: 3.1 g

Carbohydrates: 53 g

Cholesterol: 7 g

Sodium: 93 mg

Vegan option

Calories: 176

Total fat: 1 g

Protein: 4 g

Fiber: 4.1 g

Carbohydrates: 40 g

Cholesterol: 0 g

Sodium: 73 mg

Banana-Blueberry Smoothie

DAIRY / VEGAN OPTION

2 to 3 servings

Blueberries are one of the most antioxidant-rich fruits available, making this a supercharged way to start your day.

Combine all the ingredients in a food processor or blender and process until smoothly puréed. Or place in a container and process with an immersion blender. Serve at once in tall glasses.

1 medium banana, broken into several pieces
1 cup blueberries
1 tablespoon maple syrup or brown rice syrup
1 cup vanilla low-fat yogurt or soy yogurt or crumbled silken tofu
1 cup white or red grape juice

Dairy	Vegan option
Calories: 258	Calories: 213
Total fat: 2 g	Total fat: 2 g
Protein: 5 g	Protein: 3 g
Fiber: 2.8 g	Fiber: 3.5 g
Carbohydrates: 58 g	Carbohydrates: 50 g
Cholesterol: 8 g	Cholesterol: 0 g
Sodium: 70 mg	Sodium: 42 mg

Cinnamon Apple or Pear Smoothie

DAIRY / VEGAN OPTION

2 to 3 servings

Here's a blended drink for fall or winter. It's a delightful change-of-pace fruit beverage to make when summer fruit is out of season.

1 ripe banana, broken into several pieces

2 medium soft apples (such as Cortland or Golden Delicious) or ripe pears, peeled, cored, and coarsely diced

1 cup vanilla low-fat yogurt or soy yogurt

1 cup apple juice or apple cider

¼ teaspoon ground cinnamon

Combine all the ingredients in a food processor or blender and process until smoothly puréed. Or place in a container and process with an immersion blender. Serve at once in tall glasses.

Dairy

Calories: 252

Total fat: 2 g

Protein: 5 g

Fiber: 4.3 g

Carbohydrates: 57 g

Cholesterol: 8 g

Sodium: 60 mg

Vegan option

Calories: 207

Total fat: 2 g

Protein: 3 g

Fiber: 5 g

Carbohydrates: 49 g

Cholesterol: 0 g

Sodium: 32 mg

Nutty Chocolate-Banana Smoothie

This easy, filling breakfast shake is one of our favorite winter smoothies.

Combine all the ingredients in a food processor or blender and process until smoothly puréed. Or place in a container and process with an immersion blender. Serve at once in tall glasses.

VEGAN

2 servings

1 large banana, broken into several pieces
1½ cups chocolate soy milk
1 heaping tablespoon peanut butter or cashew butter

Calories: 200
Total fat: 7 g
Protein: 8 g
Fiber: 4.3 g
Carbohydrates: 29 g
Cholesterol: 0 g
Sodium: 57 mg

CHAPTER TWO

Soothing Soups and Savory Stews

DOESN'T EVERYONE FEEL nourished and comforted by soup? I doubt there is anyone who doesn't enjoy revisiting favorite childhood soups (or at least a healthier facsimile). Make sure to create cozy memories for your children by serving a repertoire of savory soups all year round.

There are lots of ways to make soups tempting to kids, including the addition of noodles or croutons and blending soups into velvety purées. As young taste buds develop, soups also provide an introduction to a variety of vegetables, grains, and beans. Finally, thick stews can be a most inviting entrée for families with older kids and teens with heartier appetites.

Soups can serve as a light beginning to family meals, but more often they can be the centerpiece, especially when chock-full of nourishing ingredients. This chapter starts with a half dozen or so simple "nursery" soups, moves on to those that offer more complex flavors, and ends with a number of stick-to-the-ribs stews. Within this range you'll find soups that can be ready in minutes, as well as longer-simmering concoctions that will fill your kitchen with enticing aromas.

• Add salt toward the end of the cooking to give the other flavors a chance to develop and thus avoid oversalting. Salt a little at a time, stir in thoroughly, and taste frequently.

• Those who need to limit their intake of salt might try adding lemon juice and/or a salt-free all-purpose seasoning (see page xxvi) for added zest.

• When appropriate, a small amount of dry wine adds nice depth of flavor. About ¼ cup is sufficient in a large pot of soup. Add it when adding the bulk of the soup's liquid.

• Most important, use the amount of seasoning given in any soup recipe as only a guide. Adjust to suit your taste.

• When the craving for soup runs high but time is short, have a few cans of vegetable stock (preferably reduced sodium), good-quality bouillon cubes, and natural soup bases on hand. Even one 15-ounce can used in a decent-size pot of soup can lend a deeper flavor. Natural foods stores offer other interesting options such as Imagine Garden Vegetable Broth in 32-ounce containers and a vegetable broth powder by the makers of Veg-It seasoning, which comes complete with B complex and nutritional yeast. Another that I like is Vogue Instant Vege Base, a powdered natural seasoning mixture that you can add generously to soups.

• Watch out for supermarket brands of bouillon cubes. Some contain MSG, partially hydrogenated fats, and other questionable ingredients. Stick with natural brands.

Cream of Broccoli Soup

A longtime favorite in our family of broccoli enthusiasts, this soup gets a thick, creamy base from puréed white beans or tofu. The addition of green peas at the end of the cooking time brightens the color and heightens the flavor of the soup.

1 Heat the oil in a soup pot and add the onion. Sauté over medium heat until golden, 5 to 7 minutes.

2 Add the broccoli, bouillon cube, and 4 cups water. Bring to a simmer, then cover and simmer gently until the broccoli is tender but not overcooked, 8 to 10 minutes.

3 Transfer the mixture to a food processor. Purée until smooth, then return to the pot. Purée the beans and add to the pot. Then purée 1 cup of the peas and add. (If using an immersion bender, simply add the beans and peas to the pot; insert the bender and purée until smooth.)

4 Add enough milk to give the soup a medium-thick consistency. Stir in the remaining peas and the dill. Season with salt and pepper. Cook over very low heat for 5 minutes, then serve.

MAKE IT A MEAL: This soup is terrific with Crispy Croutons (page 59). It makes a nice introduction to simple pasta, grain, or potato main dishes. For a soup-and-salad meal, try it with Taco Salad (page 76) and corn on the cob. For soup-and-sandwich dinner ideas, see Supper Sandwiches and Super Wraps (page 238.)

1½ tablespoons light olive oil

1 medium-large onion, coarsely chopped

2 large or 3 medium broccoli crowns, coarsely chopped

1 vegetable bouillon cube

One 16-ounce can Great Northern beans or cannellini, drained and rinsed, or one 16-ounce tub soft tofu, crumbled

2 cups frozen green peas, thawed

1 cup low-fat milk, rice milk, or soy milk

½ teaspoon dried dill, or 1 tablespoon minced fresh

Salt and freshly ground pepper to taste

Dairy	Vegan option
Calories: 181	Calories: 181
Total fat: 5 g	Total fat: 5 g
Protein: 9 g	Protein: 8 g
Fiber: 7.4 g	Fiber: 7.4 g
Carbohydrates: 27 g	Carbohydrates: 28 g
Cholesterol: 2 g	Cholesterol: 0 g
Sodium: 106 mg	Sodium: 94 mg

Alphabet Vegetable Soup

This tasty soup—a healthier version of the canned type you may have eaten as a child—can be started about 30 minutes before you want to serve it.

1 tablespoon light olive oil

2 medium carrots, peeled and cut into small dice

2 medium potatoes, any variety, peeled and cut into small dice

½ cup alphabet noodles

1 vegetable bouillon cube

¼ teaspoon paprika

¼ teaspoon dried dill, or 1 teaspoon minced fresh

1 cup frozen green peas, thawed

1 cup diced ripe tomato or canned diced tomatoes (about half of one 16-ounce can—see Notes)

1 Heat the oil in a medium saucepan. Add the carrots and sauté for 5 minutes over medium heat.

2 Add the potatoes, noodles, bouillon cube, paprika, dill, and 4 cups of water. Bring to a simmer, then cover and simmer gently until the carrots and potatoes are tender, 15 to 20 minutes.

3 Add the peas and tomatoes and simmer for another 5 minutes. Add a little more water if the broth seems crowded and cook just until heated through.

Notes

- If you like a more tomatoey soup, use the entire can of diced tomatoes, or 2 cups diced fresh tomatoes.
- If you have leftovers, you'll find that much of the broth will be absorbed by the noodles. Add water as needed, then add more paprika and/or dill, if needed. Add salt, if desired.
- Is anyone too old for alphabet noodles? I hope not! But if you prefer, substitute tiny pasta rings, pasta stars, or orzo for the alphabets.

MAKE IT A MEAL: For a perfect nursery meal for younger children, serve this with Grilled Cheese Strips (page 59). This soup is also good with Pita Cheese Calzones (page 246). In either case, pass a platter of raw veggies with Easy Dill Dip (page 256).

Calories: 137

Total fat: 3 g

Protein: 4 g

Fiber: 4 g

Carbohydrates: 24 g

Cholesterol: 0 g

Sodium: 76 mg

Creamy Corn Chowder

DAIRY / VEGAN OPTION

6 to 8 servings

Puréed silken tofu is a superb base for creamy soups like this chowder. It provides substance and a silky texture. The mild, familiar flavors will entice kids of all ages to enjoy a soothing bowl of soup.

1   Heat the oil in a soup pot. Add the onion and celery and sauté over medium heat until golden. Add the carrots and potatoes with just enough water to cover.

2   Stir in the cumin, bay leaves, and bouillon cubes. Bring to a simmer, then cover and simmer gently until the vegetables are tender, 25 to 30 minutes.

3   Stir in the corn kernels and puréed tofu. If needed, add a small amount of low-fat milk to thin the consistency, but let the base of the soup remain fairly thick. Season with salt and pepper and simmer for another 10 minutes over very low heat. Don't let it boil.

4   If time allows, let the soup stand off the heat for 1 hour or so before serving, then heat through as needed. Remove the bay leaves before serving.

EMBELLISH IT: When craving something simple and comforting, both adults and children will be pleased by this soup. But for those who like to spice things up, the soup's delicious with good-quality curry powder and/or minced fresh ginger added to taste. Another option is to top each adult serving with a generous handful of fresh herbs—minced fresh parsley, dill, or cilantro, or a combination.

MAKE IT A MEAL: For an easy meal, serve with veggie burgers or bean burgers (Chapter 6) on whole-grain buns or English muffins and a simple green salad or coleslaw (see page 68). This is also delightful paired with Mediterranean Salad-Stuffed Bread (page 249).

1$\frac{1}{2}$ tablespoons light olive oil

1 medium onion, finely chopped

1 large celery stalk, diced

2 medium carrots, peeled and thinly sliced

2 medium-large potatoes, any variety, peeled and finely diced

$\frac{1}{2}$ teaspoon ground cumin

2 bay leaves

2 vegetable bouillon cubes

3 cups cooked fresh corn kernels (from about 3 medium ears) or frozen corn kernels, thawed

One 12.3-ounce package silken tofu, puréed until smooth

Low-fat milk, soy milk, or rice milk, as needed

Salt and freshly ground pepper to taste

Calories: 166

Total fat: 4 g

Protein: 6 g

Fiber: 3.8 g

Carbohydrates: 28 g

Cholesterol: 0 g

Sodium: 105 mg

6 servings

2 tablespoons light olive oil

1 cup chopped onion

Two 16-ounce bags baby carrots

1 vegetable bouillon cube

2 bay leaves

1 teaspoon paprika

½ teaspoon good-quality curry powder

1½ cups low-fat milk, rice milk, or soy milk

Salt and freshly ground pepper to taste

1½ cups frozen green peas, warmed

Dairy	Vegan option
Calories: 170	Calories: 179
Total fat: 6 g	Total fat: 6 g
Protein: 6 g	Protein: 4 g
Fiber: 6.9 g	Fiber: 6.9 g
Carbohydrates: 26 g	Carbohydrates: 30 g
Cholesterol: 2 g	Cholesterol: 0 g
Sodium: 135 mg	Sodium: 125 mg

Cream of Baby Carrot Soup

No matter what your age, a vegetable purée is a concentrated source of nourishment and a prime form of comfort. Let's face it, though—peeling and chopping 2 pounds of carrots is a lot of work. I was pleased with the brainstorm of tossing two bags of organic baby carrots (which are usually very sweet) into a soup pot and even more pleased with how well the idea works. Make sure to use the carrots while still fresh; once they start drying out, the results aren't as good. Using an immersion blender makes the preparation a breeze.

1 Heat the oil in a soup pot. Add the onion and sauté over medium heat, stirring frequently, until golden, about 10 minutes.

2 Add the carrots and just enough water to not quite cover. Bring to a simmer, then add the bouillon cube, bay leaves, paprika, and curry powder. Cover and simmer gently until the carrots are tender, 15 to 20 minutes.

3 Remove the bay leaves. If using a food processor, purée the solid ingredients until smoothly puréed, then return to the pot, and stir into the liquid. If using an immersion blender, simply immerse into the pot and process until smoothly puréed.

4 Stir in enough milk to give the soup a slightly thick consistency. Season with salt and pepper and serve, or cover and let stand off the heat for 1 hour or so before serving, then heat through. Scatter some green peas over the top of each serving.

MAKE IT A MEAL: A versatile meal opener, this soup makes a good introduction to many types of meals, including pastas, grain and bean dishes, and casseroles. For a child-friendly meal that adults can enjoy as well, try this with a macaroni and cheese (Chapter 4) or Pasta with Enlightened Alfredo Sauce (page 124) and a generous portion of steamed broccoli.

Chinese Vegetable and Tofu Soup

This quick and colorful soup will please kids and teens who enjoy Asian flavors. Just toss everything into a soup pot and in a few moments, it's ready to eat.

1 Combine 5 cups of water with the bouillon cubes, baby corn, bell pepper, snow peas, and tofu in a large saucepan or small soup pot. Bring to a gentle simmer, then cover and simmer for 5 minutes.

2 Meanwhile, if using spinach, rinse it well, remove the stems, and chop coarsely. If using lettuce, cut into narrow shreds. Add the greens to the soup and simmer just until wilted, about 2 minutes. Season with pepper and serve at once.

MAKE IT A MEAL: Serve with Vegetable Lo Mein (page 104) or Vegetable Chow Mein (page 105). Round out the meal with streamed broccoli or, with just a little extra effort, Stir-Fried Broccoli (page 209). Another fun meal is to pair the soup with low-fat spring rolls, which can be purchased in natural foods stores, along with Stir-Fried Rice with Baby Corn and Peas (page 231) and some cherry tomatoes and bell pepper strips.

VEGAN

4 to 6 servings

2 vegetable bouillon cubes

One 15-ounce can cut baby corn, with liquid

½ medium red bell pepper, cut into short narrow strips

1 cup snow peas, cut in half

4 ounces soft tofu, sliced, well blotted, and cut into small dice

A good handful of fresh spinach or dark green lettuce leaves, shredded

Freshly ground pepper to taste

Calories: 53

Total fat: 1 g

Protein: 4 g

Fiber: 2.8 g

Carbohydrates: 6 g

Cholesterol: 0 g

Sodium: 135 mg

Simple Ramen Noodle Soup

VEGAN

4 to 6 servings

Brimming with curly noodles, this easy soup has long been one of my sons' favorites.

Two 15-ounce cans vegetable broth (preferably low-sodium) plus 1 cup water, or 5 cups water with 2 vegetable bouillon cubes
One 4-ounce package curly ramen noodles, broken up (see Note)
1 or 2 scallions, green part only, thinly sliced
1 cup sliced small white or brown mushrooms, optional
1 cup frozen green peas, thawed

Calories: 43
Total fat: 0 g
Protein: 2 g
Fiber: 1.7 g
Carbohydrates: 7 g
Cholesterol: 0 g
Sodium: 131 mg

1 Bring the broth and water to a simmer in a large saucepan. Add the noodles and cook until you can separate the strands with a fork, 1 or 2 minutes.

2 Add the scallions and mushrooms, if using, and cook until tender, 5 to 7 minutes. If you'd like to make the strands of noodles even shorter, use a pair of kitchen shears and cut the noodles here and there while still in the saucepan.

3 Add the peas. Simmer just until they're cooked through, then serve.

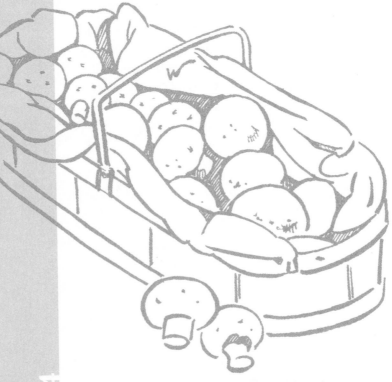

Note

Look for packages of plain curly ramen noodles (not noodle soup) in the Asian foods section of well-stocked supermarkets or natural foods stores.

MAKE IT A MEAL: This makes a nice introduction to hearty Asian tofu or seitan dishes. Try it with Tofu and Mixed Veggie Stir-Fry (page 149), Triple Jade Stir-Fry with Tofu or Seitan (page 150), or Seitan and Broccoli Stir-Fry (page 161).

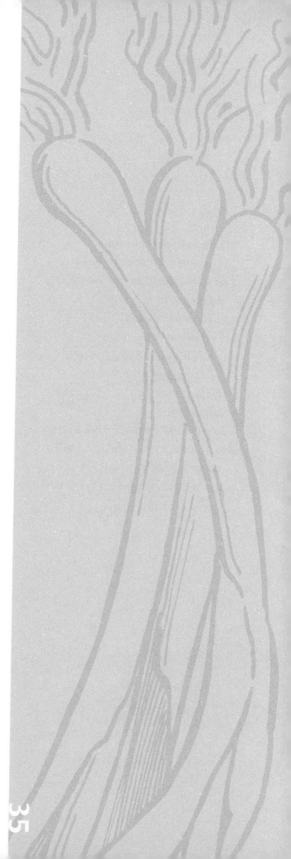

Mock Chicken Noodle Soup

VEGAN

6 servings

This simple, tasty soup might recall a childhood comfort food. Use a mild variety of baked tofu. My favorites for this soup is Soy Boy Tofu Lin and teriyaki-flavor White Wave baked tofu.

1 tablespoon light olive oil

2 large celery stalks, finely diced

3 medium carrots, peeled and thinly sliced

1 small onion, minced

2 vegetable bouillon cubes

1 teaspoon salt-free all-purpose seasoning (see page xxvi)

½ teaspoon dried dill or 1 tablespoon minced fresh

6 ounces small pasta rings (see Notes)

4 to 5 ounces baked tofu (about half a package), finely diced

Salt and freshly ground pepper to taste

1 Heat the oil slowly with 2 tablespoons of water in a large soup pot. Add the celery, carrots, and onion. Sauté over medium heat until the vegetables begin to soften, about 10 minutes.

2 Add 8 cups of water, the bouillon cubes, seasoning mix, and dill. Bring to a simmer, then cover and simmer gently until the vegetables are tender, about 15 minutes.

3 Raise the heat and bring to a rapid simmer. Add the pasta and simmer steadily until al dente, 5 to 8 minutes. Add the tofu, then season with salt and pepper and serve.

Calories: 140

Total fat: 5 g

Protein: 9 g

Fiber: 2.8 g

Carbohydrates: 18 g

Cholesterol: 0 g

Sodium: 238 mg

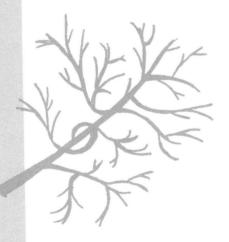

Notes

- If you can't find pasta rings, sometimes called anellini, use short, fine yolk-free egg noodles or tubetti (tiny pasta tubes).
- As the soup stands, the noodles quickly absorb the liquid. If there is leftover soup, add a cup or so of additional water before storing and adjust the seasonings. That way the soup can develop more flavor as it stands.

MAKE IT A MEAL: This soup goes well with vegetable main dishes. For a hearty cold-weather meal, pair it with a Vegetable Upside-Down Casserole (page 165) or, as a first course, with Veggie Pot Pie (page 177) or Shepherd's Pie (page 172). Complete any of these meals with a simple green salad or a Cold Vegetable Platter (page 84). Another option is to serve this as part of a soup-and-sandwich meal. See ideas for Supper Sandwiches and Super Wraps (pages 238–39).

6 servings

2 large or 3 medium sweet potatoes

4 medium-large white potatoes, preferably russet

2 to 3 cups low-fat milk, rice milk, or soy milk

1½ cups grated Cheddar cheese or Cheddar-style nondairy cheese

½ teaspoon seasoned salt

½ teaspoon dry mustard

Pinch of ground nutmeg

1 cup frozen green peas, thawed

Dairy	Vegan option
Calories: 333	Calories: 301
Total fat: 11 g	Total fat: 6 g
Protein: 15 g	Protein: 11 g
Fiber: 5 g	Fiber: 5 g
Carbohydrates: 45 g	Carbohydrates: 53 g
Cholesterol: 34 g	Cholesterol: 0 g
Sodium: 416 mg	Sodium: 477 mg

Cheesy Sweet and White Potato Soup

This soothing soup is made easy by microwaving the potatoes ahead of time. It's delicious served with Crispy Croutons (page 59).

1 Microwave the sweet potatoes and white potatoes separately on high until easily pierced with a knife. Allow 4 minutes per sweet potato and test; add another minute each until done. Allow 2 minutes per white potato; add another minute each until done.

2 When the potatoes are cool enough to handle, slip the peels off and cut into large chunks.

3 Purée the potatoes in the food processor in two batches, adding 1 cup of water to each batch, until smooth and transfer to a soup pot. Or place the potatos in a soup pot with 2 cups water. Insert an immersion blender into the pot and process until smooth.

4 Bring the mixture to a simmer. Add enough milk to make a fluid but fairly thick consistency. Add the cheese, salt, mustard, and nutmeg. Cover and simmer gently for 10 minutes. Let stand for 1 to 2 hours before serving, or serve at once. Top each serving with a sprinkling of green peas.

EMBELLISH IT: Sautéed chopped leeks make a great garnish. Pass around in a small bowl to top individual portions.

MAKE IT A MEAL: This filling soup is a good choice for a soup-and-salad meal. Pair it with Taco Salad (page 76), Green Salad with Avocado, Apples, and Baked Tofu (page 75), or Hearty Seitan Salad (page 83). For the latter two options, you can serve the salads in wraps.

Sweet Potato and Silken Tofu Bisque

DAIRY / VEGAN OPTION

6 or more servings

A velvety, golden-orange soup with two nutritious secrets (tofu and tomatoes), this is delicious topped with Crispy Croutons (page 59) or the topping suggested in "Embellish it."

1 Heat the oil in a soup pot. Add the onion and sauté over medium-low heat until golden.

2 Add the sweet potatoes, carrots, and enough broth to just cover the vegetables. Bring to a simmer, then stir in the tomatoes, bay leaves, and seasonings. Cover and simmer gently until the vegetables are tender, 20 to 25 minutes. Remove from the heat and discard the bay leaves.

3 If using an immersion blender, add the tofu, broken into a few chunks, and blend the mixture in the pot until velvety smooth. If using a food processor, process the solid ingredients in batches; add about ½ cup of the cooking liquid to each batch and add the tofu to one of the batches. Process until smooth and return to the pot.

4 Add enough milk to achieve a slightly thick consistency. Season with salt and pepper, then heat to a simmer over very low heat for 10 minutes longer.

5 Serve at once, or let stand off the heat for 1 or 2 hours before serving, then heat through as needed.

EMBELLISH IT: Sautéed corn kernels, minced fresh parsley, and pumpkin seeds make a topping that will delight the eye and palate.

MAKE IT A MEAL: Serve with Tomatoes with Black Beans or Chickpeas (page 79) and Batter-Dipped Vegetable Fritters (page 224); this meal is especially good with the batter-dipped cauliflower.

2 tablespoons light olive oil

1 large red onion, chopped

2 large or 3 medium sweet potatoes, peeled and diced

2 large carrots, peeled and sliced

Prepared vegetable broth, or water as needed

One 16-ounce can diced tomatoes

2 bay leaves

½ teaspoon salt-free all-purpose seasoning (see page xxvi)

¼ teaspoon ground cinnamon

¼ teaspoon dried basil

One 12.3-ounce package silken tofu

1 cup low-fat milk, rice milk, or soy milk

Salt and freshly ground pepper to taste

Dairy	Vegan option
Calories: 191	Calories: 196
Total fat: 7 g	Total fat: 7 g
Protein: 8 g	Protein: 6 g
Fiber: 4.3 g	Fiber: 4.6 g
Carbohydrates: 26 g	Carbohydrates: 29 g
Cholesterol: 2 g	Cholesterol: 0 g
Sodium: 179 mg	Sodium: 173 mg

VEGAN

6 or more servings

2 tablespoons light olive oil

1 medium onion, chopped

2 medium carrots, peeled and diced

**1 medium-small zucchini, quartered
lengthwise and sliced**

One 28-ounce can crushed tomatoes

**1½ teaspoons salt-free all-purpose
seasoning (see page xxvi)**

**⅔ cup small pasta such as tiny shells or
ditalini (see Note)**

**1 cup canned chickpeas, drained and
rinsed**

1 cup frozen green peas

2 tablespoons minced fresh parsley

Salt and freshly ground pepper to taste

Calories: 232

Total fat: 6 g

Protein: 7 g

Fiber: 8.3 g

Carbohydrates: 38 g

Cholesterol: 0 g

Sodium: 244 mg

Streamlined Minestrone

This simplified version of a favorite Italian soup is a good choice for families with kids who love lots of veggies. The next logical step forward from Alphabet Vegetable Soup (page 30) for budding palates, this soup keeps well and develops flavor as it stands.

1 Heat the oil in a large soup pot. Add the onion and carrots and sauté over medium-low heat until golden.

2 Add the zucchini, tomatoes, seasoning, and 4 cups of water. Bring to a simmer, then cover and simmer very gently until the vegetables are tender but not overdone, about 30 minutes.

3 Meanwhile, cook the pasta in a separate saucepan until al dente; drain.

4 When the vegetables are done, stir the cooked pasta and the chickpeas, peas, and parsley into the soup. Adjust the consistency with more water if necessary, then season with salt and pepper. Simmer over very low heat for another 5 to 10 minutes, then serve.

Note
If you will be serving this soup as a first course with a pasta meal, omit the pasta.

MAKE IT A MEAL: This soup is a meal in itself when served with a whole-grain bread and a salad. Omitting the pasta, this is a nice introduction to a light pasta dish like Angel Hair with Zucchini and Bread Crumbs (page 122) or Pasta with Enlightened Alfredo Sauce (page 124). For either pasta option, serve with steamed broccoli or green beans and diced ripe tomatoes.

Tomato-Tortellini Soup

Tortellini adds immediate appeal to an otherwise basic soup.

DAIRY / VEGAN OPTION

6 servings

1 Heat the oil in a soup pot. Add the carrots and sauté over medium heat for 5 minutes. Add the garlic and sauté until the carrots are golden, another 3 minutes or so.

2 Add the tomato sauce, tomatoes, zucchini, oregano, dill, and 3 cups of water. Bring to a simmer, then cover and simmer gently until the vegetables are tender, about 15 minutes.

3 Meanwhile, cook the tortellini in a separate saucepan, according to the package directions.

4 Stir the cooked tortellini into the soup and season with salt and pepper. Simmer gently for 2 to 3 minutes longer. Adjust the consistency with more water if necessary. Serve, passing the Parmesan for sprinkling on the soup.

MAKE IT A MEAL: A good main-dish soup, this meal can be completed with fresh bread and a colorful salad such as Mixed Greens with Green Beans, Beets, and Feta or Goat Cheese (page 81). Add steamed cauliflower if you'd like.

FOR PICKY EATERS: Set aside a few tortellini to be cooked and served plain (or with some nonhydrogenated margarine or marinara sauce). Serve with anything your child might eat from the suggested salad, such as some plain steamed green beans, beets, or chunks of the feta or goat cheese.

1½ tablespoons light olive oil
2 medium carrots, peeled and sliced
2 garlic cloves, minced
One 16-ounce can tomato sauce
One 16-ounce can diced tomatoes
1 small zucchini, quartered lengthwise
    and sliced
½ teaspoon dried oregano
½ teaspoon dried dill or 1 to 2
    tablespoons minced fresh
8 ounces fresh or frozen tortellini,
    cheese, vegetable, or tofu filled
Salt and freshly ground pepper to taste
Freshly grated Parmesan or grated
    Parmesan-style soy cheese for
    topping, optional

Dairy	Vegan
Calories: 144	Calories: 128
Total fat: 5 g	Total fat: 4 g
Protein: 6 g	Protein: 4 g
Fiber: 4 g	Fiber: 4.4 g
Carbohydrates: 21 g	Carbohydrates: 21 g
Cholesterol: 8 g	Cholesterol: 0 g
Sodium: 325 mg	Sodium: 290 mg

Basic Lentil Soup with Tasty Variations

VEGAN

6 servings

For kids who can appreciate the earthy flavor of lentils, this soup is a tasty introduction to a nourishing legume.

2 tablespoons light olive oil

1 medium-large onion, finely chopped

2 garlic cloves, minced

2 celery stalks, finely diced

2 medium carrots, peeled and sliced

1¼ cups dried lentils, rinsed and picked over

2 vegetable bouillon cubes

2 teaspoons salt-free all-purpose seasoning mix (see page xxvi)

2 bay leaves

Salt and freshly ground pepper to taste

Calories: 187

Total fat: 5 g

Protein: 10 g

Fiber: 9.5 g

Carbohydrates: 27 g

Cholesterol: 0 g

Sodium: 121 mg

1 Heat the oil in a small soup pot. Add the onion and garlic and sauté over medium heat until translucent, about 5 minutes. Add the celery and carrots and sauté for 3 to 4 minutes longer.

2 Add 6 cups of water and the remaining ingredients, except the salt and pepper. Bring to a simmer, then cover and simmer until the lentils and vegetables are tender, 30 to 40 minutes.

3 Season with salt and pepper. If time allows, this soup benefits from standing for 1 hour or so before serving to develop flavor. Heat through as needed and remove bay leaves before serving.

Variations

Lentil Barley or Lentil Rice Soup: Add ⅓ cup pearl barley or brown rice when adding the lentils along with an additional cup of water.

Lentil "Frankfurter" Soup: A retro classic brought up to date—add 4 to 6 thinly sliced soy hot dog links to the soup at the end of its cooking time.

Lentil Tomato Soup: Add one 16-ounce can diced or crushed tomatoes once the lentils are done and simmer gently for another 10 minutes.

Lentil Soup with Tiny Noodles: Cook 1 cup tiny shells or ditalini. Add to the soup with additional water as needed, and taste to correct seasonings.

MAKE IT A MEAL: Lentil soups are hearty yet leave room for more. This is a good first course for pasta, grain, potato, and vegetable dishes. For a simple meal for kids, serve with Grilled Cheese Strips (page 59). Otherwise, serve with Little Garlic Toasts (page 59) and follow with Cheesy Smashed Potatoes (page 200) or Green Noodles (page 116) and a colorful salad or a Cold Vegetable Platter (see page 84). This also works well as an accompaniment to grown-up sandwiches and wraps. See Supper Sandwiches and Super Wraps (pages 238–39).

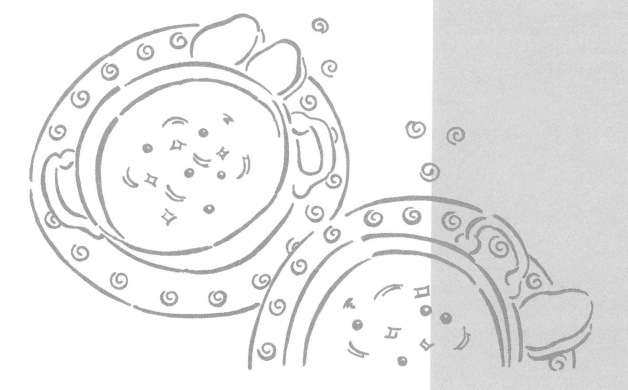

Simple Miso Tofu Soup

Many kids enjoy miso soup when eating in Japanese restaurants. Because it's an easy, nearly instant soup to re-create at home, we have this fairly often, especially as an accompaniment to Vegetable Sushi (pages 193–94).

5 cups prepared vegetable broth or 5 cups water with 1 vegetable bouillon cube

2 to 3 scallions, green and white parts, thinly sliced

2 strips kombu, each 3 by 5 inches, optional (see Note)

8 ounces soft or medium-firm tofu, cut into ¼-inch-thick slices, well blotted, and finely diced

2 to 4 tablespoons miso

1 Combine the stock with the scallions and kombu, if using, in a soup pot. Bring to a simmer, then cover and simmer gently for 5 minutes.

2 Stir in the tofu. Simmer for 1 to 2 minutes longer, then remove the kombu.

3 Dissolve the desired amount of miso in just enough warm water to make it pourable. Stir into the broth and remove from the heat. Taste and add more dissolved miso if desired. Serve at once.

Calories: 77

Total fat: 4 g

Protein: 7 g

Fiber: 1.5 g

Carbohydrates: 5 g

Cholesterol: 0 g

Sodium: 369 mg

Note
Kombu, a sea vegetable available in dried form in natural foods stores and Asian groceries, is a traditional ingredient in Japanese miso soup. If you don't care to use it, the soup is fine without it.

MAKE IT A MEAL: Miso soup makes a nice introduction to many types of Asian vegetable or noodle dishes. For a simple meal, serve with Asian Noodles with Stir-Fried Corn and Cabbage (page 106) and Cold Vegetable Platter #4 (page 84). For a fun meal, serve with sushi. See "Make it a meal" on page 195.

Miso Noodle Soup with Crisp Vegetables

If you feel like having a fresh, light soup in a hurry, here's a good choice. Once the quick-cooking noodles are done, the rest comes together in minutes.

1 Bring the broth to a simmer in a soup pot. Add the noodles and simmer until al dente, 6 to 8 minutes.

2 Add all the vegetables and cook just until everything is well heated through, 3 to 4 minutes.

3 Dissolve the desired amount of miso in just enough warm water to make it pourable. Stir into the soup and remove from the heat. Add a few grindings of pepper and serve.

Note
Do try to use whole-grain Asian noodles, but if unavailable, substitute linguine.

MAKE IT A MEAL: Serve as a first course with Asian-style tofu or seitan dishes. This complements many of these types of dishes quite nicely (see Chapter 5 for ideas), but we especially like it as a starter for Seitan and Broccoli Stir-Fry (page 161) and Asian-Flavored Coleslaw (page 70).

VEGAN

4 servings

6 cups prepared vegetable broth or 6 cups water with 1 vegetable bouillon cube

4 to 5 ounces udon or soba noodles, broken in half (see Note)

½ medium red bell pepper, sliced into very thin rings

1 medium carrot, peeled and coarsely grated

1 cup shredded dark green lettuce leaves or loosely packed watercress leaves

2 scallions, green and white parts, thinly sliced

One 15-ounce can cut baby corn, with liquid

2 to 4 tablespoons miso, to taste

Freshly ground pepper to taste

Calories: 168
Total fat: 2 g
Protein: 8 g
Fiber: 52 g
Carbohydrates: 31 g
Cholesterol: 0 g
Sodium: 933 mg

6 servings

1 large butternut squash
2 tablespoons light olive oil
1 large red onion, chopped
4 cups peeled, diced apple, any cooking
    variety
4 cups prepared vegetable broth, or 4
    cups water with 1 vegetable bouillon
    cube
½ teaspoon ground ginger
¼ teaspoon ground nutmeg
2 cups low-fat milk, rice milk, or soy milk
Salt and freshly ground pepper to taste

Dairy	Vegan option
Calories: 169	Calories: 178
Total fat: 6 g	Total fat: 6 g
Protein: 4 g	Protein: 2 g
Fiber: 5.2 g	Fiber: 5.2 g
Carbohydrates: 28 g	Carbohydrates: 33 g
Cholesterol: 3 g	Cholesterol: 0 g
Sodium: 95 mg	Sodium: 83 mg

Creamy Butternut Squash and Apple Soup

Everything about this soup says fall harvest—from its warm golden color to its slightly sweet, fresh flavor. Once the squash is baked, this soup comes together fairly quickly.

1 Preheat the oven to 400° F.

2 Halve the squash lengthwise with a sharp knife and scoop out the seeds and fibers. Place cut side up in a shallow baking dish and cover tightly with foil. Or, if you'd like a more roasted flavor, simply brush the squash halves with a little olive oil and leave uncovered. Either way, bake for 45 to 50 minutes, or until tender. Set aside until cool enough to handle.

3 Heat the oil in a soup pot. Add the onion and sauté over medium-low heat until golden, 8 to 10 minutes.

4 Add the apples, broth, and spices. Bring to a simmer, then cover and simmer gently until the apples are soft, about 10 minutes.

5 In a food processor, purée the squash with ½ cup of the milk until completely smooth. Transfer to a bowl.

6 Transfer the apple-onion mixture to the food processor and purée until completely smooth. Return to the soup pot and add the squash purée; stir together. Add the remaining milk, using a bit more if the purée is too thick.

7 Bring the soup to a gentle simmer, then cook over low heat until well heated through, 5 to 10 minutes. Season with salt and pepper. Serve at once, or let the soup stand off the heat for 1 to 2 hours, then heat through as needed before serving.

MAKE IT A MEAL: This luscious purée is a good first course for many types of cool-weather dishes. It's suitable to serve before most casseroles (Chapter 6), especially for company meals. It works nicely served before hearty pastas, including a macaroni and cheese variation (Chapter 4). Try it with Tortellini or Ravioli with Broccoli (page 119) or Mixed Mushrooms Stroganoff (page 128). For a special-occasion meal, see "Make it a meal" on page 179.

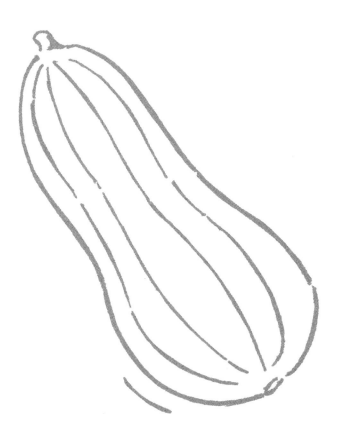

¾ cup tiny pasta (orzo, small shells,
    ditalini, or tubetti)
1 tablespoon light olive oil
1 small onion, minced
2 medium carrots, peeled and finely
    diced
2 medium celery stalks, diced
6 cups prepared vegetable broth or 6
    cups water with 2 vegetable bouillon
    cubes
1 small zucchini, finely diced
2 plum (Roma) tomatoes, finely diced
1 cup fresh peas or frozen peas, thawed
A few good handfuls of dark green
    lettuce leaves or fresh spinach leaves,
    stemmed and shredded
1 tablespoon minced fresh dill or 1
    teaspoon dried
Salt and freshly ground pepper to taste

Calories: 119
Total fat: 3 g
Protein: 4 g
Fiber: 4 g
Carbohydrates: 20 g
Cholesterol: 0 g
Sodium: 131 mg

Garden Vegetable Soup with Tiny Pasta

A light soup for spring and early summer, this is good served just warm as well as piping hot.

1   Cook the pasta according to the package directions until al dente; drain.

2   Meanwhile, heat the oil in a soup pot. Add the onion, carrots, and celery and sauté over medium heat until golden.

3   Add the broth and bring to a simmer, then add the zucchini, tomatoes, and peas. Cover and simmer gently until the vegetables are just done, about 10 minutes.

4   Add the lettuce and dill. Simmer until the greens have just started to wilt, then remove from the heat and stir in the cooked pasta. Season with salt and pepper.

5   Allow the soup to stand off the heat, uncovered, for 30 minutes or so, then serve warm.

MAKE IT A MEAL: This is a good choice for a light soup-and-sandwich meal. Youngsters may enjoy this with Grilled Cheese Strips (page 59); for more creative options, explore the ideas for Supper Sandwiches and Super Wraps (pages 238–39). A simple tossed salad, coleslaw (see page 68), or any of the Cold Vegetable Platters (page 84) complete the meal.

Navy Bean Soup with Corn and Red Peppers

Hearty yet not heavy, this soup will appeal to family members with a taste for beans, and entice others who are acquiring the taste.

1 Heat the oil in a soup pot. Add the onion and sauté over medium heat until golden. Add the potatoes, carrot, and broth. Bring to a simmer, then cover and simmer gently for 15 minutes.

2 Add the beans, bell pepper, tomatoes, corn, dill, and paprika. Simmer very gently until all the vegetables are tender and the flavors well blended, 25 to 30 minutes. Season with salt and pepper, simmer for another 5 minutes, then serve.

Note

If you'd like to give the soup a thicker base, purée one of the cans (or 2 cups) of navy beans before adding to the soup.

MAKE IT A MEAL: If you're inclined to bake a bread, Quick Three-Grain Brown Bread (page 280) is a great choice. Pop it in the oven before starting the soup and you'll have a fragrant, fresh bread by the time it's done. Otherwise, Veggie Cheese Toasts (page 245) is another good pairing. Cabbage, Apple, and Raisin Slaw (page 69) or a simple tossed salad round out the meal.

VEGAN

6 servings

2 tablespoons light olive oil

1 large onion, finely chopped

2 medium potatoes, finely diced

1 large carrot, peeled and thinly sliced

6 cups prepared vegetable broth or 6 cups water with 2 vegetable bouillon cubes

Two 16-ounce cans navy (small white) beans, drained and rinsed or 4 cups cooked (from 1⅔ cup dried) (see Note)

1 medium red bell pepper, cut into short, thin strips

2 plum (Roma) tomatoes, finely diced

2 cups cooked fresh corn kernels (from about 2 medium ears) or frozen corn kernels, thawed

1 teaspoon dried dill

1 teaspoon paprika

Salt and freshly ground pepper to taste

Calories: 331
Total fat: 5 g
Protein: 14 g
Fiber: 10.2 g
Carbohydrates: 59 g
Cholesterol: 0 g
Sodium: 112 mg

8 servings

2 tablespoons light olive oil

1 medium-large onion, finely chopped

1 to 2 garlic cloves, minced, optional

¾ cup pearl barley, rinsed

2 to 3 medium carrots, peeled and sliced

1 large potato, peeled and diced

2 large celery stalks, diced

2 bay leaves

One 16-ounce can crushed tomatoes

3 tablespoons chopped fresh dill, or to
    taste

Salt and freshly ground pepper to taste

Calories: 119

Total fat: 4 g

Protein: 2 g

Fiber: 3.3 g

Carbohydrates: 20 g

Cholesterol: 0 g

Sodium: 109 mg

Dilled Vegetable-Barley Soup

A sturdy, everyday sort of soup that's soothing and fortifying at the same time.

1 Heat the oil in a large soup pot. Add the onion and sauté over low heat until golden.

2 Add the garlic, barley, carrots, potato, celery, bay leaves, and 6 cups of water. Bring to a simmer, then cover and simmer gently, stirring occasionally, until the barley and vegetables are nearly done, 45 minutes.

3 Add the tomatoes and dill, and simmer gently, covered, until the barley is puffy and the vegetables are tender but not mushy, 20 to 30 minutes. Adjust the consistency with more water if necessary and season with salt and pepper. Remove bay leaves before serving.

TIP: This soup will thicken as it stands. Adjust the liquid and seasonings as needed, but allow the soup to remain thick.

MAKE IT A MEAL: A good choice to serve with soup-and-sandwich meals; see ideas for Supper Sandwiches and Super Wraps (pages 238–39). For a nice soup-and-salad meal, serve with Green Salad with Avocado, Apples, and Baked Tofu (page 75) or Mixed Greens with Green Beans, Beets, and Feta or Goat Cheese (page 81). For a simple meal, serve with veggie burgers and a tossed salad.

FOR PICKY EATERS: Young eaters might just go for this soup but may not appreciate the strong flavor of fresh dill. If this is the case, pass a small bowl of chopped fresh dill to stir into the soup.

Tortilla Soup

VEGAN

6 servings

This soup makes a lively start to Southwestern-style meals.

1 Preheat the oven to 400° F.

2 Heat the oil in a large soup pot. Add the onion and garlic and sauté over medium heat until golden. Add the bell pepper and broth. Bring to a simmer, then cover and simmer gently for 15 minutes.

3 Meanwhile, cut the tortillas into strips about ½ inch wide by 1½ inches long. Arrange on a baking sheet and bake about 15 minutes, or until crisp and dry. Remove from the oven and set aside.

4 Add the squash, tomatoes, green chilies, cumin, and oregano and stir to mix. Continue to simmer until the squash is tender, 10 to 15 minutes. Season with salt and pepper. If time allows, let the soup stand off the heat for 1 to 2 hours before serving, then heat through as needed.

5 When ready to serve, divide the tortilla strips among 6 serving bowls and ladle the soup over top. Serve at once.

MAKE IT A MEAL: For a soup-and-salad meal, pair this with Southwestern Rice and Black Bean Salad (page 86). This soup is also a good introduction to a meal of Black Bean Sofrito (page 188) served with brown rice. A platter of fresh raw vegetables completes either option.

1 tablespoon olive oil
1 medium onion, finely chopped
2 to 3 garlic cloves, minced
½ medium green bell pepper, finely diced
6 cups prepared vegetable broth or 6 cups water with 1 vegetable bouillon cube
Six 6-inch corn tortillas
1 medium zucchini or yellow squash, diced
2 medium firm plum tomatoes, finely diced
One 4-ounce can chopped mild green chilies
½ teaspoon ground cumin
½ teaspoon dried oregano
Salt and freshly ground pepper to taste

Calories: 117
Total fat: 3 g
Protein: 3 g
Fiber: 3.2 g
Carbohydrates: 19 g
Cholesterol: 0 g
Sodium: 141 mg

VEGAN

6 servings

1 tablespoon light olive oil

2 medium onions, chopped

2 garlic cloves, minced

1 large green bell pepper, finely chopped

4 cups cooked pinto or pink beans (about
   1⅔ cups dried) or two 16-ounce cans
   pinto or pink beans, drained and
   rinsed

One 28-ounce can crushed tomatoes

1½ cups cooked fresh corn kernels (from
   about 2 medium-small ears) or frozen
   corn kernels, thawed

One 4-ounce can mild or hot chopped
   green chilies

1 teaspoon dried oregano

2 teaspoons good-quality chili powder,
   or to taste

1 teaspoon ground cumin

Salt to taste

Calories: 266

Total fat: 3 g

Protein: 13 g

Fiber: 13.5 g

Carbohydrates: 50 g

Cholesterol: 0 g

Sodium: 223 mg

Classic
Vegetarian Chili

Long a standard in the vegetarian repertoire, this variety of chili consists of beans and vegetables in a spiced tomato base. I serve chili for everyday meals as well as for casual company dinners. It's especially welcome when the cool days of late fall arrive or when feeding people who think they don't like vegetarian food. This mildly spiced version is good in its basic form, but don't forget to try some of the embellishments.

1 Heat the oil in a large soup pot. Add the onion and garlic and sauté over medium heat until the onion is golden.

2 Add the remaining ingredients except the salt. Cover and simmer gently for 30 minutes, stirring occasionally. Season lightly with salt and adjust the other seasonings. If time allows, let stand for 1 hour or so off the heat, then heat through as needed before serving. Serve warm.

EMBELLISH IT:
- For a spicier chili, add one or two seeded and minced fresh or canned jalapeño peppers. Let the chili simmer for 5 minutes or so after adding the jalapeños. You may want to set aside the portions for those who want to keep their chili mild.
- Pass around a bowl of grated Cheddar cheese or Cheddar-style nondairy cheese for topping individual portions.
- For a "meaty" textured chili, add 2 cups or so of soy burger crumbles along with ½ cup of water, or as needed, during the last 10 minutes of cooking.

MAKE IT A MEAL: Serve with stone-ground tortilla chips and Mexican Green Rice (page 230) or hot cooked rice (if not using bulgur or couscous in the chili). Add a tossed salad or coleslaw (see page 68). Another delicious idea is to team this with Spoonbread (page 284) and Taco Salad (page 76), omitting the beans from the salad.

Quick Black Bean and Sweet Potato Chili

VEGAN

6 servings

With the addition of sweet potatoes, this easy chili is invigorating yet comforting. And it is festive enough for a last-minute company meal.

1 Bake or microwave the sweet potatoes on high until just firm, about 3 to 4 minutes per potato. When cool enough to handle, peel and cut into ¾-inch dice. Set aside.

2 Heat the oil in a large soup pot. Add the onion and garlic and sauté over medium heat until golden. Add the bell pepper, beans, tomatoes, chilies, cumin, and oregano. Bring to a simmer. Cover and simmer gently for 15 minutes. Add the sweet potatoes and continue to simmer until the vegetables are tender, 10 to 15 minutes.

3 Season lightly with salt. If time allows, let stand off the heat for 1 or 2 hours, then heat through as needed.

EMBELLISH IT: Pass a bowl of chopped fresh cilantro for sprinkling over the top of individual portions.

MAKE IT A MEAL: For an easy meal, serve this with a purchased cornbread or other hearty whole-grain bread and a bountiful tossed salad. Or, like Classic Vegetarian Chili (page 52), this is wonderful with Spoonbread (page 284) and Taco Salad (page 76), omitting the beans from the salad.

2 medium-large sweet potatoes
2 tablespoons light or extra-virgin olive oil
1 cup chopped onion
2 to 3 garlic cloves
1 medium red bell pepper, diced
One 32-ounce can black beans, drained and rinsed
One 28-ounce can diced tomatoes
1 or 2 small fresh hot chilies, minced, or one 4-ounce can chopped mild green chilies
2 teaspoons ground cumin
½ teaspoon dried oregano
Salt to taste

Calories: 202
Total fat: 5 g
Protein: 8 g
Fiber: 8.5 g
Carbohydrates: 33 g
Cholesterol: 0 g
Sodium: 222 mg

VEGAN

6 to 8 servings

1½ tablespoons light olive oil

1 large red onion, chopped

3 to 4 garlic cloves, minced

2 cups shredded white cabbage

2 medium-large sweet potatoes, peeled
and cut into ½-inch dice

One 16-ounce can diced tomatoes, with
liquid

1 teaspoon grated fresh ginger

2 cups trimmed and sliced fresh okra or
one 10-ounce package frozen sliced
okra, thawed (see Note)

½ cup natural-style smooth peanut
butter

¼ teaspoon cayenne pepper or
½ teaspoon hot red pepper flakes

Salt to taste

Garnishes
Chopped scallions, optional
Chopped peanuts, optional

Calories: 219

Total fat: 11 g

Protein: 8 g

Fiber: 5.2 g

Carbohydrates: 23 g

Cholesterol: 0 g

Sodium: 59 mg

West African Peanut Stew

This is a Westernized version of a typical African dish, made in various ways around the continent. I first made this stew as part of an African feast at my sons' school some years ago in conjunction with a class project. Privately, I doubted that any of the kids, then third- and fourth-graders, would eat this. I couldn't have been more mistaken! The kids not only loved making it but scraped every last drop from the huge pot.

1   Heat the oil in a soup pot or steep-sided stir-fry pan. Add the onion and garlic and sauté over medium heat until golden.

2   Add the cabbage, potatoes, tomatoes, ginger, and 3 cups of water. Bring to a simmer, then cover and simmer gently until the potatoes and cabbage are nearly tender, about 15 minutes.

3   Add the okra, then stir in the peanut butter, a little at a time, until it melts into the broth. Stir in the cayenne, then cover and simmer gently until all the vegetables are tender, about 10 minutes. Add a bit more water if needed for a moist but not soupy consistency.

4   Season with salt, then serve in bowls over hot cooked rice. If desired, garnish each serving with chopped scallions and/or chopped peanuts.

Note

Okra may not be everyone's favorite vegetable, but in this dish it is very good. However, if you truly want to avoid it, substitute one 10-ounce package of frozen cut green beans or 2 cups fresh green beans cut into 2-inch lengths for results that are equally delectable, if a bit less authentic.

EMBELLISH IT: To raise the heat level of this dish, slowly step up the quantities of the ginger and cayenne. You can do so in the entire stew or in individual portions.

MAKE IT A MEAL: Traditionally, this stew is eaten with a mashed root vegetable or a mushy grain. Cooked millet (see page 234) is an especially appropriate choice. Another alternative is to serve stew with Spoonbread (page 284), or Leslie's Corn Bread Cake (page 285). With any of the above options, serve with a simple seasonal salad.

Seitan "Meat and Potatoes" Stew

Seitan, a high-protein food made of wheat gluten, gives this stew a "meaty" texture. To learn more about seitan or to try making your own, see page 154.

see page 154

VEGAN

6 to 8 servings

2 tablespoons light olive oil

1 large onion, quartered and thinly sliced

2 garlic cloves, minced

5 medium potatoes, any firm variety, peeled and diced

4 medium carrots, peeled and sliced

1 vegetable bouillon cube

1 teaspoon salt-free all-purpose seasoning (see page xxvi)

1 to 1½ pounds prepared seitan or Homemade Seitan (page 154), cut into bite-size pieces

Salt and freshly ground pepper to taste

Minced fresh parsley, for garnish

Calories: 286

Total fat: 5 g

Protein: 30 g

Fiber: 3.8 g

Carbohydrates: 32 g

Cholesterol: 0 g

Sodium: 62 mg

1 Heat 1 tablespoon of the oil in a large soup pot. Add the onion and garlic and sauté over medium heat until golden.

2 Add 3 cups of water along with the potatoes, carrots, bouillon cube, and seasoning. Bring to a simmer, then cover and simmer gently until the potato and carrots are tender, 25 to 30 minutes.

3 Meanwhile, heat the remaining 1 tablespoon oil in a large skillet. Add the seitan and sauté over medium-high heat, stirring frequently, until most sides are nicely browned and crisp.

4 Once the vegetables are done, use the back of a wooden spoon to mash enough of the potatoes to thicken the base of the stew. Stir in the sautéed seitan. Add a bit more water if necessary. The consistency should be thick and moist, but not soupy.

5 Taste and season with salt and pepper, then serve in shallow bowls. Pass the parsley for garnishing individual portions.

MAKE IT A MEAL: Cabbage, Apple, and Raisin Slaw (page 69) adds a refreshing balance to the stew's substantial texture. Steamed green beans or broccoli is a good addition to the meal.

FOR PICKY EATERS: It's easy to set aside some elements from the stew for young eaters who might like them separately. Leave a small amount of sautéed seitan out of the stew to serve separately; microwave a potato to serve with it (split it open and fluff it with some nonhydrogenated margarine). Arrange a small platter with any of the ingredients that your child might enjoy, including some carrot sticks, and serve with a dip (try Easy Dill Dip, page 256).

Coconut Curried Vegetable Stew

VEGAN

6 to 8 servings

Coconut milk makes a delectable base for this delicately curried vegetable mélange. You couldn't ask for a gentler introduction to curried dishes than this.

1½ tablespoons light olive oil

2 medium onions, chopped

2 to 3 garlic cloves, minced

4 medium potatoes, any firm variety, peeled and diced

4 medium carrots, peeled and sliced

½ medium head cauliflower, cut into bite-size pieces

2 cups frozen cut green beans, thawed

1 to 2 teaspoons grated fresh ginger or to taste

2 to 3 teaspoons good-quality curry powder or to taste

½ teaspoon turmeric

One 15-ounce can light coconut milk

Salt to taste

1 cup frozen green peas, thawed

Calories: 200

Total fat: 7 g

Protein: 6 g

Fiber: 6.5 g

Carbohydrates: 33 g

Cholesterol: 0 g

Sodium: 49 mg

1 Heat the oil in a large soup pot. Add the onion and garlic and sauté over medium heat until golden. Add the potatoes, carrots, and 2 cups of water, and bring to a simmer. Cover and simmer gently until the potatoes are about half tender, 10 to 15 minutes.

2 Add the cauliflower, green beans, ginger, curry powder, and turmeric. Cover and continue to simmer very gently until the vegetables are tender, about 20 minutes.

3 Mash some of the potatoes against the side of the pot with a wooden spoon to thicken the base. Stir in the coconut milk and season with salt. If time allows, let the stew stand for 1 hour or so before serving.

4 Just before serving, heat the stew and taste to correct the seasonings. Stir in the peas and cook just until the peas are heated through, then serve in shallow bowls.

EMBELLISH IT: If your family enjoys spicer and more complex flavors, add 2 fresh mild chile peppers, seeded and minced, and ¼ cup minced fresh cilantro to the stew. Or pass the chilies and cilantro to stir into individual portions.

MAKE IT A MEAL: For a festive meal, serve with Fruited Couscous (page 227), Tomatoes and Cucumbers in Yogurt (page 79), and warm flat bread.

Grilled Cheese Strips: These are ordinary grilled cheese sandwiches cut into narrow strips, perfect for dunking into soup. Try organic American cheese or American-style rice or soy cheese on a sturdy light wheat bread for young eaters; for teens and adults, use any kind of organic or nondairy cheese you'd like. Heat nonhydrogenated margarine in a medium skillet. Cook the sandwiches on both sides until golden brown. Then cut each sandwich into four or five long, narrow strips. These are especially good with puréed and tomato-based soups

Crispy Croutons: Croutons are a good way to entice young eaters to enjoy soup and are particularly good in puréed soups. Use the ends and pieces of whole-grain bread that is several days old (but not stale), allowing about 1 slice per serving. If you'd like, brush the bread with a little olive oil and sprinkle with Parmesan or Parmesan-style soy cheese and a little oregano. Or simply leave the bread plain. Cut the bread into ½-inch dice. Arrange on a baking sheet and bake in a preheated 275° F oven or toaster oven for 20 minutes, until dry and crisp. Allow the croutons to cool on a plate. They may be used as soon as they have cooled, but if you can leave them out at room temperature for at least 30 minutes, they'll stay crisper in the soup.

Little Garlic Toasts: Cut a long, narrow French bread into ½-inch-thick slices, allowing 3 to 4 slices per serving. Arrange on a baking sheet and bake in a preheated 350° F oven for 10 to 15 minutes, turning once, until both sides are golden and crisp. Watch them carefully! Remove from the oven. Cut a clove of garlic in half lengthwise. When cool enough to handle, rub one side of each toast with the open side of the garlic. If desired, brush a bit of olive oil on the same side of the toasts as well.

Parmesan Pita Chips and Bagel Crisps: See page 262.

CHAPTER THREE

Salads and Such

I'M A HUGE FAN OF SALADS. I love concocting them, I love serving a variety of cold dishes to family and friends, and my favorite lunch is a big salad made with whatever is in the vegetable drawer. Most of us, vegetarian or not, should be eating far more fresh, raw vegetables, and salads offer an ideal way to do so.

If truth be told, salads aren't often high on the list of children's favorite food. My own sons began eating salads of all sorts only recently, as they approached adolescence. But within this quandary has always been an opportunity: Nearly any kind of salad contains ingredients that can be set aside, arranged, and placed within reach of children. Sometimes a dip makes raw veggies more enticing, but, more often than not, platters of raw vegetables get cleaned up any way they're served. In fact, since until now I've had more success serving platters of vegetables that are arranged rather than mixed, you'll find five cold vegetable platters that add color and crunch to many types of meals.

This chapter offers an array of salads to tempt everyone from the finicky to the emerging salad fan, to the true salad aficionado. Cooked salads (such as potato salads and grain salads), raw salads, slaws, and composed salads offer a range of possibilities to inspire the use of bountiful fresh produce each and every day. And, of course, as always, I urge you to use organic versions of vegetables and other salad ingredients as often as you possibly can.

Serving small portions of salad in their own edible "bowls" gives them immediate appeal to young eaters. The containers can be hollowed-out tomato halves, red or green bell pepper halves, avocado halves (with all but a ½-inch shell scooped out), or even a whole-wheat kaiser roll (or other sturdy roll), also hollowed out to a ½-inch thickness. All but the avocado can be eaten out of hand. You can fill these with a simple, finely chopped lettuce and tomato salad with your child's favorite dressing. If this form of salad proves to be a hit, try experimenting with other salads. Note that this works best with salads consisting of small or finely chopped ingredients. Stuffed salads aren't just for little ones—there's no reason why everyone in the family wouldn't enjoy this fun option. Grain and bean salads are particularly good for this purpose. Here are some ideas to try:

- **Southwestern Rice and Black Bean Salad** (page 86) in avocado halves
- **Spring Barley Salad** (page 90) in red bell pepper halves
- **Tomato and Corn Relish** (page 79) in avocado, green bell pepper, or whole-wheat roll halves
- **Tomatoes with Black Beans or Chickpeas** (page 79) in tomato, avocado, or green bell pepper halves

Pasta Salad with Southwestern Flavors

A quick main-dish salad, this is made with convenient canned beans and bottled salsa.

1 Cook the pasta in plenty of rapidly boiling water until al dente. Drain and rinse until cool, then drain well.

2 Meanwhile, combine the remaining ingredients in a serving container. Add the pasta and toss together. Serve at once.

Variation

Add one or two diced ripe tomatoes to give the salad a fresher flavor, especially in the summer.

MAKE IT A MEAL: For a soup-and-salad meal with a Southwestern theme, precede this with Tortilla Soup (page 51), then serve with corn on the cob and avocado wedges. Or, instead of soup, serve the salad with any of the Easy Quesadillas or Soft Tacos (page 242) that don't themselves contain beans.

EMBELLISH IT: Pass around some chopped fresh cilantro and thinly sliced scallions in small bowls for topping individual portions.

VEGAN

6 servings

10 to 12 ounces uncooked pasta, any short shape

One 16-ounce can pinto beans, drained and rinsed

1 cup cooked fresh corn kernels (from about 1 medium ear) or frozen corn kernels, thawed

½ medium green bell pepper, finely diced

1 cup bottled salsa, mild or medium-hot

2 tablespoons extra-virgin olive oil

Juice of ½ lemon or lime, or more to taste

Salt and freshly ground pepper to taste

Calories: 203

Total fat: 5 g

Protein: 7 g

Fiber: 5.1 g

Carbohydrates: 33 g

Cholesterol: 0 g

Sodium: 249 mg

Macaroni Salad with Vegetable Confetti

A mild and simple macaroni salad, this is reminiscent of the kind sold at deli counters—but with more going for it. This pasta salad goes well with many types of bean and vegetable dishes.

8 ounces uncooked elbow macaroni, or your favorite short chunky shape

½ red bell pepper, finely diced

½ cup frozen green peas, thawed

½ cup cooked fresh corn kernels (from about 1 medium-small ear) or frozen corn kernels, thawed

1 medium carrot, peeled and finely diced

½ cup soy mayonnaise

1 teaspoon prepared mustard

Salt to taste

Calories: 232

Total fat: 5 g

Protein: 7 g

Fiber: 2.9 g

Carbohydrates: 38 g

Cholesterol: 0 g

Sodium: 383 mg

1   Cook the macaroni in plenty of rapidly boiling water until al dente, then drain. Rinse under cool water, then drain again and transfer to a serving container.

2   Combine half of the vegetables with the cooked pasta. Add the mayonnaise and mustard and stir together.

3   Season gently with salt, then scatter the remaining vegetables over the top. Serve at once or cover and refrigerate until needed.

TIP: Pack leftover portions in thermoses to use as part of portable lunches. This also makes a delightful picnic dish, packed in a shallow storage container.

EMBELLISH IT: Embellish adult portions with minced scallions and/or fresh herbs such as parsley and dill. Toasted sunflower seeds scattered over the top also add a nice touch. For a slightly more sophisticated yet still kid-friendly salad, use elbow twists (cavatappi or celantani).

MAKE IT A MEAL: For a colorful summer meal, serve with Southwestern Summer Succotash (page 218) and Italian Bread-and-Tomato Salad (page 80). It's a good side dish with veggie burgers, bean burgers (Chapter 6), sandwiches, or wraps (see Supper Sandwiches and Super Wraps, pages 238–39).

Family-Friendly Pasta Salad

VEGAN

6 servings

Small, fun pasta shapes (such as wagon wheels and small shells) and colorful veggies make this pasta salad appealing to all ages. Leftovers are easy to pack into small containers or shallow thermoses for a change-of-pace lunch. Feel free to substitute other vegetables that you think your family would enjoy—such as green peas instead of broccoli.

1 Cook the pasta according to package directions. Just before it's done, add the broccoli and carrots to the simmering water and allow to cook for 1 to 2 minutes, just until the broccoli turns bright green.

2 Drain the pasta and vegetables and rinse under cold running water until cool. Drain well.

3 Combine with the olives, corn, and dressing in a large bowl. Season with salt. If you make this the night before, taste and add more dressing, if needed, before packing into containers.

EMBELLISH IT: Pass around thinly sliced strips of sun-dried tomatoes and top individual portions with minced fresh parsley or thinly sliced basil leaves.

MAKE IT A MEAL: See "Make it a meal" on page 64. This salad is good for lunch-box thermoses and for picnics. Another possibility is to serve this with Skillet Baked Beans (page 189) and sautéed or batter-dipped zucchini and yellow squash (see page 225).

FOR PICKY EATERS: You might try serving this to children who are new to pasta salads. But if the time is not yet right, cook some extra pasta to serve plain. Serve with some of the cooked broccoli florets and some raw carrot sticks (serve with Easy Dill Dip, page 256, if you'd like). Cook a little extra corn to serve plain as well.

8 ounces uncooked rotelle (wagon wheels), small pasta shells, or elbow twists

2 cups small broccoli florets

2 medium carrots, peeled and sliced diagonally

$\frac{1}{2}$ cup pitted black olives, halved

$\frac{1}{2}$ cup cooked fresh corn kernels (from about 1 medium-small ear) or frozen corn kernels

$\frac{1}{3}$ cup Basic Vinaigrette (page 92) or other dressing of your choice, as needed to moisten

Salt to taste

Calories: 160

Total fat: 8 g

Protein: 3 g

Fiber: 2.8 g

Carbohydrates: 19 g

Cholesterol: 0 g

Sodium: 183 mg

4 to 6 servings

8 ounces uncooked soba (Japanese
    buckwheat noodles)
1 large cucumber
1 tablespoon light olive oil
2 teaspoons sesame oil
1 tablespoon mild vinegar (such as rice
    or white wine)
2 tablespoons natural soy sauce
2 tablespoons sesame seeds, optional
Parsley or Cilantro Sauce (page 67),
    optional

Calories: 212
Total fat: 5 g
Protein: 8 g
Fiber: 2.1 g
Carbohydrates: 34 g
Cholesterol: 0 g
Sodium: 403 mg

Cold Soba and Cucumber Salad

My sons enjoy this refreshing cold pasta dish in its basic form; my husband and I like to embellish it with the optional invigorating herb sauce.

1 Cook the noodles in plenty of rapidly boiling water until al dente. Drain and rinse under cold running water until cool, then drain well.

2 Meanwhile, peel the cucumber and quarter it lengthwise. If the seeds are watery, cut them away. Cut the cucumber into narrow strips, approximately 2 inches in length, and place in a mixing bowl.

3 Add the remaining ingredients, except the Parsley or Cilantro Sauce, and toss together. Serve as is or topped with sauce, if desired.

Parsley or Cilantro Sauce

Combine all the ingredients in a food processor with ¼ cup water. Process until fairly smooth but not completely puréed. Transfer to a small bowl. Pass around to serve over noodles.

MAKE IT A MEAL: This cold noodle dish is a fantastic accompaniment for many types of tofu or seitan dishes and stir-fries. Try it with Teriyaki Tofu Triangles (page 148) or Two Kinds of Tofu in a Sweet-and-Savory Sauté (page 147). Complete the meal with either Wilted Sesame Spinach (page 213) or Sesame Stir-Fried Green Beans (page 212). It's also a wonderful accompaniment to sushi; see "Make it a meal" on page 195.

VEGAN

Makes about ³/₄ cup

¾ cup parsley or cilantro leaves (or a combination)
2 tablespoons cashew, almond, or natural peanut butter
1 tablespoon freshly squeezed lemon juice, rice vinegar, or other mild vinegar
Pinch of salt

Per 2-tablespoon serving
Calories: 33
Total fat: 2.5 g
Protein: 1 g
Fiber: 0.15 g
Carbohydrates: 1.5 g
Cholesterol: 0 g
Sodium: 1.5 mg

Simple Slaws

Preshredded coleslaw, available in 8- and 16-ounce bags, is quite possibly the only nonorganic vegetable I still buy—I can't resist its convenience and versatility. And I take comfort in never having seen cabbage listed on a most-contaminated vegetable list. I prefer the kind that includes shredded carrots. With coleslaw vegetables on hand, a simple salad is just moments away. That's a nice option to look forward to when you don't have the time or energy to make a fancier salad.

Make sure to examine the coleslaw vegetables in the bag carefully. They should look crisp and fresh. If they look wilted, slightly yellowed, or watery, steer clear. For my family of four, I use 8 ounces to make a slaw; at its simplest, soy mayonnaise to moisten and a splash of vinegar or lemon juice is all that's needed. But usually I toss in an extra ingredient or two to liven things up. Here are some easy ways to embellish a simple slaw. Use one or two of the following:

- ½ cup cooked fresh corn kernels, or frozen corn kernels, thawed
- 2 scallions, thinly sliced
- 1 medium tart apple, diced
- ⅓ cup dried cranberries or raisins
- ¼ cup toasted sunflower seeds
- ⅓ cup toasted slivered or sliced almonds
- ½ medium green or red bell pepper, thinly sliced
- Minced fresh parsley and/or dill to taste

You can vary the dressings, as well. Natural ranch or vinaigrette dressings are both suitable (prepared or homemade; see pages 93 and 92); for an offbeat flavor, try Tangy Tahini Dressing (page 97).

A simple coleslaw is a versatile salad that goes well with many types of meals. It's especially nice served with casseroles, bean dishes (such as chili), and vegetable main dishes with which you may not need a mixed salad.

Cabbage, Apple, and Raisin Slaw

VEGAN

6 servings

For older kids and teens whose palates welcome interesting textures, this colorful and naturally sweet medley has an appealing crunch.

Combine all the ingredients in a serving bowl and toss together well. Cover and let stand for 15 minutes or so before serving.

EMBELLISH IT: Pass around a bowl of toasted sunflower or pumpkin seeds and/or minced fresh parsley to sprinkle on top.

MAKE IT A MEAL: This provides a pleasant textural contrast to creamy dishes, such as Baked Risotto (page 178) and Ultimate Macaroni and Cheese (page 109). It's refreshing served with spiced dishes such as Classic Vegetarian Chili (page 52) and Coconut Curried Vegetable Stew (page 58).

FOR PICKY EATERS: Peel and slice some extra apple and cut up a few celery sticks; arrange on a small plate with a handful of raisins.

3 to 4 cups green cabbage, coarsely shredded
1 large Granny Smith or other tart, crisp apple, cut into $\frac{1}{2}$-inch dice
2 large celery stalks, cut diagonally
$\frac{1}{3}$ cup raisins
$\frac{1}{2}$ cup soy mayonnaise
Juice of $\frac{1}{2}$ lemon or lime

Calories: 104
Total fat: 4 g
Protein: 1 g
Fiber: 2.7 g
Carbohydrates: 15 g
Cholesterol: 0 g
Sodium: 175 mg

VEGAN

6 to 8 servings

Asian-Flavored Coleslaw

If you'd like something fresh and crunchy to go along with Asian-style recipes, this salad serves the purpose nicely.

5 to 6 cups thinly shredded red, white, or Napa cabbage, or a combination

2 large celery stalks, sliced thinly on the diagonal

2 to 3 scallions, sliced

¼ cup minced fresh cilantro, optional

⅓ to ½ cup Asian Sesame Salad Dressing (page 96)

Freshly ground pepper to taste

1 Combine the cabbage, celery, scallions, and cilantro, if using, in a serving bowl.

2 Pour the dressing over the vegetables. Season with pepper, and toss well. Let the salad stand for 10 minutes or so before serving.

Variation

For a shortcut, use a 16-ounce bag preshredded coleslaw.

MAKE IT A MEAL: This salad is a refreshing accompaniment to Asian-style stir-fries, such as Tofu and Mixed Veggie Stir-Fry (page 149), Hearty Seitan Buddhist's Delight (page 160), or Sweet-and-Sour Seitan and Vegetables (page 158).

Calories: 72

Total fat: 6 g

Protein: 1 g

Fiber: 1 g

Carbohydrates: 4 g

Cholesterol: 0 g

Sodium: 162 mg

Tri-Color Coleslaw

VEGAN

6 servings

I buy two batches of broccoli almost every week. Most of the time I trim the stalks and turn them into tasty vegetable sticks (see page 211), perfect for snacking or dipping; and occasionally I'll use them to make this terrific slaw. This slaw is good with many types of dressings, and I've recommended my favorites (see below). This teams nicely with pastas, tofu dishes, casseroles, and sandwiches.

2 large or 3 medium broccoli stalks, prepared as directed on page 211
3 medium carrots, peeled and cut into large chunks
¼ small head red cabbage
1 tablespoon minced fresh chives or 1 scallion, thinly sliced, optional
½ cup natural prepared or homemade dressing (see Note)
Salt and freshly ground pepper to taste

1 Grate the broccoli, carrots, and cabbage in a food processor using a coarse grating blade.

2 Combine the vegetables with the remaining ingredients in a serving container. Stir together. Let the salad stand for 10 to 15 minutes before serving.

Calories: 125
Total fat: 9 g
Protein: 2 g
Fiber: 2.3 g
Carbohydrates: 11 g
Cholesterol: 0 g
Sodium: 35 mg

Note
This is good dressed with vinaigrette, ranch, or tahini dressings. For homemade versions, see Basic Vinaigrette (page 92), Ranch Dressing (page 93), and Tangy Tahini Dressing (page 97).

DAIRY / VEGAN OPTION

6 servings

**5 medium-large red-skinned or Yukon
   Gold potatoes**
½ cup soy mayonnaise
2 teaspoons prepared yellow mustard
1 large celery stalk, finely diced
1 cup frozen green peas, thawed
Salt and freshly ground pepper to taste

Optional additions
½ medium red bell pepper, finely diced
Crumbled feta or goat cheese
1 to 2 scallions, thinly sliced
Toasted sunflower seeds, to taste
Minced fresh dill, to taste
Chopped fresh parsley, to taste

For basic salad, without additions
Calories: 187
Total fat: 4 g
Protein: 4 g
Fiber: 3.8 g
Carbohydrates: 31 g
Cholesterol: 0 g
Sodium: 186 mg

Expandable Potato Salad

Here's an essential potato salad recipe that's a great addition to many types of meals—including picnics. The basic recipe will appeal to a wide range of tastes; to make it more interesting, stir in any combination of the optional additions you wish to add, or arrange them in small bowls and let everyone add his or her own.

1 Microwave the potatoes on high in their skins until done but still firm. Allow 2 to 3 minutes per potato, test for doneness, then add a little more time as needed. When cool enough to handle, peel the potatoes and cut into ½ - to ¾-inch chunks. Place them in a serving container.

2 Combine the mayonnaise and mustard in a small bowl and stir together. Add to the potatoes, along with the celery and peas; mix well. Season with salt and pepper.

3 Add any of the optional ingredients you'd like; mix well. Cover and refrigerate until needed or serve at once.

MAKE IT A MEAL: This is the perfect companion to veggie burgers and sandwich meals (see Supper Sandwiches and Super Wraps, pages 238–39) and Easy Quesadillas or Soft Tacos (page 242). For a nice warm-weather meal, serve with Taco Salad (page 76) or Hearty Seitan Salad (page 83) and corn on the cob.

FOR PICKY EATERS: Prepare an extra potato or two, and sauté the chunks in a little olive oil. Serve with ketchup and some peas on the side. Arrange a few extra raw veggies that you used for the salad (such as celery and red bell pepper) on the plate.

Golden Potato Salad

Combining Yukon Gold and sweet potatoes gives this salad a pleasant twist and an enticing color.

1   Bake or microwave the potatoes in their skins until done but still firm. Allow 2 to 3 minutes per potato, test for doneness, then add a little time as needed. Let them cool to room temperature. Slip their skins off and cut into ½- to ¾-inch chunks and place in a serving container with the peas, bell pepper, and scallions.

2   Combine the dressing ingredients in a small bowl and stir together. Stir into the potato mixture.

3   Season with salt and pepper. Add parsley to taste, or put in a small bowl and pass for topping individual portions.

MAKE IT A MEAL: An ideal side dish for wraps (see Supper Sandwiches and Super Wraps, pages 238–39), this is also good with Skillet Baked Beans (page 189) or Black Bean and Zucchini Chilaquiles (page 168) and a bountiful tossed salad.

FOR PICKY EATERS: Prepare an extra potato and/or sweet potato or two. Serve in any way your child might enjoy them. Cook some peas to serve plain as well. Set aside a few strips of bell pepper and a small amount of the dressing to dip them in.

DAIRY / VEGAN OPTION

6 servings

1 large sweet potato
4 medium Yukon Gold potatoes
1 cup frozen green peas, thawed
1 medium red bell pepper, cut into
    narrow strips
2 scallions, thinly sliced

Dressing:
½ cup soy mayonnaise
½ cup low-fat yogurt or soy yogurt
2 teaspoons prepared yellow mustard
Juice of ½ lemon or lime

Salt and freshly ground pepper to taste
Minced fresh parsley and/or dill, to taste

Dairy	Vegan option
Calories: 185	Calories: 182
Total fat: 5 g	Total fat: 4 g
Protein: 5 g	Protein: 4 g
Fiber: 3.8 g	Fiber: 4 g
Carbohydrates: 29 g	Carbohydrates: 30 g
Cholesterol: 1 g	Cholesterol: 0 g
Sodium: 196 mg	Sodium: 187 mg

Marinated Potato-Tofu Salad

With the addition of tofu, this becomes a flavorful main-dish salad. Simple though this is, it's always a hit with guests and is a good potluck dish.

5 medium Yukon Gold or red-skinned potatoes

One 16-ounce tub extra-firm tofu

1 tablespoon olive oil

½ medium green pepper, cut into short thin strips

½ medium red bell pepper, cut into short thin strips

¼ to ½ cup sun-dried tomatoes (oil-cured or not), thinly sliced

½ cup prepared vinaigrette or Basic Vinaigrette (page 92), or as needed

Salt and freshly ground pepper to taste

1 Bake or microwave the potatoes in their skins until done but still firm. Let them cool to room temperature. Slip their skins off and cut into ½- to ¾-inch chunks and place in a serving container.

2 Meanwhile, cut the tofu into ½-inch-thick slices. Blot well between clean tea towels or several layers of paper towels and cut into ½-inch dice.

3 Heat just enough oil to coat the bottom of a wide skillet. Add the tofu and sauté over medium-high heat, stirring frequently until golden on most sides.

4 Add the tofu to the potatoes. Add the remaining ingredients and stir together gently. Cover and allow the salad to marinate at room temperature for 30 to 60 minutes. If needed, add a bit more vinaigrette to moisten, then stir again and serve.

Calories: 327

Total fat: 18 g

Protein: 15 g

Fiber: 4.5 g

Carbohydrates: 31 g

Cholesterol: 0 g

Sodium: 175 mg

Variation

Substitute one large sweet potato for two of the potatoes.

EMBELLISH IT: If your younger eaters will accept it, add ¼ to ½ cup minced fresh parsley to the salad. Otherwise, garnish individual portions with some minced parsley. This salad is also delicious topped with toasted pine nuts or sunflower seeds.

Green Salad with Avocado, Apples, and Baked Tofu

This luscious salad adds substance to a meal based on a light main dish and makes a nice at-home lunch on weekends and holidays.

1   Combine the tofu, bell pepper, and lettuce in a serving bowl.

2   Just before serving, toss the avocado and apples with the lemon juice in another bowl, then add to the salad and toss together. Moisten with the dressing of your choice, then serve, passing additional dressing.

Note
I especially recommend either French Dressing (page 95) or Tangy Tahini Dressing (page 97).

MAKE IT A MEAL: This is a tasty salad to stuff into a pita or to wrap up. Wrapped or not, this makes a nice early fall meal with Golden Potato Salad (page 73). For a more substantial meal, start with Cream of Baby Carrot Soup (page 32). Or serve with Dilled Vegetable-Barley Soup (page 50) and fresh bread for an easy soup-and-salad meal.

FOR PICKY EATERS: This salad has several tasty ingredients that can be served to kids who enjoy eating things separately. Cut up some extra apple, red bell pepper, and the remaining tofu from the package. Add a few pieces of diced avocado to the plate if your kids like it.

VEGAN

6 servings

4 to 6 ounces baked tofu (half of an 8- or 12-ounce package), diced or cut into strips

1 medium red bell pepper, diced

1 medium head dark green lettuce, or as desired

1 medium-large firm, ripe avocado, diced

2 medium Granny Smith apples, cored and diced

Juice of ½ large lemon

Any prepared or homemade salad dressing (see Note)

Calories: 188

Total fat: 10 g

Protein: 7 g

Fiber: 5.2 g

Carbohydrates: 21 g

Cholesterol: 0 g

Sodium: 321 mg

2 medium firm ripe tomatoes, chopped

1 medium red or green bell pepper,
    diced

¼ cup black or green olives, sliced

2 scallions, thinly sliced, optional

1 cup grated Cheddar, Monterey Jack, or
    nondairy soy cheese

1 cup canned pinto or kidney beans (see
    Note)

1 small head dark green lettuce, torn

Two good handfuls stone-ground tortilla
    chips, lightly crushed

Taco Salad Dressing or prepared low-fat
    Catalina or French salad dressing, to
    taste

Dairy	Vegan option
Calories: 225	Calories: 190
Total fat: 12 g	Total fat: 8 g
Protein: 10 g	Protein: 9 g
Fiber: 4.9 g	Fiber: 4.9 g
Carbohydrates: 20 g	Carbohydrates: 20 g
Cholesterol: 24 g	Cholesterol: 0 g
Sodium: 317 mg	Sodium: 329 mg

Taco Salad

Here's a hearty green salad for a family that enjoys Southwestern flavors.
I prefer using organic stone-ground tortilla chips that contain no
hydrogenated oils.

Combine tomatoes, bell pepper, olives, scallions, if using, cheese, and
beans in a serving bowl. Add lettuce as needed, according to the number
of servings. Add the tortilla chips. Use enough dressing to moisten and
serve at once.

Note
Omit the beans if you plan on serving this with another dish that contains
beans.

TIP: For a festive look, serve in small salad bowls and tuck five or so
triangular tortilla chips in along the edges, point side up.

MAKE IT A MEAL: Omitting the beans, this salad is a lively partner to
Southwestern-style bean dishes. For a warm-weather meal, pair this
with Southwestern Rice and Black Bean Salad (page 86) or Pasta Salad with
Southwestern Flavors (page 63). Try it with one of the Easy Quesadillas or Soft
Tacos (page 242), with the addition of baked or microwaved sweet potatoes.
Or see "Make it a meal" with Classic Vegetarian Chili (page 52).

Taco Salad Dressing

If you have a little extra time and inclination, make this tasty dressing for taco salad and other types of green salads, too.

Combine all the ingredients in a small bowl and stir together until smooth.

VEGAN

Makes about ²/₃ cup

½ cup salt-free puréed tomatoes
¼ cup soy mayonnaise
1 tablespoon red wine vinegar
½ teaspoon chili powder
Pinch of salt

Per 2-tablespoon serving
Calories: 33
Total fat: 2 g
Protein: 0 g
Fiber: 0.1 g
Carbohydrates: 1 g
Cholesterol: 0 g
Sodium: 95 mg

Five Easy Ways to Serve Fresh Tomatoes

When tomatoes are at their peak of flavor in mid to late summer, serve them as often and as simply as possible. They're an abundant source of vitamin C and lycopene (the substance that gives them their red color, which has been found to be a powerful antioxidant). Whether you grow your own or purchase them from a local market, here's a tip for maximizing that blissful tomato taste and scent: Don't refrigerate them. Buy or pick only as many as you need for a few days and store them on the counter, away from direct sun. Refrigerating tomatoes compromises their flavor and gives them a mealy texture. Here are some wonderful ways to serve them, each requiring only a few moments to prepare:

Tomato and Corn Relish: Combine 2 or 3 medium ripe tomatoes, finely diced, with 1 cup cooked corn kernels (preferably fresh, from about 1 large ear) in a small serving container. Stir in minced fresh dill to taste and moisten with a good prepared vinaigrette or Basic Vinaigrette (page 92).

Tomatoes with Olive Oil and Fresh Herbs: Here's one of the best yet simplest things to do with tomatoes when their flavor is at its peak. Dice any number of tomatoes you wish and place in a serving bowl. Moisten generously with extra-virgin olive oil and add your favorite minced fresh herbs (basil is most welcome in the summer, but use whichever herbs you prefer). Add a splash of balsamic vinegar or lemon juice if you'd like, and make sure to have a crusty whole-grain bread on hand to soak up the delicious juices.

Tomatoes with Goat Cheese or Feta Cheese and Black Olives: Dice 3 or 4 large tomatoes and combine in a serving bowl with ½ cup or so of crumbled goat or feta cheese and ¼ to ½ cup small cured black olives, pitted. Drizzle with extra-virgin olive oil to moisten.

Tomatoes and Cucumbers in Yogurt: Finely dice 3 or 4 medium tomatoes and combine with 1 medium cucumber, peeled and seeded, finely diced. Add ½ to 1 cup low-fat yogurt or soy yogurt and ¼ cup or so minced fresh cilantro and stir together. This preparation is similar to an Indian raita, a palate-cooling relish, and is excellent served with curries and other spicy dishes.

Tomatoes with Black Beans or Chickpeas: Dice 3 or 4 medium tomatoes and combine with one 16-ounce can black beans or chickpeas, drained and rinsed. Moisten as needed with a prepared vinaigrette or Basic Vinaigrette (page 92). Stir in 1 or 2 thinly sliced scallions and/or 2 tablespoons or so minced fresh dill.

4 to 6 servings

Italian Bread-and-Tomato Salad

Crisp cubes of Italian bread mingle with fresh tomatoes in this interpretation of a popular Mediterranean salad. Use only the most flavorful of summer tomatoes for best results. The unexpected addition of bread to a salad might be just what it takes to tempt reluctant salad eaters.

4 cups Italian bread, preferably whole grain, cut into 1-inch cubes

2 pounds flavorful ripe tomatoes, diced

¼ cup chopped fresh basil, or more to taste

⅓ cup chopped green olives

2 tablespoons extra-virgin olive oil

2 tablespoons white balsamic or white wine vinegar

Salt and freshly ground pepper to taste

1   Preheat the oven to 300° F.

2   Arrange the bread cubes on a baking sheet and bake about 15 minutes, until dry and lightly golden. Remove from the oven and allow to cool.

3   Mix the remaining ingredients with the bread cubes and toss together. Serve at once.

Variation

Make the salad more substantial by adding one 16-ounce can chickpeas, drained and rinsed.

Calories: 140

Total fat: 8 g

Protein: 3 g

Fiber: 3.7 g

Carbohydrates: 16 g

Cholesterol: 0 g

Sodium: 225 mg

MAKE IT A MEAL: This salad pairs nicely with light pasta dishes like Angel Hair with Zucchini and Bread Crumbs (page 122) and Green Noodles (page 116). Add color to the plate with baby carrots.

Mixed Greens with Green Beans, Beets, and Feta or Goat Cheese

Proving that simple can be splendid, this dazzling salad will dress up most any dinner plate.

Combine all the ingredients in a serving bowl and toss together. Serve at once.

Variation

Use yellow wax beans or a combination of green and yellow beans.

Note

For tips on cooking beets, see Unbeatable Beets (page 217).

MAKE IT A MEAL: This salad adds color to the plate when served with mild, pale dishes like Baked Risotto (page 178) and Pasta with Enlightened Alfredo Sauce (page 124). Sweet Cinnamon-Maple Glazed Baby Carrots (page 214) completes the meal.

FOR PICKY EATERS: Place some cheese, green beans, and beets separately on a plate for young eaters.

DAIRY

6 servings

1½ cups green beans, cut into 1-inch lengths and steamed until tender-crisp

5 to 6 ounces mixed baby greens (mesclun)

3 to 4 medium beets, cooked, peeled, and diced (see Note) or one 12- to 16-ounce jar sliced pickled beets, drained

½ cup crumbled feta or goat cheese

2 tablespoons toasted sunflower seeds, optional

Extra-virgin olive oil, to taste

Fresh lemon juice, to taste

Calories: 78
Total fat: 4 g
Protein: 4 g
Fiber: 2 g
Carbohydrates: 7 g
Cholesterol: 17 g
Sodium: 241 mg

Middle Eastern Pita Bread Salad

Not as well known in our culture as is tabouli (which, like this, is a Lebanese salad), this fattouche salad is just as delicious. It gets its characteristic touch from the use of small bits of toasted pita bread.

2 large pita breads

4 ripe flavorful plum tomatoes, or 3 medium tomatoes

1 medium cucumber, peeled, quartered lengthwise, and sliced (remove seeds if large and watery)

3 to 4 scallions, white and green parts, minced

¼ cup chopped fresh parsley, or to taste

2 tablespoons extra-virgin or light olive oil

Juice of 1 lemon

½ small head dark green lettuce, torn

Salt and freshly ground pepper to taste

1 Preheat the oven or toaster oven to 375° F.

2 Cut the pita breads into 1-inch squares with kitchen shears or a sharp knife. Place on a baking sheet and bake about 8 minutes, or until golden and just beginning to become crisp.

3 Combine the remaining ingredients in a serving bowl. Add the pita and toss again. Serve at once.

MAKE IT A MEAL: Warm up some extra pita breads to serve with White Bean Hummus (page 260) as an accompaniment to this salad for a light dinner or a special lunch. Or serve this with Quick Couscous and Black Bean Pilaf (page 233), purchased stuffed grape leaves, and cured black olives. With either option, add fresh corn on the cob.

Calories: 185

Total fat: 7 g

Protein: 6 g

Fiber: 5.3 g

Carbohydrates: 27 g

Cholesterol: 0 g

Sodium: 202 mg

Hearty
Seitan Salad

VEGAN

Here's a delectable main-dish salad featuring strips of high-protein seitan.

6 servings

1 Cut the seitan into strips, about $\frac{1}{2}$ by 2 inches. Heat the oil in a wide skillet. Sauté, stirring frequently, until golden, then remove from the heat.

2 Combine the lettuce, bell pepper, tomatoes, avocado, olives, and optional scallions in a mixing bowl and toss together. Add the seitan strips and enough dressing to moisten the salad, and toss again. Serve at once.

1 pound seitan or Homemade Seitan (page 154)

1 tablespoon light olive oil

1 small head dark green lettuce, thinly shredded

1 medium green or red bell pepper, cut into narrow strips

2 medium firm ripe tomatoes, diced

1 medium avocado, sliced

$\frac{1}{4}$ cup sliced black olives

2 scallions, sliced, optional

Any prepared or homemade dressing (see Note)

Note

Try dressing this with Basic Vinaigrette (page 92) or French Dressing (page 95). Another zippy option is Tangy Tahini Dressing (page 97).

MAKE IT A MEAL: This salad is delicious served in wraps, as suggested on page 229. Wrapped or not, serve with Expandable Potato Salad (page 72) or Golden Potato Salad (page 73). For a more substantial meal, precede with a light soup such as Creamy Butternut Squash and Apple Soup (page 46) or Cream of Baby Carrot Soup (page 32).

FOR PICKY EATERS: Set aside a few strips of seitan and any of the other elements of the salad that might appeal to your younger eaters. Consider threading small chunks of seitan, avocado, and tomato on small skewers for them.

Without dressing

Calories: 307

Total fat: 18 g

Protein: 27 g

Fiber: 33 g

Carbohydrates: 12 g

Cholesterol: 0 g

Sodium: 64 mg

Cold Vegetable Platters

Often, it takes some time before even adventurous young eaters appreciate tossed or mixed salads. I've always found more success (with my own and other children) serving a platter of nicely arranged, mostly raw vegetables. In some cases, vegetables that are lightly steamed and cooled, such as green beans, broccoli, and cauliflower, are more appealing to kids than when served raw, but either can work, according to preference. Use your creativity and combine four or five items with a variety of colors, textures, and shapes on a platter. You can include a favorite dressing for dipping, too.

- **Platter #1:** Chickpeas, baby carrots, green and red bell pepper strips (or any other colorful bell peppers, including yellow, orange, or purple), and black olives or organic pickle spears

- **Platter #2:** Beets (jarred pickled beets or cooked, peeled, and sliced fresh beets), kidney beans, cauliflower florets (raw or lightly steamed), and carrot and celery sticks

- **Platter #3:** Cherry tomatoes, cucumber or zucchini spears or slices, baby carrots, and broccoli florets (raw or very lightly steamed)

- **Platter #4:** Turnip, kohlrabi, or jicama sticks; celery sticks; baby corn; lightly steamed green beans; and red bell pepper strips (this combination goes particularly well with Asian-style dishes)

- **Platter #5:** Green and/or red bell pepper strips, cured black olives, cucumber rounds, tomato wedges, chunks of feta cheese or tofu, and even purchased stuffed grape leaves (this combination makes a Greek-style platter)

Pineapple Rice Salad

VEGAN

6 servings

The first time I made this, I followed the "For picky eaters" suggestions, though I no longer considered my sons finicky. Still, I didn't think they'd like a salad with such diverse ingredients. I was wrong—everyone loved this luscious main-dish salad from the start, and it continues to be a family favorite.

1 If using long-grain rice, simmer in 2½ cups water in a medium saucepan until water is absorbed. If using quick-cooking rice, cook according to package directions.

2 Combine the mayonnaise, lemon juice, and curry powder in a small bowl and whisk together; set aside.

3 When the rice is done, combine it with the remaining ingredients, except the mayonnaise mixture, and stir together. Stir in the mayonnaise mixture. Allow to cool to room temperature, then serve.

EMBELLISH IT: Pass ½ cup toasted chopped cashews and ¼ cup minced fresh cilantro or parsley for topping individual portions.

MAKE IT A MEAL: Serve with Cream of Baby Carrot Soup (page 32) as a first course. Pair with a simple salad of mixed greens and cherry tomatoes. Or, for a truly hearty meal, team with West African Peanut Stew (page 54).

FOR PICKY EATERS: This dish consists of many appealing components that younger kids can enjoy separately. Cook extra rice and serve it with a bit of nonhydrogenated margarine, seasoned salt, and some of the steamed broccoli. Serve with some baked tofu strips, at room temperature or slightly warmed. Finish the plate with some extra pineapple chunks, red bell pepper strips, and raisins. Served with soup, this makes a fun and varied meal.

1 cup long-grain brown rice, or 6-serving portion quick-cooking brown rice
½ cup soy mayonnaise
Juice of ½ lemon or lime
½ teaspoon good-quality curry powder, or more to taste
One 16-ounce can unsweetened pineapple chunks, well drained
2 cups bite-size broccoli florets, steamed until bright green
1 medium red bell pepper, cut into short, narrow strips
One 8-ounce package baked tofu, cut into narrow strips
2 scallions, green parts only, thinly sliced
½ cup raisins
Salt and freshly ground pepper to taste

Calories: 312
Total fat: 9 g
Protein: 12 g
Fiber: 4.5 g
Carbohydrates: 45 g
Cholesterol: 0 g
Sodium: 330 mg

6 or more servings

1 ½ to 2 cups cold cooked brown rice (see
    Note)
One 16-ounce can black beans, drained
    and rinsed
1 ½ cups cooked fresh corn kernels (from
    2 medium ears) or frozen corn
    kernels, thawed
1 medium red bell pepper, cut into
    narrow 2-inch strips
1 medium firm ripe avocado, diced
Juice of ½ lemon or lime, or to taste
2 tablespoons extra-virgin or light olive
    oil
½ teaspoon dried oregano
½ teaspoon ground cumin
2 tablespoons apple cider vinegar
Salt and freshly ground pepper to taste

Calories: 252
Total fat: 10 g
Protein: 7 g
Fiber: 8 g
Carbohydrates: 36 g
Cholesterol: 0 g
Sodium: 9 mg

Southwestern Rice and Black Bean Salad

Here's a tempting way to use leftover cooked rice.

1 Combine the rice, beans, corn, and bell pepper in a serving container.

2 Toss the avocado with the lemon juice, then add to the rice mixture along with the remaining ingredients. Toss to combine. Serve at once or cover and refrigerate until needed.

Note
If you need rice in a hurry, cook a 4-serving portion of quick-cooking brown rice.

EMBELLISH IT: Pass chopped fresh cilantro and thinly sliced scallions for topping individual portions.

MAKE IT A MEAL: Serve with one of the Easy Quesadillas or Soft Tacos (page 242) and add a side dish of steamed broccoli, green beans, or Brussels sprouts. Also, see "Make it a meal" on p. 51.

FOR PICKY EATERS: Serve bell pepper strips, corn kernels, black beans, and diced avocado arranged separately on a small platter. Save out a little rice to serve with nonhydrogenated margarine.

VEGAN

6 servings

Composed Couscous and Corn Salad

This colorful main-dish salad is simple to prepare yet has a festive "company's coming" look.

4 medium potatoes, any firm variety, or 2 medium-large sweet potatoes

Prepared ranch dressing or vinaigrette, or Ranch Dressing (page 93) or Basic Vinaigrette (page 92)

¾ cup couscous

2 cups cooked fresh corn kernels (from 2 to 3 medium ears) or frozen corn kernels, thawed

1 tablespoon light olive oil

Salt to taste

Minced fresh parsley for topping, optional

1 red or green bell pepper (or half of each), cut into narrow strips

1 cup baby carrots, or to taste

½ cup black olives, preferably cured and pitted

1 cup red or yellow cherry tomatoes, halved

1 Bake or microwave the potatoes or sweet potatoes until done but still firm. When cool enough to handle, peel and cut into bite-size chunks and place in a small mixing bowl. Toss with enough dressing to moisten.

2 Meanwhile, pour 1½ cups boiling water over the couscous in a heatproof container. Let stand for 10 minutes, then fluff with a fork.

3 Combine the couscous with the corn in a mixing bowl. Drizzle in the oil and toss well. Season gently with salt.

4 Mound the couscous mixture in the center of a large platter. Sprinkle with minced fresh parsley, if desired.

5 Arrange alternating piles of potatoes, bell pepper, baby carrots, olives, and tomatoes around the couscous mixture. Each person can make up his or her own plate. Pass additional dressing to drizzle on the raw vegetables as desired.

Calories: 261
Total fat: 6 g
Protein: 6 g
Fiber: 5 g
Carbohydrates: 48 g
Cholesterol: 0 g
Sodium: 141 mg

MAKE IT A MEAL: This salad makes a bountiful accompaniment to veggie burgers or quesadillas (see Easy Quesadillas or Soft Tacos, page 242).

FOR PICKY EATERS: This salad may seem too sophisticated for kids, but honestly, it's perfect for picky eaters since it has so many tempting separate elements. Children can take whatever appeals to them, and leave the rest.

Spring Barley Salad

Make this delectable salad when the first crop of asparagus appears in spring.

1 cup pearl or pot (unhulled) barley

6 to 8 ounces slender asparagus, trimmed, bottoms cut into 1-inch pieces

1 cup fresh peas, steamed, or substitute 1 cup frozen green peas, thawed

1 medium red bell pepper, finely diced

1 cup finely shredded green cabbage

1 celery stalk, finely diced

¼ to ½ cup sliced black olives

2 tablespoons minced fresh dill, or more to taste

½ cup prepared low-fat vinaigrette or Basic Vinaigrette (page 92), or as needed to moisten

Salt and freshly ground pepper to taste

1 Combine the pearl barley with 3 cups water or the pot barley with 3¾ cups water in a deep saucepan. Bring to a simmer, then cover and simmer gently, until the water is absorbed, 40 to 50 minutes. Let cool to room temperature.

2 Combine the barley with all the remaining ingredients in a mixing bowl. Toss together thoroughly. If time allows, let stand for 1 hour or so before serving to allow the flavors to blend.

MAKE IT A MEAL: This teams nicely with Eggless Tofu Quiche (page 136). Add a platter of cherry tomatoes and baby carrots. For a more substantial meal, serve a potato dish as well, such as Sautéed Skillet Potatoes (page 200) or some baked or microwaved potatoes or sweet potatoes.

FOR PICKY EATERS: Set aside some of the components that you think your child might enjoy. You can choose from among the asparagus, peas, cucumber, celery, and olives to prepare an attractive platter. See if your picky eater might try some warm cooked barley with a little nonhydrogenated margarine.

Calories: 158

Total fat: 2 g

Protein: 4 g

Fiber: 5.8 g

Carbohydrates: 33 g

Cholesterol: 0 g

Sodium: 68 mg

Salads can be more enticing to both adults and youngsters when served with flavorful dressings. For some years, I used only store-bought, natural dressings, which are tasty as well as convenient. Recently, though, I've returned to making my own. It's surprisingly easy and fun to make dressings, and their flavors surpass those of store-bought versions. Here are a few of my family's favorites.

Makes about 1 cup

½ cup extra-virgin olive oil

¼ to ⅓ cup balsamic or apple cider
  vinegar

1 tablespoon Dijon mustard

1 tablespoon honey, maple syrup, or
  brown rice syrup

1 teaspoon Italian or salt-free all-
  purpose seasoning (see page xxvi)

Per 2-tablespoon serving

Calories: 128

Total fat: 14 g

Protein: 0 g

Fiber: 0 g

Carbohydrates: 3 g

Cholesterol: 0 g

Sodium: 19 mg

Basic Vinaigrette

An all-purpose dressing for salads, slaws, and marinating. Increase the proportion of vinegar if you prefer a more pungent taste.

Combine all ingredients in a tightly lidded bottle and shake thoroughly. Shake well before each use. Keeps for up to 2 weeks, refrigerated; bring to room temperature before using.

Ranch Dressing

It's easy to make a good homemade version of this versatile dressing.

Combine all ingredients in a small bowl with ¼ cup water and whisk together until smooth. Transfer to a tightly lidded bottle. Shake well before each use. Keeps up to 1 week, refrigerated.

Variations

- Use ¾ cup puréed silken tofu in place of the yogurt/mayonnaise combination.
- Eliminate the water and use as a dip.

DAIRY / VEGAN OPTION

Makes about 1 cup

½ cup low-fat yogurt or soy yogurt
¼ cup soy mayonnaise
Juice of ½ lemon or 1½ tablespoons white wine vinegar or rice vinegar, or to taste
1 teaspoon salt-free all-purpose seasoning (see page xxvi)
½ teaspoon dried dill

Per 2-tablespoon serving

Dairy	Vegan option
Calories: 28	Calories: 26
Total fat: 2 g	Total fat: 2 g
Protein: 1 g	Protein: 0 g
Fiber: 0 g	Fiber: 0.1 g
Carbohydrates: 1 g	Carbohydrates: 2 g
Cholesterol: 1 g	Cholesterol: 0 g
Sodium: 69 mg	Sodium: 62 mg

Thousand Island Dressing

This is the first dressing that enticed my sons to try salad when they were young. It's a good bet for your young children, too.

DAIRY / VEGAN OPTION

Makes about 1 cup

½ cup soy mayonnaise

¼ cup low-fat yogurt or soy yogurt

¼ cup natural ketchup

1 tablespoon sweet pickle relish, or to taste

Combine all ingredients in a small bowl and whisk together until smooth. Transfer to a small lidded container. Spoon onto salads. This is also good for use as a sandwich dressing. Keeps up to 1 week, refrigerated.

Per 2-tablespoon serving

Dairy	Vegan option
Calories: 50	Calories: 49
Total fat: 3 g	Total fat: 3 g
Protein: 1 g	Protein: 0 g
Fiber: 0.1 g	Fiber: 0.2 g
Carbohydrates: 3 g	Carbohydrates: 3 g
Cholesterol: 0 g	Cholesterol: 0 g
Sodium: 225 mg	Sodium: 221 mg

French Dressing

My sons seem to have made the natural segue from Thousand Island Dressing (page 94) to this one as their current favorite. I hope you'll agree that this is better than the store-bought variety.

Combine all the ingredients in a small mixing bowl and whisk together until smoothly blended. Transfer to a tightly lidded bottle. Shake well before each use. Keeps up to 2 weeks, refrigerated.

HONEY / VEGAN OPTION

Makes about 1 cup

¼ cup good-quality ketchup
½ cup soy mayonnaise
3 tablespoons light olive oil
2 tablespoons red wine vinegar
1 tablespoon honey or maple syrup
½ teaspoon paprika, or to taste

Per 2-tablespoon serving
Calories: 96
Total fat: 8 g
Protein: 0 g
Fiber: 0 g
Carbohydrates: 4 g
Cholesterol: 0 g
Sodium: 214 mg

Makes about 1 cup

1/3 cup light olive oil

2 tablespoons dark sesame oil

1/3 cup rice vinegar or white wine vinegar

1 tablespoon honey or maple syrup

1 tablespoon reduced-sodium natural
   soy sauce

1/2 teaspoon grated fresh ginger or pinch
   of ground ginger

1 tablespoon sesame seeds

Per 2-tablespoon serving

Calories: 120

Total fat: 12 g

Protein: 0 g

Fiber: 0.1 g

Carbohydrates: 2 g

Cholesterol: 0 g

Sodium: 87 mg

Asian Sesame Salad Dressing

Salty and tangy, this is the perfect dressing for salads served with Asian-style meals. I call for this in Asian-Flavored Coleslaw (page 70).

Combine all ingredients in a tightly lidded bottle. Shake well before each use. Keeps up to 2 weeks, refrigerated.

Tangy Tahini Dressing

This one is hands-down my personal favorite. It makes even the simplest salad shine.

Combine all ingredients in a tightly lidded bottle and shake thoroughly. Shake well before each use. Keeps up to 2 weeks, refrigerated.

VEGAN

Makes about 1 cup

½ cup extra-virgin or light olive oil

¼ cup sesame tahini

2 to 3 tablespoons apple cider vinegar

Juice of ½ lemon

2 tablespoons reduced-sodium natural soy sauce

1 teaspoon dried dill

1 teaspoon dried chives, optional

Per 2-tablespoon serving

Calories: 168

Total fat: 17 g

Protein: 2 g

Fiber: 0.7 g

Carbohydrates: 3 g

Cholesterol: 0 g

Sodium: 180 mg

CHAPTER FOUR

Pasta
and
Noodles

WHERE WOULD PARENTS be without pasta? It's the perfect food when you want dinner in a hurry and need to accommodate both adults and children. Most varieties cook quickly enough to satisfy ravenous hunger yet allow enough cooking time to prepare a simple sauce and a salad, with perhaps time to spare to cut some bread. It's hard not to love pasta, and I wonder if there is any child (except those with an intolerance to wheat) who won't gladly eat it, plain or embellished. That said, there are several varieties of wheat-free pastas available, so no one has to lead a noodle-deprived life. Some of these varieties are detailed in A Pasta Primer on page 100.

I encourage you to explore the wide variety of whole-grain pastas available to make these kinds of meals more nourishing. Whole-grain Asian noodles, Italian whole-wheat pastas, and mixed-flour pastas are especially good and offer a change of pace and variety to an already-beloved staple. I have no quibble with refined pastas, so long as they are used in moderation and especially if used as vehicles for vegetables and nourishing sauces.

In this concise chapter, you'll find comforting classics given contemporary twists, quick Asian-style noodle dishes, and pastas that are amazingly hearty one-dish meals.

A Pasta Primer

Nutrition Notes

Pastas and noodles have at last shed their old "fattening" image—it's not what's in them, after all, it's what you put on them. An average serving of 2 ounces of plain cooked pasta contains only 1 to 2 grams of fat, depending on the composition of flours. Still, with questions being raised about high-carbohydrate diets, some wonder what role pasta should play. We all need sources of good-quality carbohydrates, for that food group is still considered a prime source of energy for the body. The good news is that even refined durum wheat pasta is considered a complex carbohydrate food by most experts because its carbs enter the bloodstream slowly, unlike the simple, system-shocking carbohydrates of refined sugars and other sweeteners.

Nutritional qualities of the different varieties of pastas and noodles depend on the particular flours used in making them. In general, most pastas and noodles are good sources of complex carbohydrates (starches, complex sugars, and fiber), good sources of protein (ranging from about 6 grams in a 2-ounce serving of refined pasta to 10 grams per 2-ounce serving in whole-grain pastas), and are rich in iron and B vitamins. Though ordinary durum wheat pastas can claim the aforementioned benefits owing to the enrichment process, pastas and noodles made from whole-grain flours provide greater amounts of protein and fiber and contain a wider range of vitamins and minerals, including calcium, magnesium, phosphorus, zinc, vitamin B_6, and vitamin E.

For children and adults whose diets are already high in fiber, using some refined pasta can actually help with mineral absorption. It may be beneficial for those who are trying to gain weight or who have delicate appetites. If your family has a definite preference for refined pasta but otherwise has a diet rich in whole grains, fruits, and vegetables, no problem. However, for those whose diets include mostly refined grains, eating whole-grain pasta, at least some of the time, is a step in the right direction.

Please note that unless a specialty pasta (such as soba or udon) is called for in a recipe, the nutritional analysis assumes the use of ordinary durum wheat pasta. Protein and fiber content will be higher if you use whole-grain pasta.

Expand Your Pasta Horizons

Pastas and noodles available in well-stocked supermarkets, natural food stores, ethnic groceries, and specialty food shops come in all manner of flours, flavors, shapes, and sizes. And those who are wheat intolerant need not feel deprived, with all the wheat-free varieties to choose from. Easy and quick to cook, easy to digest, low in fat, rich in nutrients, and versatile and tasty, pasta and noodles should be perfectly at home in every busy, health-conscious cook's pantry.

Following are descriptions of some varieties of pastas and noodles to explore. Look for these products in natural foods stores, Asian groceries, and natural foods mail-order sources. When first trying a variety, buy it in packaged form to become familiar with the manufacturer's suggestions for cooking time and other tips. Then, if available, you might buy these pastas in more economical bulk form.

ASIAN NOODLES

Though Asian markets and specialty food shops are good sources for these noodles, natural foods stores are more likely to carry the whole-grain versions, when available. This is not an exhaustive list of Asian noodles; I've included only the ones used in this book's recipes.

Buckwheat noodles (soba): These are spaghetti-like noodles that combine hearty-tasting buckwheat flour with wheat or whole-wheat flour. They come in varying percentages of buckwheat, from 20 percent buckwheat/80 percent whole wheat to 100 percent buckwheat. The greater percentage of mineral-rich buckwheat, the more pronounced the flavor. Note that 100 percent buckwheat noodles are wheat-free. *Uses:* With sweet-and-sour sauces, soy sauce and sesame oil, spicy peanut sauce, spaghetti sauces, and soy-flavored vinaigrettes; broken into shorter lengths for soups and broths; with stir-fried vegetables, and cold with Asian vegetables (such as snow peas, daikon radish, and mung bean sprouts).

Ramen noodles: These thin, wavy noodles, available in whole-grain varieties such as buckwheat, are best known for their use in soup mixes commonly available in natural foods stores. They are occasionally available on their own in small packages or bundles. *Uses:* In miso or vegetable broths and combined with tender-crisp vegetables and tofu or with chopped sea vegetables and soy sauce.

Rice noodles (also called bifun, rice vermicelli): These long, fine noodles are made of white rice flour and have the same mild flavor and tender texture of white rice. Though not a whole-grain product, these wheat-free noodles lend an offbeat touch to Asian recipes. These come in bundles and cook very quickly. *Uses:* Simmered in brothy soups, served cold with matchstick-cut vegetables and soy vinaigrette, fried in hot oil as a crisp garnish, and substituted for rice as a bed for vegetable dishes or adzuki beans.

Somen: These spaghetti-like noodles are usually imported from Japan, where they are traditionally eaten cold during the summer months. A smooth-textured whole-wheat version is available in natural foods stores. *Uses:* With spicy peanut sauce, sesame sauce, and spaghetti sauces and cold with crisp vegetables (such as daikon radish, carrot, and turnip) with a light soy vinaigrette.

Udon: These long, somewhat thick noodles are akin to linguine. The whole-wheat variety of this Japanese import (available in natural foods stores) has a smooth texture and mild flavor. *Uses:* With spaghetti sauces, pesto sauce, and miso-based sauces, with diced tofu or tempeh, scallions, and soy sauce; and with ginger-flavored dressing and crisp vegetables.

SPECIALTY WHOLE-GRAIN PASTAS AND NOODLES

Many of the pasta varieties listed below are available in organic form. Some may be suitable for wheat-free diets; check the labels carefully.

Artichoke pasta: This pasta is made of a blend of durum semolina or whole-wheat flour and Jerusalem artichoke flour or artichoke flour alone in a wheat-free version. Artichoke pasta is mild and flavorful, with a pleasant texture, and is available in almost all standard shapes such as angel hair spaghetti, shells, elbows, and fettuccine. It also comes in flavors, such as garlic-parsley and tomato-basil. *Uses:* In Italian-style recipes, especially with light, fresh tomato sauces and pestos; in pasta salads and macaroni and cheese; and combined with beans in hot or cold dishes.

Corn pasta: Made of natural blends of corn flour, this wheat-free product allows those with wheat intolerance to enjoy traditional pasta dishes. The spaghetti tends not to hold up as well in cooking, but the small shapes such as shells and elbows do fine and have the slightly grainy texture and pleasant flavor of cornmeal. *Uses:* With spaghetti sauces and pesto; with steamed vegetables and olive oil; with beans in hot or cold dishes; and with fresh corn kernels and tomatoes.

Quinoa pasta: These noodles, combining whole-wheat flour with the flour of quinoa, a super-nutritious ancient grain, come primarily in the form of flat fettuccine noodles or elbows. The nutty flavor of quinoa comes through lightly. Also available are quinoa-corn elbows, a great combination of two flavorful grains. *Uses:* Fettuccine-shaped noodles with Italian-style sauces and creamy milk- or soy milk–based sauces and with steamed fresh greens (such as kale and spinach). Quinoa-corn elbows with olive oil or nonhydrogenated margarine, in macaroni salad, and in macaroni and cheese casserole.

Soy pasta: This is a combination of wheat flour with 10 to 20 percent soy flour and comes in a variety of shapes. The flavor and texture are smoother than 100 percent whole-wheat pasta. *Uses:* Substitute for similarly shaped ordinary pastas.

Spelt pasta: Spelt, a nutritious ancient grain, is used to make a variety of pastas that have a more delicate, nutty flavor and texture than whole-wheat pastas. This pasta is available in the gamut of popular shapes from spaghetti, elbows, and shells to lasagna noodles. *Uses:* Substitute for similarly shaped ordinary pastas.

Vegetable pastas: Natural foods stores are host to a variety of pastas that combine whole or refined durum wheat flour with vegetable flours. Spinach pasta is perhaps the most widely used and imparts the most pronounced flavor, but beet, carrot, and tomato pastas are also common. It is available in spirals, shells, and elbows, often in packages of mixed colors. *Uses:* With light sauces (such as garlic and olive oil) or puréed fresh tomato sauce; particularly good in cold marinated salads with a light vinaigrette.

Whole-wheat pastas: Domestic whole durum wheat pastas are dark, hearty flavored, and often have a grainy texture, in contrast to whole-wheat Asian noodles. Higher in protein and fiber than refined durum wheat pasta, whole-wheat pastas come in a wide range of shapes and sizes, from alphabets to lasagna noodles. Look for products imported from Italy as well. These also tend to be smoother and more tender than domestic brands. *Uses:* Substitute for similarly shaped ordinary pasta for a more robust flavor and texture; with pesto sauce, spicy peanut sauce, and sesame sauce; with beans in hot or cold dishes; in winter soups and stews.

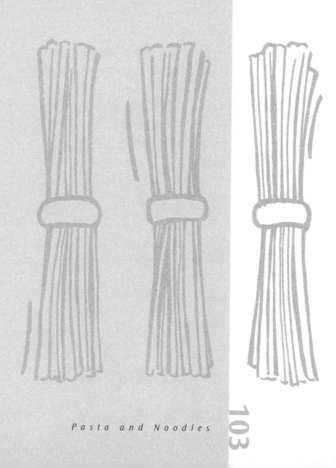

Vegetable Lo Mein

This Chinese-restaurant favorite is a fun dish to create at home and has the advantage of being far less oily than its carry-out counterpart. Udon or soba noodles work well; using whole-grain varieties makes the dish nutritious as well as authentic.

8 ounces narrow Chinese wheat noodles, udon, or soba (if unavailable, substitute linguini)
1 tablespoon light olive oil
8 ounces preshredded coleslaw (preferably with carrots included)
1½ cups sliced brown or white mushrooms or one 15-ounce can cut baby corn, drained
1 cup snow peas or frozen green beans, thawed
2 to 3 scallions, cut into 1-inch-long pieces
Reduced-sodium soy sauce, to taste
1 tablespoon dark sesame oil
Freshly ground pepper, to taste

1 Cook the noodles in plenty of rapidly boiling water until al dente, then drain.

2 Meanwhile, heat the olive oil in a wok or stir-fry pan. Add the coleslaw and stir-fry over medium-high heat for 5 minutes, then add the mushrooms, snow peas, and scallions. Continue to stir-fry until the vegetables are all just tender-crisp, adding just enough water to keep the bottom of the pan moist, 5 to 7 minutes more.

3 Combine the cooked noodles with the vegetables in a serving bowl and toss together. Season with soy sauce, sesame oil, and pepper. Serve at once.

MAKE IT A MEAL: Serve with Orange-Glazed Tofu and Broccoli (page 146). Another pleasing combination is to team this with Asian Succotash (page 219) and Stir-Fried Broccoli (page 209). In either case, add raw vegetables, such as carrots and bell peppers, to the plate.

Calories: 314
Total fat: 8 g
Protein: 13 g
Fiber: 6.1 g
Carbohydrates: 51 g
Cholesterol: 0 g
Sodium: 20 mg

Vegetable Chow Mein

Here's a Chinese-restaurant classic that's easy to make at home.

1   Combine the liquid from the baby corn and water chestnuts in a large cup or other container. Dissolve the cornstarch in a small amount of the reserved liquid and then pour it back into the larger cup; add the soy sauce. Set aside.

2   Cook the noodles in plenty of rapidly boiling water until al dente, then drain.

3   Meanwhile, heat the oil in a wok or stir-fry pan. Add the onion and sauté over medium heat until soft and lightly browned.

4   Add the celery and bell pepper, turn the heat up to medium-high, and stir-fry for 2 to 3 minutes.

5   Add the baby corn, water chestnuts, and bean sprouts along with the reserved cornstarch liquid. Cook until all the ingredients are well heated through and the sauce is thickened. Season with pepper, then serve at once. Pass extra soy sauce.

EMBELLISH IT: Pass chopped toasted cashews or chopped walnuts and minced cilantro for sprinkling over individual portions.

MAKE IT A MEAL: Begin the meal with Chinese Vegetable and Tofu Soup (page 33). Serve baby carrots and pickled beets with the chow mein, and finish the meal with sliced oranges.

VEGAN

4 to 6 servings

One 15-ounce can baby corn, drained, liquid reserved
One 6- to 8-ounce can sliced water chestnuts, liquid reserved
2 tablespoons cornstarch or arrowroot
2 tablespoons reduced-sodium soy sauce
8 ounces wide Chinese wheat noodles or fettuccine, broken in half
$1\frac{1}{2}$ tablespoons light olive oil
1 large onion, quartered and thinly sliced
3 large celery stalks or bok choy stalks, sliced diagonally
1 medium red bell pepper, cut into narrow strips
4 ounces mung bean sprouts
Freshly ground pepper to taste

Calories: 177
Total fat: 5 g
Protein: 6 g
Fiber: 7.3 g
Carbohydrates: 30 g
Cholesterol: 0 g
Sodium: 316 mg

Asian Noodles with Stir-Fried Corn and Cabbage

VEGAN

4 to 6 servings

One 8-ounce package udon or soba
   noodles, preferably whole grain
2 tablespoons light olive oil
4 cups thinly sliced green cabbage
1 cup frozen corn kernels, thawed
3 scallions, cut into 1-inch pieces
1 to 2 tablespoons reduced-sodium
   soy sauce
1 to 2 teaspoons dark sesame oil
Freshly ground pepper to taste

Calories: 292
Total fat: 10 g
Protein: 10 g
Fiber: 3.9 g
Carbohydrates: 43 g
Cholesterol: 0 g
Sodium: 222 mg

This quick and tasty noodle dish teams well with Asian-style tofu and seitan dishes.

1 Cook the noodles in plenty of rapidly boiling water until al dente, then drain.

2 Meanwhile, heat the olive oil in a wide skillet or stir-fry pan. Add the cabbage, corn, and scallions and stir-fry over medium-high heat until the cabbage is slightly wilted but still crisp, 3 to 5 minutes.

3 Stir in the noodles, then season with soy sauce, sesame oil, and pepper. Serve at once.

EMBELLISH IT: Pass a bottle of Szechwan or other Asian hot sauce and/or a small dish of grated fresh ginger to stir into individual portions. It's also nice topped with a sprinkling of sesame seeds.

MAKE IT A MEAL: Serve with Orange-Glazed Tofu and Broccoli (page 146) or Seitan and Broccoli Stir-Fry (page 161). Teriyaki Tofu Triangles (page 148) and purchased good-quality spring rolls (look for these in the frozen foods section of natural foods stores) make this a most enjoyable meal as well. With any of these options, serve a platter of alternating strips of red and green bell pepper.

Gingery Japanese Noodles with Mushrooms and Snow Peas

This noodle dish is served Japanese-style in a small portion of broth. Different varieties of soba noodles are available in natural foods stores and well-stocked supermarkets (see pages 101–2).

1 Bring the broth or water with bouillon cube to a simmer in a large saucepan. Add the noodles and cook at a rapid boil until al dente.

2 Meanwhile, heat the oils plus ¼ cup water in a stir-fry pan. Stir in the ginger and soy sauce, then add the snow peas and mushrooms. Cook over medium-high, stirring frequently, until the snow peas are tender-crisp and the mushrooms are wilted, 3 to 4 minutes.

3 Add the cooked noodles and their broth and the scallions. Season with pepper. Cook for 2 to 3 minutes longer. Serve at once in shallow bowls, including some of the broth with each serving.

MAKE IT A MEAL: Serve with Teriyaki Tofu Triangles (page 148) and a platter of crisp raw vegetables (for some ideas, see page 84) or a simple salad of greens, orange sections, and toasted almond slices. This also makes a nice accompaniment to Vegetable Sushi (page 193).

VEGAN

4 to 6 servings

5 cups prepared vegetable broth or 5 cups water with 1 vegetable bouillon cube
One 8-ounce package soba (Japanese buckwheat noodles) or somen
2 tablespoons light olive oil
1 teaspoon dark sesame oil
1 to 2 teaspoons grated fresh ginger
1 tablespoon reduced-sodium soy sauce, or to taste
2 cups (about 4 ounces) snow peas
6 to 8 ounces fresh shiitake, cremini, or baby bella mushrooms, stemmed and sliced
2 to 3 scallions, thinly sliced
Freshly ground pepper to taste

Calories: 271
Total fat: 7 g
Protein: 10 g
Fiber: 4.1 g
Carbohydrates: 43 g
Cholesterol: 0 g
Sodium: 203 mg

VEGAN

4 servings

8 ounces soba (Japanese buckwheat
   noodles)
One 16-ounce tub firm or extra-firm tofu
1½ tablespoons light olive oil
1½ pounds firm ripe tomatoes, diced
1 teaspoon dark sesame oil
¼ to ½ cup thinly sliced fresh basil
   leaves
1 teaspoon good-quality curry powder
1 teaspoon natural granulated sugar
   (see page 283)
2 to 3 scallions, minced
2 tablespoons reduced-sodium soy sauce,
   or to taste

Calories: 471
Total fat: 18 g
Protein: 30 g
Fiber: 6.7 g
Carbohydrates: 55 g
Cholesterol: 0 g
Sodium: 381 mg

Soba with Tofu, Tomatoes, and Basil

Here's a lively summer dish with an Asian and Italian fusion. Flavorful ripe tomatoes are a must!

1 Cook the noodles in plenty of rapidly boiling water until al dente, then drain.

2 Meanwhile, cut the tofu into ½-inch-thick slices. Blot between clean tea towels or several layers of paper towels to remove excess moisture. Cut into ½-inch dice.

3 Heat the olive oil in a wide skillet or stir-fry pan. Add the tofu and stir-fry over medium-high heat until most sides are golden. Add the tomatos and cook just until they are warmed.

4 Combine the cooked noodles and tofu-tomato mixture in a serving bowl. Add the remaining ingredients, toss well, and serve.

EMBELLISH IT: For a spicier version, add hot red pepper flakes or any kind of Asian hot sauce, to taste.

MAKE IT A MEAL: Fresh corn on the cob, a platter of crisp garden vegetables or simple salad, and a crusty whole-grain bread are enough to make this a light and satisfying warm-weather meal.

Ultimate Macaroni and Cheese

A most beloved comfort food, macaroni and cheese can be a good option for grown-up kids to enjoy along with the youngsters, especially if their portions can be jazzed up. Use the toppings on page 111 as a springboard for your own innovations.

1 Cook the pasta in plenty of rapidly boiling water until al dente, then drain.

2 Meanwhile, dissolve the flour in ½ cup of the milk, and combine with the remaining milk, margarine, and cheese in a saucepan. Slowly bring to a gentle simmer, stirring often. Cook over low heat until the sauce is smooth and thick, 4 to 5 minutes.

3 Combine the cooked macaroni and sauce in a serving container and stir together. Season with salt and serve.

EMBELLISH IT: See suggestions on page 112.

MAKE IT A MEAL: See "Make it a meal" on page 111.

DAIRY / VEGAN OPTION

4 to 6 servings, or more for kid-size portions

10 to 12 ounces cavatappi (tubular twists) or elbow macaroni
3 tablespoons unbleached white flour
1½ cups low-fat milk, rice milk, or soy milk
2 tablespoons nonhydrogenated margarine
1½ to 2 cups grated Cheddar cheese or Cheddar-style nondairy cheese
Salt to taste

Dairy	Vegan option
Calories: 497	Calories: 445
Total fat: 19 g	Total fat: 12 g
Protein: 22 g	Protein: 18 g
Fiber: 2.5 g	Fiber: 2.5 g
Carbohydrates: 60 g	Carbohydrates: 65 g
Cholesterol: 44 g	Cholesterol: 0 g
Sodium: 675 mg	Sodium: 769 mg

Macaroni and Cheese with Secret Silken Tofu Sauce

DAIRY / VEGAN OPTION

4 to 6 servings, or more for kid-size portions

10 to 12 ounces elbow macaroni, or
    other short tubular pasta shape such
    as cavatappi
One 12.3-ounce package silken tofu
2 tablespoons nonhydrogenated
    margarine
1½ to 2 cups firmly packed grated
    Cheddar cheese or Cheddar-style
    nondairy cheese
Salt to taste

Dairy	Vegan option
Calories: 489	Calories: 428
Total fat: 20 g	Total fat: 14 g
Protein: 22 g	Protein: 20 g
Fiber: 2.9 g	Fiber: 2.9 g
Carbohydrates: 55 g	Carbohydrates: 56 g
Cholesterol: 41 g	Cholesterol: 0 g
Sodium: 642 mg	Sodium: 747 mg

Using puréed silken tofu as a base for the sauce lends the dish a dose of soy goodness. When I first developed this recipe, I wanted to test it out on the two very particular sons of my dear friend Stacie. Skeptical, she warned me that "They won't eat macaroni and cheese unless it comes out of a box." I'm happy to report that not only was it love at first bite but now, years later, the boys still request this dish each time they visit.

1 Cook the pasta in plenty of rapidly boiling water until al dente, then drain.

2 Meanwhile, purée the tofu until perfectly smooth in a food processor or blender. Transfer to a medium saucepan and add the margarine and cheese. Slowly bring to a gentle simmer, stirring often, then cook over low heat until the cheese is thoroughly melted.

3 Combine the cooked macaroni and sauce in a serving container and stir together. Season with salt and serve at once.

Toppings

Try these toppings over any macaroni and cheese recipe.

- **Wilted greens and sun-dried tomatoes:** Steam a good-size bunch of spinach, Swiss chard, or arugula until tender in a large saucepan (spinach and arugula need only the water clinging to their leaves and 1 or 2 minutes of cooking; chard needs a bit of water and 5 to 8 minutes). Drain well, chop coarsely, and serve with sliced sun-dried tomatoes (oil-packed or rehydrated).
- **Sautéed onions, garlic, and herbs:** Slowly sauté 1 large onion, chopped, and 3 to 4 garlic cloves, minced, in a small amount of light olive oil until golden brown. Stir in ¼ cup or more of your favorite chopped fresh herbs (parsley, dill, oregano, or a combination).
- **Salsa, corn kernels, and black beans:** Combine 1 cup cooked black beans, 1 cup cooked corn, and ½ cup salsa, or to taste. Stir in some minced fresh cilantro, if desired. Warm until heated through.
- **Wild mushrooms, mustard, and dill:** Slice a good-size batch of shiitake, cremini, portabella, or baby bella mushrooms (or a combination). Cook in a skillet with just a bit of water, covered, until tender. Drain, leaving just a small amount of liquid. Stir in 2 teaspoons prepared grainy mustard and ¼ cup minced fresh dill.

MAKE IT A MEAL: You can serve any macaroni and cheese variation with a number of vegetable side dishes and salads. When I make it, I'm geared to a simple meal, so I often serve just steamed broccoli and a bountiful green salad. Other good accompaniments are Orange and Maple-Glazed Beets (page 216) and Cabbage, Apple, and Raisin Slaw (page 69).

Macaroni and cheese with a hint of sweet potato: Add ½ cup very well mashed sweet potato to either the Ultimate Macaroni and Cheese (page 109) or the Macaroni and Cheese with Secret Silken Tofu Sauce (page 110) for added body and flavor.

Baked macaroni and cheese with crisp bread crumbs: Transfer macaroni and cheese to a lightly oiled 2-quart casserole dish. Top with ½ to ¾ cup fresh bread crumbs. Bake at 400°F for 20 to 25 minutes, until the top is golden and crusty.

Cincinnati Chili Mac

A vegetarian take on a unique recipe from the American Midwest, this "chili mac" can be made with a variety of ingredients and seasonings, the common denominator being that it's always served over spaghetti and contains a hint of sweet spice (such as cinnamon or allspice). This is great for older kids who have developed a taste for chili, hungry teens, and adults who like heartier pasta dishes.

1 Heat the oil in a large saucepan or stir-fry pan. Add the onion and sauté over medium heat until translucent. Add the green and red bell peppers and continue to sauté until the onion is golden.

2 Stir in the remaining ingredients except the spaghetti and bring to a simmer. Cover and simmer gently for 20 minutes, or until the vegetables are tender and the flavorings completely blended.

3 Meanwhile, cook the spaghetti in plenty of rapidly boiling water until al dente, then drain.

4 For each serving, place a small amount of spaghetti in a wide shallow bowl and top with some of the chili. If desired, top with any or all of the suggested garnishes.

EMBELLISH IT: Top individual portions with any or all of the following:

- Diced ripe tomatoes
- Chopped onion or thinly sliced scallions
- Grated Cheddar cheese or Cheddar-style nondairy cheese

MAKE IT A MEAL: This is a hefty one-dish meal; all you need to complete it is a bountiful green salad and, if desired, some natural stone-ground tortilla chips.

VEGAN

6 servings

1 tablespoon light olive oil

1 cup chopped onion

1 medium green bell pepper, diced

1 medium red bell pepper, diced

1 small fresh hot chile, minced, or one 4-ounce can chopped mild green chilies

One 28-ounce can diced tomatoes

4 cups cooked kidney or red beans (from $1\frac{2}{3}$ cups dried) or two 16-ounce cans kidney or red beans, drained and rinsed

1 to 2 teaspoons good-quality chili powder

1 teaspoon ground cumin

1 teaspoon dried oregano

$\frac{1}{2}$ teaspoon ground cinnamon

12 to 16 ounces spaghetti (use a whole-grain variety if desired)

Calories: 496

Total fat: 5 g

Protein: 22 g

Fiber: 13.4 g

Carbohydrates: 94 g

Cholesterol: 0 g

Sodium: 223 mg

6 to 8 servings

Mom's "Tuna"-Noodle Casserole

Here's a vegan version of an old-fashioned family favorite straight from the 1950s. Pack a leftover portion of this casserole as part of a brown-bag lunch or picnic—it's just as tasty at room temperature as right out of the oven. Baked tofu does an awesome job standing in for tuna.

12 ounces ribbon-style noodles (see Note)
1 tablespoon light olive oil
3 medium celery stalks, diced
1 cup sliced white or cremini mushrooms, optional
2 cups rice milk or soy milk
3 tablespoons unbleached white flour
One 10- to 12-ounce package baked tofu, finely diced
2 to 3 scallions, sliced
Salt and freshly ground pepper, to taste
Wheat germ, for topping
1 cup grated Cheddar-style nondairy cheese for topping, optional

Calories: 361
Total fat: 8 g
Protein: 19 g
Fiber: 36 g
Carbohydrates: 53 g
Cholesterol: 0 g
Sodium: 229 mg

1 Preheat the oven to 350° F. Oil a wide, shallow 2-quart casserole dish.

2 Cook the noodles in plenty of rapidly boiling water until al dente, then drain.

3 Meanwhile, heat the oil in a medium saucepan. Add the celery and sauté over medium heat for 3 to 4 minutes. Add the mushrooms, if using, and continue to sauté until wilted, about 5 minutes longer.

4 Pour 1½ cups of the milk into the saucepan and bring to a simmer. Combine the remaining milk with the flour in a small bowl and stir until the flour is smoothly dissolved. Slowly pour into the saucepan, whisking constantly. Simmer gently until the sauce has thickened, then remove from the heat.

5 In a large mixing bowl, combine the noodles, sauce, tofu, and scallions. Mix gently but thoroughly. Season with salt and pepper and toss again.

6 Transfer the mixture to the prepared casserole. Sprinkle generously with wheat germ. If desired, sprinkle cheese over the top as well. Bake for 35 minutes, or until the top is golden brown and beginning to get crusty. Allow to cool for 5 minutes, then cut into squares to serve.

Note

You can use any sort of ribbon noodle (try a nutritious variety like quinoa or spelt ribbons) or use fettuccine or pappardelle, broken into thirds.

MAKE IT A MEAL: Bake a batch of Scalloped Cauliflower or Broccoli (page 206) at the same time, using the broccoli option to add color to the plate. Complete the meal with a bountiful tossed salad. Another option is to serve this with Sweet Cinnamon-Maple Glazed Baby Carrots (page 214) and Cold Vegetable Platter #1 or #2 (page 84). Add fresh corn on the cob when in season.

Green Noodles

Kids who enjoy green vegetables will appreciate this mild pasta dish, and adults can dress it up as suggested below.

10 to 12 ounces pasta (any shape)

1 tablespoon nonhydrogenated margarine

1½ cups finely chopped broccoli florets

1 cup frozen green peas, thawed

½ cup low-fat cottage cheese or crumbled silken tofu

½ cup low-fat milk, rice milk, or soy milk

Salt to taste

Grated fresh Parmesan or Parmesan-style soy cheese for topping, optional

1 Cook the pasta in plenty of rapidly boiling water until al dente, then drain. Transfer to a serving container and toss with the margarine.

2 Meanwhile, steam the broccoli florets with a small amount of water in a saucepan or microwave in a heatproof container, until tender but still bright green. Add the peas and steam or microwave until the peas are heated through, about 1 minute.

3 Combine the vegetables with cottage cheese and milk in a food processor or blender and process until smoothly puréed or add the cottage cheese and milk to the saucepan and purée with an immersion blender.

4 Pour the sauce over the cooked pasta and toss to combine. Stir in a little additional milk if needed for a moist consistency. Season gently with salt and serve at once, passing Parmesan cheese, if desired, to top individual portions.

Dairy	Vegan option
Calories: 334	Calories: 336
Total fat: 4 g	Total fat: 4 g
Protein: 15 g	Protein: 13 g
Fiber: 5.4 g	Fiber: 5.6 g
Carbohydrates: 60 g	Carbohydrates: 62 g
Cholesterol: 2 g	Cholesterol: 0 g
Sodium: 132 mg	Sodium: 39 mg

Tip

When reheating any leftovers of this dish, add a little more milk to moisten the sauce.

EMBELLISH IT: Top individual portions with lots of chopped fresh herbs (dill is particularly good), chopped scallions, and/or toasted sliced or slivered almonds. Another good way to top this is with nicely browned onions and garlic.

MAKE IT A MEAL: For a comforting meal, serve with Skillet Baked Beans (page 189) and Sweet Cinnamon-Maple Glazed Baby Carrots (page 214). Add some diced ripe tomatoes or cherry tomatoes and green bell pepper strips. See also "Make it a meal" on page 80.

4 to 6 servings

**10 to 12 ounces rotini or cavatappi
(spirals or macaroni twists)**
2 cups frozen green peas, thawed
**1½ tablespoons nonhydrogenated
margarine**
**One 15-ounce container part-skim
ricotta cheese**
½ cup low-fat milk, rice milk, or soy milk
¾ cup dark raisins
Salt to taste

Calories: 512
Total fat: 11 g
Protein: 24 g
Fiber: 7.4 g
Carbohydrates: 81 g
Cholesterol: 27 g
Sodium: 154 mg

Ricotta Pasta with Raisins and Peas

This is one of the first pasta dishes with "things in it" that my boys enjoyed when they were young. It's a mild dish made enticing with peas and raisins.

1 Cook the pasta in plenty of rapidly boiling water until al dente. Just before draining, add the peas to the pot, and simmer for a few more seconds.

2 Drain the pasta and pea mixture, then transfer to a serving container and toss with the margarine to melt.

3 Combine the ricotta cheese and milk in a smaller mixing bowl. Stir well until smooth, then add to the pasta and stir together until the pasta is evenly coated.

4 Stir in the raisins, then season gently with salt. Serve.

EMBELLISH IT: Adults may enjoy giving this dish a curried spin after young eaters take their portions. It's wonderful with good-quality curry powder and grated or minced fresh ginger stirred in. Scatter toasted almonds over the top.

MAKE IT A MEAL: For a simple, well-rounded meal, serve with a fresh whole-grain bread and Tomatoes with Black Beans or Chickpeas (page 79), steamed broccoli, and raw carrot sticks.

FOR PICKY EATERS: Cook some extra pasta and toss it with margarine. Cook or microwave a small portion of peas. Serve each item separately; offer some of the fresh bread, and a few carrot sticks and raisins.

Tortellini or Ravioli with Broccoli

Filled pastas always seem festive, even as part of easy everyday meals. Consider trying varieties other than the standard ricotta-filled, just for fun. Look for tofu-, spinach-, or vegetable-filled varieties in natural foods stores or Italian groceries. Young eaters will appreciate this in its simplest form, and adults will love it with the suggested embellishments.

1 Cook the pasta according to package directions until al dente, then drain. Transfer to a large serving bowl and toss with the margarine until melted.

2 Meanwhile, heat the oil in a large skillet. Add the garlic and sauté over low heat until golden, 2 to 3 minutes. Add the broccoli and ¼ cup water. Cover and cook until the broccoli is bright green and tender-crisp to your liking, about 5 minutes.

3 Combine the broccoli mixture with the pasta in a serving bowl. Season with salt and pepper and toss together. Serve at once, passing Parmesan cheese, if desired.

EMBELLISH IT: Adults will enjoy topping their pasta with sun-dried tomatoes (oil or dry packed) and fresh basil, both cut into strips. Toasted pine nuts are also a welcome topping.

MAKE IT A MEAL: Serve with Sweet Cinnamon-Maple Glazed Baby Carrots (page 214) and Italian Bread-and-Tomato Salad (page 80) for a delightful meal.

FOR PICKY EATERS: Set aside some of the tortellini or ravioli (or cook extra) to serve with nonhydrogenated margarine. Steam some small broccoli florets to serve on the side.

DAIRY / VEGAN OPTION

4 to 6 servings

One 16-ounce bag frozen tortellini or ravioli (ricotta-, tofu-, or vegetable-filled)
1 tablespoon nonhydrogenated margarine
1 tablespoon extra-virgin olive oil
2 to 3 garlic cloves, minced
4 cups bite-size broccoli florets
Salt and freshly ground pepper to taste
Grated fresh Parmesan or Parmesan-style soy cheese, optional

Dairy	Vegan option
Calories: 232	Calories: 199
Total fat: 9 g	Total fat: 11 g
Protein: 10 g	Protein: 10 g
Fiber: 2.7 g	Fiber: 4.3 g
Carbohydrates: 27 g	Carbohydrates: 20 g
Cholesterol: 19 g	Cholesterol: 0 g
Sodium: 165 mg	Sodium: 700 mg

Pasta with Sneaky Marinara Sauce

VEGAN

6 servings

1 pound pasta, cooked (any shape)

2 tablespoons extra-virgin olive oil

3 to 4 garlic cloves, minced

1 medium onion, finely chopped

One 28-ounce can salt-free puréed tomatoes

One 14- to 16-ounce can salt-free diced tomatoes

One 14- to 16-ounce can salt-free tomato sauce

¼ cup dry red wine, optional

2 teaspoons Italian seasoning

2 cups well-cooked vegetables, puréed (see Note)

Salt and freshly ground pepper to taste

Calories: 266

Total fat: 6 g

Protein: 9 g

Fiber: 9.3 g

Carbohydrates: 49 g

Cholesterol: 0 g

Sodium: 60 mg

There are many excellent pasta sauces on the market, and they can't be beat for convenience. But they can't compare to a homemade marinara, with the wonderful aroma that will permeate your kitchen as it cooks! If young eaters in your home balk at vegetables (and there are plenty of little vegetarians who do so), pasta sauce provides great camouflage for puréed cooked vegetables.

1   Cook the noodles in plenty of rapidly boiling water until al dente, then drain.

2   Heat the oil in a large saucepan. Add the garlic and onion and sauté over low heat until golden, 2 to 3 minutes.

3   Add all the tomato purée, tomatoes, tomato sauce, wine, seasoning, and vegetable purée and bring to a simmer. Cover and simmer very gently over low heat for 30 minutes. Season with salt and pepper. Serve over hot pasta.

Note

Use about 2 cups of well-cooked (but not overcooked), high-nutrient vegetables such as broccoli, carrots, cauliflower, spinach and other greens, and winter squash—preferably a mixture of two or three kinds. Purée them well in a food processor or with an immersion blender.

EMBELLISH IT: Sauté any combination of finely diced bell peppers, sliced mushrooms, and finely diced eggplant as an optional topping. Near the end of the cooking time, add chopped fresh herbs such as parsley, basil, and/or oregano to the sauce if your family is ready for more complex flavors.

MAKE IT A MEAL: Keep it simple by serving with a bountiful tossed salad with chickpeas tossed in, or a Cold Vegetable Platter (page 84). For a larger meal, add a steamed green vegetable such as broccoli or green beans and a crusty whole-grain bread.

Angel Hair with Zucchini and Bread Crumbs

VEGAN

4 to 6 servings

Great for warm weather, but welcome any time you crave a light yet satisfying pasta dish. I like it with some of the recommended embellishments, especially sun-dried tomatoes and parsley.

4 slices whole-grain bread

10 to 12 ounces angel hair pasta (cappellini)

3 tablespoons extra-virgin olive oil

3 to 4 garlic cloves, crushed

4 small zucchini, sliced, or 2 medium zucchini, quartered lengthwise and sliced (about 1½ pounds total)

¼ cup dry white wine, vegetable stock, or water

Salt and freshly ground pepper to taste

Calories: 407

Total fat: 11 g

Protein: 12 g

Fiber: 6.4 g

Carbohydrates: 64 g

Cholesterol: 0 g

Sodium: 91 mg

1 Place the bread in a food processor and whirl until it becomes fine crumbs.

2 Cook the pasta in plenty of rapidly boiling water until al dente, then drain.

3 Meanwhile, heat 2 teaspoons of the oil in a wide skillet. Add the bread crumbs and cook over medium-high heat until they turn toasty brown and crisp. Transfer to a bowl.

4 Heat the remaining oil in the same skillet. Add the garlic and sauté over low heat for 1 to 2 minutes, until golden. Stir in the zucchini and wine. Raise the heat to medium, and cook, stirring frequently, until the zucchini is tender-crisp, about 4 minutes. When done, remove the garlic cloves.

5 Combine the pasta and zucchini in a large bowl. Season with salt and pepper and serve, topping each serving with some of the bread crumbs.

EMBELLISH IT: In its simplest form, this dish is tasty enough for all to enjoy, but I highly recommend passing any or all of the following in small bowls to top individual portions or to stir in before sprinkling on the bread crumbs.

- ½ cup sliced sun-dried tomatoes (oil or dry packed)
- ¼ to ½ cup sliced black olives
- ¼ to ½ cup chopped fresh parsley
- ¼ cup thinly sliced basil leaves
- Grated fresh Parmesan or Parmesan-style soy cheese

MAKE IT A MEAL: Begin this meal with Streamlined Minestrone (page 40) and serve a green salad with the pasta. If you'd like to serve this meal with an interesting salad, try Mixed Greens with Green Beans, Beets, and Feta or Goat Cheese (page 81) or Tomatoes with Black Beans or Chickpeas (page 79). In either case, add a nutritious steamed vegetable like spinach or broccoli.

FOR PICKY EATERS: Cook a little extra pasta to serve with a little nonhydrogenated margarine or olive oil, and perhaps a sprinkling of Parmesan cheese or Parmesan-style soy cheese. Set aside a few sautéed zucchini slices to serve separately.

Pasta with Enlightened Alfredo Sauce

6 servings

If you've been looking for a healthier Alfredo sauce, you've come to the right place! This one's mild and creamy but harbors a fraction of the fat and calories of the traditional cream-based sauce.

12 ounces pasta (see Note)
2 tablespoons nonhydrogenated
    margarine
2 garlic cloves, minced
One 12.3-ounce package silken tofu
½ cup low-fat milk, rice milk, or soy milk
1 teaspoon salt
Freshly ground pepper to taste
Freshly grated Parmesan cheese or
    Parmesan-style soy cheese for
    topping, optional

1 Cook the pasta in plenty of rapidly boiling water until al dente, then drain.

2 Meanwhile, heat the margarine in a small skillet. Add the garlic and sauté over low heat until golden, 2 to 3 minutes. Remove from the heat.

3 Combine the garlic (and margarine) with the tofu, milk, and salt in a food processor. Process until completely smooth and creamy.

4 Combine the pasta and sauce in a large serving bowl and toss together. Season with pepper and taste to see if you'd like to add more salt. If the mixture needs to be moister, add a small amount of additional milk and toss again. Serve at once, passing Parmesan for topping, if desired.

Dairy	Vegan option
Calories: 155	Calories: 157
Total fat: 6 g	Total fat: 6 g
Protein: 6 g	Protein: 6 g
Fiber: 1.1 g	Fiber: 1.1 g
Carbohydrates: 19 g	Carbohydrates: 20 g
Cholesterol: 1 g	Cholesterol: 0 g
Sodium: 514 mg	Sodium: 511 mg

Note

This works well with traditional fettuccine and is also nice with spinach ribbons, pappardelle, whole-wheat pastas, medium or small seashells, and vegetable-filled tortellini.

EMBELLISH IT: This is delicious topped with oil-packed sun-dried tomatoes and/or steamed fresh spinach or Swiss chard.

MAKE IT A MEAL: This is splendid with Tri-Color Coleslaw (page 71) and steamed green beans or Brussels sprouts. Another option is to serve Streamlined Minestrone (page 40) as a first course, then serve the pasta with a colorful green salad or a crisp raw vegetable platter with a dip, such as Easy Dill Dip (page 256). For another simple and colorful meal, serve this with Sautéed Broccoli, Baby Carrots, and Yellow Squash (page 210), plus cherry tomatoes and olives and fresh whole-grain bread.

Curried Pasta with Cauliflower and Chickpeas

DAIRY / VEGAN OPTION

4 to 6 servings

I've always loved the offbeat combination of pasta and curry. The addition of chickpeas makes this a filling meal. This is a good dish to try out on older kids and teens open to new adventures at the dinner table.

8 to 10 ounces pasta twists (cavatappi or cellantani), rotini (spirals), or medium shells

1 tablespoon light olive oil

1 medium onion, quartered and thinly sliced

2 garlic cloves, minced, optional

4 cups bite-size cauliflower florets and stems

One 16-ounce can diced tomatoes

2 teaspoons good-quality curry powder, or to taste

One 16- to 20-ounce can chickpeas, drained and rinsed

½ cup dark raisins

1 cup frozen green peas

2 tablespoons unbleached white flour

1 cup low-fat milk, rice milk, or soy milk

Salt and freshly ground pepper to taste

1 Cook the pasta in plenty of rapidly boiling water until al dente, then drain.

2 Meanwhile, heat the oil in a wide skillet or stir-fry pan. Add the onion and garlic and sauté over medium heat until golden.

3 Add the cauliflower, tomatoes, and curry powder, plus ½ cup water. Bring to a simmer, then cover and simmer gently until the cauliflower is just tender, 15 to 20 minutes.

4 Stir in the chickpeas, raisins, and peas.

5 Dissolve the flour in just enough milk to make a smooth paste. Stir into the skillet with the remaining milk. Cook until the liquid has thickened and everything is well heated, about 5 minutes.

6 In a large serving bowl, combine the cooked pasta with the cauliflower mixture. Season with salt and pepper and toss together. Serve at once.

EMBELLISH IT: Pass a small bowl of minced fresh cilantro or parsley for topping individual portions. If you'd like, pass some spicy chutney to add extra spark to the plate.

MAKE IT A MEAL: Serve with Tomatoes and Cucumbers in Yogurt (page 79) and fresh flatbread (chapatis or pita) to complete this meal simply.

Dairy	Vegan option
Calories: 543	Calories: 548
Total fat: 7 g	Total fat: 7 g
Protein: 2.3 g	Protein: 2.2 g
Fiber: 14.3 g	Fiber: 14.3 g
Carbohydrates: 100 g	Carbohydrates: 103 g
Cholesterol: 2 g	Cholesterol: 0 g
Sodium: 210 mg	Sodium: 203 mg

Pasta with Hearty Lentil and Spinach Sauce

This filling and nourishing pasta dish needs little else to make a complete meal.

1   Rinse and sort the lentils and put them in a small saucepan with 1½ cups water. Slowly bring to a simmer, then cover and simmer very gently until they are tender but still hold their shape, 30 to 40 minutes. Drain any excess water. This step can be done up to a day ahead of time.

2   Cook the pasta in plenty of rapidly boiling water until al dente, then drain.

3   Meanwhile, heat the oil in a large saucepan. Add the onion and garlic and sauté over medium-low heat until the onion is translucent. Add the bell pepper and mushrooms, if using, and continue to sauté until the onion is golden.

4   Stir in the cooked lentils, spinach, and marinara sauce. Slowly bring to a simmer, then cover and simmer gently for 10 minutes.

5   Combine the lentil sauce with the cooked pasta in a large serving container and toss together thoroughly. Season with salt and pepper and serve.

MAKE IT A MEAL: With this filling dish, you need serve only a big green salad and a steamed green vegetable such as broccoli or green beans to make a satisfying meal.

VEGAN

Serves 6

¾ cup lentils
8 to 10 ounces penne, ziti, or other short, chunky pasta
2 tablespoons extra-virgin olive oil
1 medium onion, chopped
3 to 4 garlic cloves, minced
1 medium green bell pepper, diced
1 cup sliced white or cremini mushrooms, optional
One 10-ounce package frozen chopped spinach, thawed and lightly drained
One 28-ounce jar good-quality marinara sauce
Salt and freshly ground pepper to taste

Calories: 339
Total fat: 6 g
Protein: 15 g
Fiber: 10.1 g
Carbohydrates: 60 g
Cholesterol: 0 g
Sodium: 636 mg

Mixed Mushrooms Stroganoff

If you have mushroom fans in your family, this contemporary take on a classic pasta dish is bound to please. High-calorie sour cream is replaced with a healthy dose of soy.

10 to 12 ounces ribbon-style noodles (see Note)

1½ tablespoons light olive oil

1 large onion, chopped

12 to 16 ounces white mushrooms, sliced (see Tip)

4 to 6 ounces fresh shiitake mushrooms, sliced

4 to 6 ounces cremini or baby bella mushrooms, sliced

½ cup dry white wine, vegetable stock, or water

One 12.3-ounce container silken tofu, puréed

1 tablespoon freshly squeezed lemon juice

Freshly ground pepper

2 tablespoons nonhydrogenated margarine

Salt, to taste, optional

Minced fresh parsley for topping, optional

Paprika for topping, optional

1 Cook the noodles in plenty of rapidly boiling water until al dente.

2 Meanwhile, heat the oil in a large skillet or stir-fry pan. Add the onion and sauté over medium heat until golden.

3 Add all the mushrooms and the wine to the pan. Cover and simmer over low heat until the mushrooms are tender, about 10 minutes. Stir in the tofu and lemon juice and heat gently just until heated through, then remove from the heat. Season to taste with pepper.

4 Drain the noodles and transfer to a serving dish. Stir in the margarine and season with salt, if desired.

5 To serve, place a bed of noodles on each plate, then top with some of the mushroom mixture. Garnish each serving with a sprinkling of parsley, if desired, plus a dusting of paprika.

Calories: 431

Total fat: 11 g

Protein: 17 g

Fiber: 6.2 g

Carbohydrates: 64 g

Cholesterol: 0 g

Sodium: 67 mg

Tip

To save time, use two 8-ounce packages presliced white mushrooms. Make sure they look fresh!

Note

Use spinach noodles, whole-grain ribbons made of quinoa or spelt flour, or pappardelle, broken into halves or thirds.

MAKE IT A MEAL: Serve with a tossed green salad with added chickpeas or pink beans. Steamed broccoli, green beans, or asparagus will round out the meal. Add some fresh whole-grain bread, if you'd like.

DAIRY / VEGAN OPTION

6 or more servings

Harvest Medley Pasta

Though this dish calls for only a half pound of pasta, the variety of vegetables included makes for a generous quantity. It's a great dish to make in late summer or early fall. Having all the vegetables cut and ready before cooking the pasta simplifies preparation.

½ pound pasta, any short chunky shape

2 tablespoons extra-virgin olive oil

3 to 4 garlic cloves, minced

2 large carrots, peeled and sliced
    diagonally

1 medium red bell pepper, cut into strips

2 cups fresh corn kernels (cut from 2
    large ears)

½ cup dry white wine, vegetable stock,
    or water

1 small yellow summer squash, sliced

1 small zucchini, sliced

6 firm, ripe plum tomatoes, sliced

One 16-ounce can kidney beans, drained
    and rinsed

1 teaspoon dried oregano or 1
    tablespoon fresh minced oregano
    leaves

Parsley

Salt and freshly ground pepper

Grated fresh Parmesan or Parmesan-
    style soy cheese for topping, optional

1 Cook the pasta in plenty of rapidly boiling water until al dente, then drain.

2 Meanwhile, heat the oil in a steep-sided stir-fry pan. Add the garlic and carrots and sauté over low heat until garlic is golden, 2 to 3 minutes. Add the bell pepper, corn kernels, and wine. Raise the heat to medium and cook, covered, stirring once or twice, for 5 minutes.

3 Add the squashes, tomatoes, beans, and oregano. Cover and cook until the vegetables are just tender, 4 to 5 minutes, then remove from the heat.

4 Combine the pasta with the vegetable mixture in a large serving container. Stir in the parsley; then season with salt and pepper and toss together. Serve at once, passing Parmesan cheese for topping if desired.

Calories: 386

Total fat: 6 g

Protein: 15 g

Fiber: 9.8 g

Carbohydrates: 68 g

Cholesterol: 0 g

Sodium: 237 mg

EMBELLISH IT: Pass chopped fresh cilantro and/or toasted pumpkin seeds for topping individual portions.

MAKE IT A MEAL: All that's needed to complete this one-dish pasta meal is fresh whole-grain bread and a green salad or coleslaw (see page 68).

FOR PICKY EATERS: This is an ideal pasta dish to take apart for the particular eater. Cook a small amount of extra pasta to be served with just a little nonhydrogenated margarine; place small amounts of some of the veggies (and perhaps a few kidney beans) separately on the plate. In addition, offer a few raw vegetables from the salad.

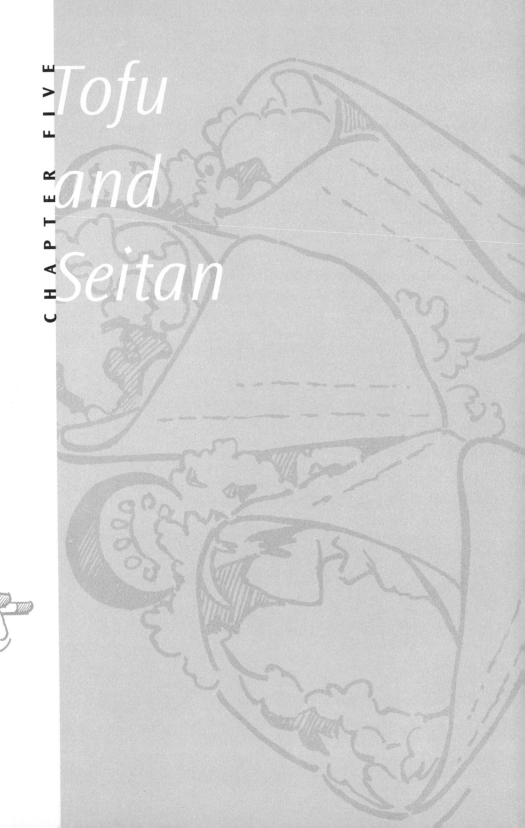

CHAPTER FIVE

Tofu and Seitan

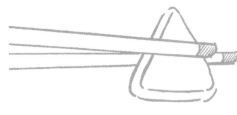

I OFFICIALLY BEGAN experimenting with child- and family-friendly tofu dishes some years ago when I wrote an article for *Vegetarian Times* titled "Soy, Boys and Girls." I could hardly use my own sons to experiment on, since they had grown up with the stuff. In fact, tofu has always been, and continues to be, one of their favorite foods, no matter how it's prepared. So I enlisted some of my friends' kids as guinea pigs, and let me tell you, these moms were skeptical.

When I asked my friend Nancy, for example, if I could try some of my kid-friendly tofu recipes out on her daughters, then ages 10 and 8, she was game. "But maybe you shouldn't actually say the 'T' word," she suggested, concerned about their reaction. She need not have worried. The "T" word didn't faze them. "Oh, so this is tofu," the girls said casually as they tasted the baked tofu headed for their sizzling fajitas (page 156).

Creamy Corn Chowder (page 31), Macaroni and Cheese with Secret Silken Tofu Sauce (page 110), and all the other tofu-based recipes I tried out on kids were embraced and devoured. Evidently, children often have fewer preconceived notions about tofu than do many adults. Surprise your family—and perhaps yourself—with the many guises of this amazingly versatile food.

Another valuable protein food explored in this chapter is seitan, which is cooked wheat gluten. An Asian staple, this has long been used as a "meaty" ingredient, especially in stir-fries. Tofu and seitan are used in many recipes throughout this book; consult the index to find even more delectable dishes for these versatile staples.

Tofu is a superb food to add to the repertoire of growing children, and pays bountiful dividends in women's and men's diets as well. Many experts recommend completely eliminating meat and high-fat dairy products as protein sources and getting more from plant-based foods such as grains, legumes, and soy foods.

Four ounces of tofu, for example, has only 100 to 120 calories and 5 to 8 grams of fat, but supplies 9 to 10 grams of protein. Tofu made with calcium sulfate provides up to 20 percent of average daily calcium requirement. It's high in easily digestible protein, low in fat, and is a good source of iron and B vitamins. To increase your chances of family-pleasing results, combine tofu with familiar flavors. Here's a brief lexicon of the most common tofu varieties:

Silken tofu: Available in 16-ounce tubs or 12.3-ounce aseptic packages, this type of tofu is soft and smooth. It's ideal to purée and use as a base for soups and sauces. It also makes wonderful dessert puddings and pie fillings. This may be the best type of tofu to use when you need to be sneaky!

Soft tofu: This comes in 16-ounce tubs and is good for using crumbled, as in faux scrambled-egg recipes, imitation egg salad, and patties. Finely crumbled, this is also a good substitute for ricotta cheese. Like silken tofu, soft tofu can be puréed and used as a soup or sauce base, with a somewhat heftier, less creamy consistency.

Firm and extra-firm tofu: Available in 16-ounce tubs, use one of these when you want the tofu to hold its shape. Either kind is ideal for use in stir-fries and stews and as cutlets or nuggets.

Baked tofu: Of the tofu varieties listed here, this one is least likely to be found in conventional supermarkets. It's a pity, since it's one of the most tasty and versatile of the tofu varieties and is the one that might most appeal to those who think they don't like tofu. Look for baked tofu in natural foods stores. It comes in 8- to 12-ounce packages and in various flavors, like Thai, Italian, Teriyaki, and Caribbean. Soy Boy and White Wave are just two brands that offer delicious baked tofu varieties. Sliced, diced, or (with some effort) crumbled, it can be used as a chicken or tuna substitute and in stir-fries and sautés, and in salads, casseroles, and tortilla dishes. Sliced and used just as is, baked tofu is also a quick, convenient sandwich filling.

Savory Tofu Burgers

This versatile burger can be enjoyed in several ways—served on whole-grain rolls with your favorite condiments or served plain. Plan on one burger for lighter eaters and two burgers for heartier eaters.

1 Place the oats in a medium mixing bowl and cover with ½ cup boiling water. Let stand 5 minutes.

2 Add the remaining ingredients except the oil and stir together until completely combined.

3 Heat enough of the oil to coat the bottom of a wide nonstick skillet or griddle. Ladle the tofu mixture onto the skillet by the ¼ cupful and flatten. Cook the patties in batches on both sides over medium heat until golden brown. Drain on paper towels and serve warm or at room temperature.

MAKE IT A MEAL: Serve on whole-grain rolls or English muffins with your favorite condiments. A slaw (pages 68) makes a nice accompaniment, as do Mashed Sweet Potatoes with Leeks, Peas, and Walnuts (page 223) or microwaved sweet potatoes. These burgers can also be served without rolls and paired with grain or pasta dishes such as Seashells in the Sand (page 228) or Rice or Bulgur with Fine Noodles (page 229). Complete with a bountiful tossed salad and a steamed green vegetable. Whether served on rolls or not, Quick Tartar Sauce (page 145) is a good sauce for dressing these burgers.

VEGAN

Makes 12

½ cup quick-cooking oats
One 16-ounce tub soft tofu, crumbled
½ cup wheat germ or oat bran, or half of each
2 tablespoons grated onion
¼ cup good-quality ketchup
2 tablespoons reduced-sodium soy sauce
1 teaspoon paprika
1 teaspoon salt-free all-purpose seasoning (see page xxvi)
1 teaspoon natural granulated sugar (see page 283)
2 tablespoons ground flaxseeds, optional
Freshly ground pepper to taste
Light olive oil

Calories: 69
Total fat: 3 g
Protein: 5 g
Fiber: 15 g
Carbohydrates: 8 g
Cholesterol: 0 g
Sodium: 179 mg

Eggless Tofu Quiche

This quiche is so tasty and easy to prepare that you may come to prefer it over the heavy egg-and-cheese variety. It's good with or without the crust.

1½ tablespoons light olive oil

1½ cups chopped onion

2 garlic cloves, minced

One 16-ounce tub silken tofu, drained and coarsely crumbled

1 teaspoon good-quality curry powder

Vegetables and embellishments of your choice (see Variations)

Salt and freshly ground pepper to taste

Wheat germ

One 9-inch good-quality whole-grain crust, optional

1 Preheat the oven to 350° F. Oil a 9-inch quiche pan or nonstick pie plate, if making a crustless quiche.

2 Heat the oil in a skillet. Add the onion and garlic and sauté until the onion is just beginning to brown. Remove from the skillet.

3 Transfer half of the onion mixture to the container of a food processor along with the tofu and curry powder and process until smooth.

4 In a mixing bowl, combine the tofu purée with the remaining onion mixture. Add vegetables as desired. Season with salt and pepper and mix thoroughly.

5 For a crustless quiche, sprinkle the bottom of the prepared pan with a generous layer of wheat germ. Pour in the tofu mixture and pat down. Top with another sprinkling of wheat germ. If using a crust, pour the mixture in and sprinkle with wheat germ.

6 Bake for 40 minutes, or until set. Let stand for 10 to 15 minutes, then cut into wedges to serve.

Crustless	With crust
Calories: 155	Calories: 262
Total fat: 10 g	Total fat: 17 g
Protein: 12 g	Protein: 9 g
Fiber: 25 g	Fiber: 2.2 g
Carbohydrates: 7 g	Carbohydrates: 19 g
Cholesterol: 0 g	Cholesterol: 0 g
Sodium: 12 mg	Sodium: 169 mg

Variations

Use about 1½ cups steamed or sautéed vegetables (2 cups for a deep-dish pie) of your choice, or a combination of two.

- Broccoli, finely chopped and steamed
- Cooked fresh corn kernels or frozen corn kernels, thawed (best used in combination with another vegetable)
- Zucchini or yellow summer squash, sliced and lightly sautéed (best to use small squashes)
- Asparagus, cut into 2-inch lengths and steamed
- Spinach or Swiss chard steamed until just wilted, well drained and coarsely chopped. (A 10-ounce package frozen greens, thawed and well drained, works nicely, too.)
- Mixed bell peppers, cut into strips, and Japanese eggplant, thinly sliced, sautéed in olive oil until fragrant and starting to brown
- 2 to 4 tablespoons chopped fresh herbs and/or scallions (try parsley and chives or parsley with dill, oregano, and/or thyme)
- ¼ cup sun-dried tomatoes, cut into strips (oil or dry packed)
- Fresh tomato slices (place on filling before sprinkling on the wheat germ topping)

MAKE IT A MEAL: Microwave some potatoes ahead of time so you can make Sautéed Skillet Potatoes (page 200) as a quick accompaniment. Or bake Scalloped Corn (page 207) at the same time. A tossed salad rounds out the meal. If you'd like a more interesting salad, consider Italian Bread-and-Tomato Salad (page 80), Golden Potato Salad (page 73), or Spring Barley Salad (page 90).

A few years ago, I was assigned to bring a vegetarian "fake meat" dish to a medieval feast at my sons' school. Since I was really short on time when the day came, I decided to roast a huge batch of diced tofu in a hot oven with barbecue sauce and then thread the chunks on skewers. I can't begin to tell you how many people asked for the recipe. It was a bit embarrassing, since after all I do have some reputation as a cookbook writer. I was forced to come clean—there was no recipe to give! A lot of kids and parents realized, however, that maybe there is something to this tofu thing after all.

Combining tofu (which has been very well drained and blotted and cut into large dice) with a good-quality natural barbecue, teriyaki, or Thai peanut sauce and applying a substantial amount of heat yields delectable results. All you need to do is coat the pieces gently and evenly with your chosen sauce, and then roast in a 425° F oven or stir-fry over high heat, until the tofu is sizzling and slightly seared. Either method takes 10 to 15 minutes.

The tofu chunks can be served on their own or threaded on skewers. Try alternating the tofu with roasted potatoes. You can also mix the cooked tofu with vegetables that have been roasted at the same time (bell peppers and onions are especially good), and serve them over brown rice or other cooked whole grain.

Stewed Tofu with Corn and Tomatoes

VEGAN

6 servings

Fresh corn and tomatoes are highlighted in this easy skillet stew, making it a great way to serve tofu in the summer and early fall. It's such a delightful quick dish that I've provided an option for using frozen corn and canned tomatoes, so that it can be enjoyed any time of year.

1 Cut the tofu into ¾-inch-thick slices and blot well between layers of paper towels or clean tea towels, then cut into dice.

2 Heat the oil in a wide skillet. Sauté the tofu over medium-high heat until golden on most sides. Add the tomatoes, corn, scallions, and paprika. Heat gently, just until heated through. Season with salt and pepper. Serve warm or at room temperature with parsley or cilantro sprinkled over the top of individual servings, if desired.

Variation

To make this when fresh corn and tomatoes are out of season, substitute one 28-ounce can diced tomatoes and 3 cups frozen corn kernels, thawed.

MAKE IT A MEAL: This is delicious with fresh whole-grain bread and a steamed green vegetable such as broccoli or green beans. With a little extra effort, Sesame Stir-Fried Green Beans (page 212) makes a tasty counterpoint to this mild dish.

FOR PICKY EATERS: Set aside some of the sautéed tofu (or better yet, sauté a little extra) and cook an extra ear of corn (or corn kernels) to serve separately.

One 16-ounce tub firm tofu
2 tablespoons light olive oil
4 large or 6 medium ripe tomatoes, diced
3 cups cooked fresh corn kernels (from about 4 medium ears)
4 scallions, sliced
1 teaspoon paprika
Salt and freshly ground pepper to taste
¼ cup minced fresh parsley or cilantro for topping, optional

Calories: 188
Total fat: 9 g
Protein: 10 g
Fiber: 4.2 g
Carbohydrates: 24 g
Cholesterol: 0 g
Sodium: 20 mg

2 generous or 4 modest servings

One 16-ounce tub soft or silken tofu
1½ tablespoons nonhydrogenated
   margarine
Pinch of good-quality curry powder or
   turmeric
Salt and freshly ground pepper to taste

Calories: 155
Total fat: 12 g
Protein: 12 g
Fiber: 1.8 g
Carbohydrates: 3 g
Cholesterol: 0 g
Sodium: 56 mg

Tofu Scrambles Galore

This makes an easy offering for breakfast, lunch, or dinner. When my husband and I have some leftovers to finish, my sons are always happy to have this as a quick dinner. Be forewarned, though, that since soft tofu loses a lot of its water as it cooks, this quantity will not serve as many as a tub of tofu usually does.

1 Crumble the tofu in a small mixing bowl. If using soft tofu, place in a colander to drain for a few minutes, until the excess moisture stops dripping.

2 Heat the margarine in a skillet and add the tofu. Sprinkle in the curry powder. Cook over medium-high heat, stirring frequently, until the liquid cooks off (soft tofu tends to be watery) and the mixture has a scrambled egg consistency, 8 to 10 minutes. Season with salt and pepper and serve.

Variations

- **Cheesy scramble:** When completely done, sprinkle ½ cup grated mild cheese or soy cheese over the top, and cover for 1 minute or so to melt the cheese.

- **Scrambled tofu burrito:** Serve in a warm flour tortilla. Flavor with a little salsa and, if desired, sprinkle on a small amount of grated cheese or nondairy cheese of your choice.

- **Veggie scramble:** Before adding the tofu to the skillet, sauté any kind of vegetable you'd like. Peppers, onions, and/or broccoli florets are particularly good.

- **Mixed mushrooms scramble:** Before adding the tofu to the skillet, sauté 6 to 8 ounces of two different types of sliced mushrooms. A little sliced scallion and/or minced fresh dill brightens this dish.

- **Fresh herb scramble:** Sprinkle with or stir in finely chopped fresh herbs of your choice (parsley, dill, cilantro, scallions, chives, or any combination).

- **Double tomato scramble:** Stir in 1 or 2 medium tomatoes, diced, and a small amount of sliced sun-dried tomatoes (oil or dry packed) once the tofu is done. Continue to sauté until the tomato is heated through. This is also delicious with a small amount of chopped fresh dill.

MAKE IT A MEAL: For a quick, light dinner, serve with Sautéed Skillet Potatoes (page 200) and whole-grain bread. Provide a platter of cherry tomatoes and sliced bell peppers and/or seedless orange sections.

Tofu and Potato Hash Browns

4 to 6 servings

Cook the potatoes ahead of time, and this easy and tasty dish will have your family eating in short order. Leftovers are wonderful for breakfast. Or, if you make this expressly to serve in the morning, make sure to microwave the potatoes the night before for a head start.

4 to 5 medium or 3 large potatoes, any variety
One 16-ounce tub extra-firm tofu
1½ tablespoons light olive oil
1 medium onion, finely chopped (see Tip)
½ medium green bell pepper, minced, optional
Paprika, to taste
Salt and freshly ground pepper to taste

1 Bake or microwave the potatoes in their skins until done but still firm. When cool enough to handle, peel and cut into ¼- to ½-inch dice.

2 Cut the tofu into ¼-inch-thick slices. Blot well between paper towels or clean tea towels, then cut into approximately ¼-inch dice.

3 Heat the oil in a large, wide skillet. Add the onion and sauté until translucent. Add the potatoes, tofu, and bell pepper, if using. Sauté over medium-high heat, stirring frequently, until the mixture is golden brown all over.

4 Sprinkle in a small amount of paprika, season with salt and pepper, and serve.

Calories: 286
Total fat: 12 g
Protein: 17 g
Fiber: 4.9 g
Carbohydrates: 31 g
Cholesterol: 0 g
Sodium: 19 mg

Tip
If anyone who will be eating this does not care for onions, sauté them separately and top individual portions.

MAKE IT A MEAL: Start with a colorful vegetable soup such as Streamlined Minestrone (page 40) or Dilled Vegetable-Barley Soup (page 50) as a first course. Then serve the hash browns with a salad or slaw of your choice and a steamed green vegetable (green beans, broccoli, or Brussels sprouts).

Creamy Tofu and Broccoli Skillet

A mild, comforting skillet dish that never fails to delight, this is on the table in less than 30 minutes. I like to use White Wave brand baked tofu for this, either teriyaki or Italian flavored.

DAIRY / VEGAN OPTION

4 to 6 servings

1 Heat the oil in a large skillet or stir-fry pan. Sauté the garlic over medium-low heat until just turning golden, about 1 minute. Add the bell pepper, broccoli, and ½ cup water. Cover and cook over medium heat until the broccoli is tender-crisp, about 4 minutes.

2 Use a little of the milk to dissolve the flour until it's smooth and flowing. Stir it into the skillet along with the remaining milk and baked tofu.

3 Stir in the cheese, and simmer gently until everything is well heated through, about 5 minutes. Season to taste with salt and pepper. Serve at once.

1½ tablespoons light olive oil

2 to 3 garlic cloves, minced

1 large red bell pepper, cut into short narrow strips

2 large broccoli crowns, cut into bite-size pieces

1 cup low-fat milk, rice milk, or soy milk

2 tablespoons unbleached white flour

Two 8-ounce packages baked tofu, cut into short, narrow strips

½ cup grated Monterey Jack cheese or Jack-style nondairy cheese

Salt and freshly ground pepper to taste

Variation
If your family likes mushrooms, add 1 cup of sliced mushrooms when adding the bell peppers and broccoli.

EMBELLISH IT: This is delicious with thinly sliced sun-dried tomatoes and/or basil leaves. Pass in small bowls to top individual portions.

MAKE IT A MEAL: For a simple meal, serve over cooked brown rice, couscous, or other grain of your choice (see Beyond Brown Rice, pages 234–35). Accompany with fresh corn on the cob during warmer seasons or baked sweet potatoes in fall and winter. A simple salad or a Cold Vegetable Platter (page 84) completes the meal.

Dairy	Vegan option
Calories: 316	Calories: 305
Total fat: 18 g	Total fat: 16 g
Protein: 27 g	Protein: 25 g
Fiber: 3 g	Fiber: 3 g
Carbohydrates: 12 g	Carbohydrates: 16 g
Cholesterol: 14 g	Cholesterol: 0 g
Sodium: 487 mg	Sodium: 510 mg

VEGAN

4 servings

One 16-ounce tub extra-firm tofu
1 tablespoon light olive oil
2 tablespoons cornmeal
2 tablespoons whole-wheat or
**   whole-wheat pastry flour**
½ teaspoon seasoned salt
1 tablespoon nutritional yeast, optional
Quick Tartar Sauce (recipe follows) or
**   prepared marinara, barbeque, or**
**   teriyaki sauce**

Calories: 221
Total fat: 13 g
Protein: 19 g
Fiber: 3.3 g
Carbohydrates: 11 g
Cholesterol: 0 g
Sodium: 188 mg

Baked Tofu Nuggets

These disappear quickly, so you may want to double the recipe for more servings or larger appetites. Make sure to use two baking pans if you do.

1   Preheat the oven to 425° F. Lightly oil a nonstick baking sheet.

2   Cut the tofu into ½-inch-thick slices crosswise to get 6 slabs. Blot well between clean tea towels or several layers of paper towels. Cut each slab crosswise into 4 sections to get ½- by 2-inch nuggets.

3   In a large mixing bowl, gently toss the tofu with the oil until evenly coated.

4   Combine the remaining ingredients in a large plastic freezer bag or produce bag and shake to combine. Add the tofu and shake gently until evenly coated.

5   Arrange in a single layer in the prepared pan. Bake 15 minutes, then turn carefully and bake another 10 minutes, or until golden and firm. Serve with the Quick Tartar Sauce, or other sauce of your choice.

Quick Tartar Sauce

VEGAN

Makes about ⅔ cup

Combine all the ingredients in a small bowl and stir together until well blended.

MAKE IT A MEAL: With the oven running at 425° F, consider roasting a few vegetables at the same time (see pages 201–2). This is good with Roasted Sweet Potatoes and Apples (page 203) or Roasted Root Vegetable Medley (page 205). Complete the meal with a green salad or a simple slaw (page 68).

½ cup soy mayonnaise
1 tablespoon pickle relish
1 to 2 teaspoons prepared mustard

Per 2-tablespoon serving
Calories: 62
Total fat: 4 g
Protein: 0 g
Fiber: 0.1 g
Carbohydrates: 2 g
Cholesterol: 0 g
Sodium: 116 mg

Orange-Glazed Tofu and Broccoli

VEGAN

4 to 6 servings

Many of the same ingredients that went into the previous mild skillet dish add up here to a zippy stir-fry. This is good with Thai- or teriyaki-flavored baked tofu.

Sauce:

2 tablespoons cornstarch

2 tablespoons reduced-sodium soy sauce

¼ cup undiluted orange juice concentrate

1 tablespoon rice vinegar or other mild white vinegar

2 teaspoons dark sesame oil

1 teaspoon grated fresh ginger or ¼ teaspoon ground ginger

Vegetables:

1 tablespoon light olive oil

2 large broccoli crowns, cut into bite-size pieces

2 garlic cloves, minced

1 medium red bell pepper, cut into short, thin strips

Two 8-ounce packages baked tofu, cut into narrow strips

1 To make the sauce, combine the cornstarch with ¼ cup water in a small mixing bowl and stir to dissolve. Stir in the remaining sauce ingredients, then set aside until needed.

2 Combine the oil with 2 tablespoons of water in a stir-fry pan or wok. Add the broccoli and garlic and stir. Cover and cook over medium heat until the broccoli is bright green and tender-crisp, 3 to 4 minutes.

3 Stir in the bell pepper and tofu and stir-fry over high heat for 2 to 3 minutes. Pour in the sauce and cook just until it has thickened and everything is well heated through. Serve at once.

EMBELLISH IT: Pass some toasted slivered almonds or chopped toasted cashews for topping, and garnish each serving with seedless orange sections.

MAKE IT A MEAL: For a tempting Asian-style meal, pair this with Vegetable Lo Mein (page 104) or Asian Noodles with Stir-Fried Corn and Cabbage (page 106). In either case, serve with a platter of raw vegetables.

Calories: 355

Total fat: 18 g

Protein: 29 g

Fiber: 3.9 g

Carbohydrates: 21 g

Cholesterol: 0 g

Sodium: 676 mg

Two Kinds of Tofu in a Sweet and Savory Sauté

VEGAN

6 servings

This is a favorite family soy dish. For years I made a similar preparation with a 16-ounce tub of extra-firm tofu, but once my sons hit the double-digit ages, it seemed that this alone wasn't enough for the four of us. On a whim, I once added a package of baked tofu and found that it not only yielded better volume but added interest to the dish. I've been making it this way ever since.

One 16-ounce tub extra-firm tofu
One 8- to 12-ounce package baked tofu
1½ tablespoons light olive oil
2 tablespoons pure maple syrup
2 tablespoons reduced-sodium soy sauce

1 Cut both kinds of tofu into ½-inch-thick slices. Blot the extra-firm well between clean tea towels or several layers of paper towels. Cut all the tofu into ½-inch dice.

2 Slowly heat the oil, syrup, and soy sauce together in a wide skillet, stirring together as they heat. Add the tofu and stir quickly to coat with the liquid. Sauté over medium-high heat until golden brown and crisp on most sides, about 10 minutes. Serve.

Calories: 262

Total fat: 15 g

Protein: 23 g

Fiber: 26 g

Carbohydrates: 11 g

Cholesterol: 0 g

Sodium: 442 mg

Variation

If you have something baking in a hot oven, try making a baked version of this dish. Preheat the oven to 400° F. Line a shallow 2-quart baking pan with foil. Combine the oil, syrup, and soy sauce in a mixing bowl and stir together. Stir in the tofu to coat with the sauce. Bake in the prepared pan, stirring occasionally, until the tofu is golden brown and the liquid has been absorbed, 30 to 40 minutes. Serve.

MAKE IT A MEAL: When I make this dish, I often accompany it with an improvisational stir-fry based on what's in the vegetable drawer and serve it over hot cooked rice or noodles. For a nice meal, try this with Stir-Fried Rice with Baby Corn and Peas (page 231). Add Stir-Fried Broccoli (page 209) or, to keep it simple, steamed broccoli.

Teriyaki marinade:

2 tablespoons reduced-sodium soy sauce

1 tablespoon light olive oil

1 teaspoon dark sesame oil

1 tablespoon honey or maple syrup

2 teaspoons rice vinegar or white wine vinegar

½ teaspoon grated fresh ginger or a good pinch of ground ginger

2 teaspoons hoisin sauce, optional

One 16-ounce tub extra-firm tofu

1 or 2 scallions, thinly sliced, optional

Calories: 226

Total fat: 14 g

Protein: 19 g

Fiber: 2.7 g

Carbohydrates: 10 g

Cholesterol: 0 g

Sodium: 365 mg

Teriyaki Tofu Triangles

Transforming tofu into crisp, teriyaki-flavored triangles is a simple thing to do, yet the fun shape gives it immediate appeal. These go quickly, so for more servings, simply double the recipe for both the tofu and marinade, and cook in batches.

1 Combine all the ingredients for the marinade in a small bowl and stir together.

2 Cut the tofu into ½-inch-thick slices. Blot well between clean tea towels or several layers of paper towels, then cut each slice through the thickness again to make ¼-inch-thick slices. Blot briefly again.

3 Cut each slice into 2 squares, then each square on the diagonal into 2 triangles. Place in a shallow pan and drizzle with the marinade. Gently turn the tofu pieces over so that both sides are coated with marinade. Let stand for 10 minutes or so.

4 Heat a wide nonstick skillet. Transfer the tofu and marinade into the skillet. Cook over medium-high heat, stirring gently and frequently, until the tofu is nicely browned on most sides. Scatter scallions over the tofu if desired, and serve at once.

MAKE IT A MEAL: Serve with Stir-Fried Rice with Baby Corn and Peas (page 231) and Wilted Sesame Spinach (page 213). Another pleasant combination is to team this with Asian Noodles with Stir-Fried Corn and Cabbage (page 106). With either combination, add a platter of raw carrots and red bell pepper strips.

Tofu and Mixed Veggie Stir-Fry

VEGAN

4 servings

When we're in the mood for Asian flavors, this simple stir-fry tops our list of choices. Vary the vegetables according to seasons and your family's preferences.

1 Make the sauce using the liquid from the baby corn and water chestnuts and set aside.

2 Cut the tofu into ½-inch-thick slices. Blot well between clean tea towels or several layers of paper towels, and cut into dice.

3 Heat half of the oil in a stir-fry pan or wok. Add the tofu and stir-fry over medium-high heat until golden on most sides, about 15 minutes. Remove from the pan and set aside.

4 Heat the remaining oil in the same pan. Add the garlic, carrots, broccoli, and ¼ cup water. Cover and cook over high heat, stirring once or twice, until the carrots and broccoli are brightly colored and just tender-crisp, about 5 minutes.

5 Add the baby corn, water chestnuts, and mushrooms. Stir-fry until all the vegetables are tender-crisp and well heated through, 2 to 3 minutes. Pour in the sauce and cook, stirring, until it has thickened, about 1 minute. Serve at once.

EMBELLISH IT: Pass Asian hot sauce and/or grated fresh ginger, plus some chopped toasted cashews or slivered almonds for topping.

MAKE IT A MEAL: Serve the stir-fry over hot cooked rice or noodles. Asian-Flavored Coleslaw (page 70) makes a crunchy accompaniment. For fun, add good-quality purchased spring rolls, which you can find in the freezer section of natural foods stores.

Basic Chinese Sauce (page 152)
One 16-ounce tub extra-firm tofu
2 tablespoons light olive oil
1 garlic clove, cut in half
2 large carrots, peeled and sliced diagonally
2 large broccoli crowns, cut into bite-size florets
One 15-ounce can baby corn, drained, liquid reserved
One 6- to 8-ounce can sliced water chestnuts, drained, liquid reserved
1 cup sliced mushrooms, diced zucchini, sliced celery, or bok choy

Calories: 343

Total fat: 18 g

Protein: 23 g

Fiber: 9.7 g

Carbohydrates: 28 g

Cholesterol: 0 g

Sodium: 405 mg

4 to 6 servings

Basic Chinese Sauce (recipe follows)

One 16-ounce tub extra-firm tofu or seitan, or 1 pound Homemade Seitan (page 154)

2 tablespoons light olive oil

2 garlic cloves, cut in half

8 ounces fresh green beans, cut in half (see Tip)

2 large broccoli crowns, cut into bite-size pieces

1 medium-small zucchini, cut into ¼-inch slices

2 scallions, cut into 1-inch lengths

Calories: 239

Total fat: 14 g

Protein: 17 g

Fiber: 5.2 g

Carbohydrates: 14 g

Cholesterol: 0 g

Sodium: 306 mg

Triple Jade Stir-Fry with Tofu or Seitan

This hearty green stir-fry is especially good to make when slender green beans are in season.

1 Make the sauce and set aside.

2 If using tofu, cut into ½-inch thick slices. Blot well between clean tea towels or several layers of paper towels, and cut into dice. If using seitan, cut into bite-size pieces.

3 Heat half of the oil in a stir-fry pan or wok. Add the tofu and stir-fry over medium-high heat until golden on most sides. Remove from the pan and set aside.

4 Heat the remaining oil in the same pan. Add the garlic, green beans, and ¼ cup water. Cook over high heat, covered, for 3 minutes, then stir in the broccoli. Cover and cook, stirring once or twice, until the vegetables are brightly colored and just tender-crisp, about 5 minutes.

5 Add the zucchini and scallions. Stir-fry until all the vegetables are tender-crisp, 2 to 3 minutes. Stir in the tofu. Pour in the sauce, and cook, stirring, until it has thickened, about 1 minute. Serve at once.

Tip

If fresh green beans are not in season, use good-quality frozen green beans, thawed. Add the beans and broccoli to the pan at the same time.

EMBELLISH IT: Add 1 to 2 teaspoons grated fresh ginger to the pan, or pass it separately for stirring into individual portions. Pass a small bowl of chopped toasted cashews to sprinkle over individual portions.

MAKE IT A MEAL: Serve this stir-fry over hot cooked rice. Asian-Flavored Coleslaw (page 70) made with red cabbage adds color and crunch to the plate. Or serve a Cold Vegetable Platter (page 84).

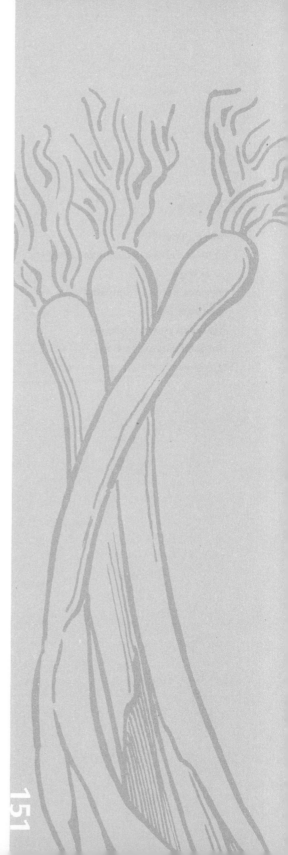

Basic Chinese Sauce

Use this for tofu and seitan stir-fries. Pour it into the hot stir-fry during the 1 to 2 last minutes of cooking, and it will thicken up quickly.

1 Combine all the ingredients except the cornstarch in a mixing bowl.

2 Dissolve the cornstarch in just enough water to make it smooth and flowing. Stir completely into the stock mixture.

Tip
Use canned low-sodium vegetable broth. Or use the liquid drained from any canned vegetables used in the main dish plus enough water to equal 1 cup (the liquid from baby corn is particularly tasty).

Makes just over 1 cup

1 cup stock (see Tip)
**2 tablespoons reduced-sodium soy sauce,
    or to taste**
**1 teaspoon natural granulated sugar
    (see page 283)**
½ teaspoon grated fresh ginger
1 teaspoon dark sesame oil
2 tablespoons cornstarch or arrowroot

Calories: 30
Total fat: 1 g
Protein: 1 g
Fiber: 0.1 g
Carbohydrates: 4 g
Cholesterol: 0 g
Sodium: 279 mg

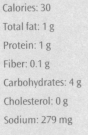

Seitan is a traditional Asian food used as a meat substitute; you may have encountered it in dishes like Buddhist's Delight in Chinese restaurants. Dense and chewy, this product of cooked wheat gluten is almost pure protein—you can see that by observing the high protein content of the recipes that use it. Clearly, though, seitan is not for anyone with gluten sensitivity. Store-bought seitan usually comes in 8-ounce packages or 16-ounce tubs.

Traditionally made by rinsing wheat-flour dough of its starch, then cooking it in a broth of soy sauce and ginger, seitan's meaty texture lends itself to numerous preparations. It's great as a substitute for beef chunks in stews and stir-fries and for fajitas and kebabs. Explore the uses of seitan if you're looking for ways to add more protein to your family's diet other than, or in addition to, soy foods. For more seitan recipes, see Seitan "Meat and Potatoes" Stew (page 56) and Hearty Seitan Salad (page 83).

Homemade Seitan

VEGAN

Makes about 2 pounds
(about 10 servings)

2 tablespoons reduced-sodium soy sauce
2¼ cups gluten flour (vital wheat gluten)

Broth:
2 vegetable bouillon cubes
2 tablespoons reduced-sodium soy sauce
3 to 4 slices fresh ginger

Calories: 112
Total fat: 0 g
Protein: 21 g
Fiber: 0 g
Carbohydrates: 0 g
Cholesterol: 0 g
Sodium: 0 mg

Store-bought seitan can be excellent or disconcertingly tough. Either way, it's expensive. Making seitan completely from scratch (which involves making a whole-wheat dough and then rinsing and rinsing to get rid of the starch) is time-consuming and messy. Using pure gluten flour provides a clever shortcut to a great homemade version that is not difficult to make. This recipe works well for me, and with practice you can produce seitan that is chewy but not overly so. Whenever I make this, I freeze half and am always happy to use it 2 to 3 weeks later.

1 Combine the soy sauce with 1 cup of water in a small mixing bowl. Place the gluten flour in a medium mixing bowl. Gradually add the liquid to form a stiff dough, stirring with a spoon at first, and then working together with your hands.

2 Turn out onto a floured board and knead 30 times, then return the dough to the bowl, cover with a clean tea towel, and let it rest for 15 minutes.

3 Meanwhile, bring 10 cups water to a simmer in a large soup pot. Add the bouillon cubes, soy sauce, and ginger.

4 Once the water is close to a simmer, divide the dough into two pieces and pull into long, narrow loaves the shape of miniature French breads.

5 With a sharp, serrated knife, cut each section of dough crosswise into approximately ½-inch sections. When the water comes to a simmer, add the dough. Simmer gently and steadily for 30 minutes. Drain (if desired, save the tasty stock to use for soup or some other purpose) and let cool. Use in recipes calling for seitan.

Simple Sautéed Seitan

VEGAN

4 servings

Much as my sons like seitan in most any dish, one of their preferred way of eating it is sautéed simply and eaten on its own, with everything else served on the side.

1 Cut the seitan into bite-size pieces.

2 Heat the oil in a large skillet or stir-fry pan. If using soy sauce or teriyaki sauce, heat gently with the oil. Add the seitan and stir to combine. Stir-fry over medium-high heat until the seitan is lightly browned on most sides, 4 to 5 minutes.

3 If using barbecue sauce, add once the seitan is done and stir-fry for just 1 or 2 minutes. Serve at once, or cover and set aside until ready to serve.

MAKE IT A MEAL: Serve with Vegetable Lo Mein (page 104) and Wilted Sesame Spinach or Swiss Chard (page 213) or Sautéed Broccoli, Baby Carrots, and Yellow Squash (page 210). Add a refreshing platter of sliced red bell pepper and orange sections.

1 to 1½ pounds seitan or Homemade Seitan (page 154)
1½ tablespoons light olive oil
1 tablespoon reduced-sodium soy sauce or teriyaki sauce, or ¼ cup good-quality natural barbecue sauce

Calories: 275

Total fat: 6 g

Protein: 48 g

Fiber: 0 g

Carbohydrates: 8 g

Cholesterol: 0 g

Sodium: 174 mg

Sizzling Seitan or Tofu Fajitas

DAIRY / VEGAN OPTION

Serves 6

What I like about serving fajitas is that everyone participates in creating his or her own meal. It's less work for the cook, and it's fun for all those at the table. In addition, everyone can tailor the ingredients to suit personal tastes.

12 to 16 ounces seitan or Homemade Seitan (page 154) or one 12-ounce package baked tofu

1 tablespoon freshly squeezed lemon or lime juice

2 tablespoons olive oil

½ teaspoon salt

1 medium green bell pepper, cut into strips

1 medium red bell pepper, cut into strips

Twelve 8-inch flour tortillas

Garnishes:

Diced fresh tomatoes

Shredded lettuce

Prepared salsa or picante sauce

Low-fat sour cream, yogurt, or soy yogurt

Grated Cheddar cheese or Cheddar-style soy cheese, optional

1 Preheat the broiler. Line a baking sheet with foil and lightly oil.

2 Cut the seitan into narrow strips, about 2 inches in length. In a mixing bowl, gently toss with the lemon juice, olive oil, and salt.

3 Arrange the seitan and bell peppers in the pan. Broil about 6 to 8 inches from heat source for 5 to 8 minutes, until golden. Carefully stir and broil another 5 to 8 minutes, until the mixture is lightly browned.

4 Meanwhile, stack the tortillas and wrap in foil. Warm in the oven for 5 minutes while seitan finishes baking.

5 Place the garnishes in separate serving bowls. Place the hot seitan and peppers in a serving platter.

6 Distribute two warmed flour tortillas to each person. To assemble a fajita, place a few strips of the seitan and peppers in the center of a tortilla and garnish as you wish. Roll up and eat out of hand.

Dairy	Vegan option
Calories: 313	Calories: 299
Total fat: 11 g	Total fat: 6 g
Protein: 19 g	Protein: 28 g
Fiber: 5.3 g	Fiber: 4.3 g
Carbohydrates: 45 g	Carbohydrates: 45 g
Cholesterol: 0 g	Cholesterol: 0 g
Sodium: 759 mg	Sodium: 520 mg

MAKE IT A MEAL: A quick grain accompaniment is Mexican Green Rice (page 230); or serve with an easy potato dish (see pages 200–1 for ideas). Slices of seedless orange add a refreshing note to the plates.

FOR PICKY EATERS: This is a good recipe for finicky kids, since they can prepare fajitas with their own choice of ingredients.

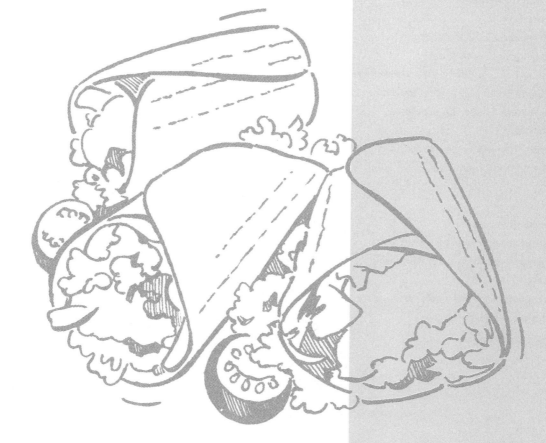

1½ tablespoons light olive oil

1 medium onion, chopped

2 medium broccoli crowns, cut into
   bite-size pieces

2 medium red bell peppers, cut into
   1-inch dice

1 medium zucchini, halved lengthwise
   and cut into ½-inch chunks

2 medium Roma (plum) tomatoes, diced

One 16-ounce can pineapple chunks in
   unsweetened juice, drained, juice
   reserved

1 pound seitan or Homemade Seitan
   (page 154), cut into strips

Sauce:

Reserved pineapple juice

2 tablespoons reduced-sodium soy sauce

3 tablespoons rice vinegar or white wine
   vinegar

2 tablespoons honey or maple syrup

2 tablespoons cornstarch

Calories: 400

Total fat: 6 g

Protein: 42 g

Fiber: 4 g

Carbohydrates: 48 g

Cholesterol: 0 g

Sodium: 368 mg

Sweet-and-Sour Seitan and Vegetables

This easy stir-fry makes a delicious and nourishing one-dish meal.

1 Heat the oil in a stir-fry pan or wok. Add the onion, then cover and cook over medium-high heat until translucent. Add the broccoli and ¼ cup water and cook, covered, for 3 minutes, or until bright green. Add the bell peppers and zucchini, cover, and cook, stirring occasionally, 5 minutes. Stir in the tomatoes, pineapple, and seitan.

2 Combine the ingredients for the sauce in a small bowl and stir until the cornstarch has dissolved. Pour into the pan, bring it to a simmer, and cook at a steady simmer for 5 minutes. Taste, and if needed, adjust the sweet and sour balance with more honey or vinegar. Serve at once.

Variation

This recipe is also excellent using a 10- to 12-ounce package of baked tofu, cut into strips, in place of seitan.

EMBELLISH IT: Pass some minced fresh cilantro and chopped roasted peanuts or toasted cashews for topping.

MAKE IT A MEAL: Serve over hot cooked brown rice, whole-grain couscous, or noodles. For a dazzling dinner plate, serve with a Simple Slaw (page 68) and steamed spinach or Swiss chard.

FOR PICKY EATERS: This dish has many interesting elements that can be pulled apart. You can try serving a few raw broccoli florets, bell pepper strips, and zucchini rounds with a dip like Easy Dill Dip (page 256). Serve a few chunks of seitan and pineapple separately (spearing them onto a skewer could make the endeavor more fun), along with a small bowl of plain rice or noodles.

Hearty Seitan "Buddhist's Delight"

VEGAN

4 to 6 servings

If you're a longtime vegetarian, you've likely ordered a version of this Chinese restaurant standard. It's easy to make at home, and always a treat for families who love Asian-style meals.

1½ tablespoons light olive oil

1 tablespoon reduced-sodium soy sauce

1 to 1½ pounds seitan or Homemade Seitan (page 154), cut into bite-size chunks

2 cups stock (see Note)

2 large broccoli crowns, cut into bite-size pieces

1 cup baby carrots

2 garlic cloves, minced

3 tablespoons cornstarch or arrowroot

One 15-ounce can baby corn, drained, liquid reserved (see Note)

1 cup small white or brown mushrooms, stemmed and cut in half

2 scallions, cut into 1-inch pieces

1 Heat the oil and soy sauce slowly in a stir-fry pan or wok. Add the seitan and stir-fry over medium-high heat until lightly browned on most sides. Remove to a plate and set aside.

2 Add half of the stock to the pan along with the broccoli, carrots, and garlic. Bring to a simmer and cook, stirring frequently, until the broccoli is bright green and the carrots are tender-crisp.

3 Dissolve the cornstarch in a small amount of the remaining stock. Add it and the remaining stock to the pan along with the reserved seitan and the baby corn, mushrooms, and scallions.

4 When the liquid thickens and everything is nicely heated through, season to taste with additional soy sauce and serve.

Note
Use the cooking liquid from Homemade Seitan (page 154) or from the baby corn. Or use low-sodium canned vegetable broth.

MAKE IT A MEAL: This hearty dish needs little else to make a complete meal. Serve over hot cooked rice or noodles, and accompany with Asian-Flavored Coleslaw (page 70), a tossed green salad with orange sections and toasted almond slices or walnuts, or a simple platter of raw red bell pepper and turnip strips.

Calories: 276

Total fat: 5 g

Protein: 40 g

Fiber: 3.4 g

Carbohydrates: 18 g

Cholesterol: 0 g

Sodium: 165 mg

Seitan and Broccoli Stir-Fry

This simple stir-fry showcases seitan's unique flavor and texture.

1 Heat the oil plus 2 tablespoons water in a stir-fry pan or wok. Add the garlic and broccoli. Turn the heat to medium-high and stir-fry until the broccoli is bright green, 4 to 5 minutes.

2 Add the remaining ingredients and continue to stir-fry until everything is sizzling hot, 3 to 4 minutes. Add a small amount of additional water if the mixture gets dry. Serve at once.

Tip
Use the broth from Homemade Seitan instead of the water in steps 1 and 2.

EMBELLISH IT: Pass additional soy sauce for seasoning individual portions.

MAKE IT A MEAL: Serve over hot cooked brown rice or hearty Asian noodles such as soba or udon. Or accompany with Stir-Fried Rice with Baby Corn and Peas (page 231). Cold Vegetable Platter #4 (page 84) provides welcome cool, crisp elements to the meal.

FOR PICKY EATERS: Try alternating chunks of the cooked seitan, broccoli, and bell pepper on skewers to make this more enticing to youngsters.

VEGAN

4 to 6 servings

2 tablespoons light olive oil

2 garlic cloves, minced, optional

2 large broccoli crowns, cut into bite-size pieces

1 medium red bell pepper, cut into thin strips

1 to 1½ pounds seitan or Homemade Seitan (page 154), cut into bite-size chunks

2 tablespoons reduced-sodium soy sauce, plus more for seasoning

1 teaspoon dark sesame oil

1 teaspoon grated fresh ginger

1 teaspoon natural granulated sugar (see page 283)

Calories: 260

Total fat: 7 g

Protein: 40 g

Fiber: 1.4 g

Carbohydrates: 10 g

Cholesterol: 0 g

Sodium: 289 mg

CHAPTER SIX

Vegetable, Grain, and Bean Main Dishes:

Comforting Casseroles, Savory Skillets, Bean Burgers, and More

HERE'S A COLLECTION of hearty main dishes based on a triumvirate of staples in the vegetarian repertoire: vegetables, grains, and beans. You'll find full-flavored recipes suited for hearty appetites as well as comfort foods that can be dressed up or kept simple to suit varying preferences within the same meal. Risotto and polenta are prime examples of dishes that can be tailored to please a variety of tastes. They're perfect for younger children, who can enjoy them in their basic form, with nutritious side dishes served separately. Adults and older kids can choose from a number of ways to dress up these simple dishes.

Included in this chapter are some of our favorite comfort foods. Shepherd's pie, pot pie, and savory bread puddings straight from the oven do much to create a cozy haven in our hectic lives. This chapter is rounded out by several lively (and quick) one-dish skillet meals, bean-based veggie burgers, and a step-by-step guide to making vegetable sushi, one of the treats most requested by my sons' friends.

If you want your family to eat more vegetables, grains, and beans (and who doesn't?), the recipes in this chapter, defined by fun and comfort, are a good place to start.

Cozy Casseroles

In this age of hurried meals, when even the most avid cooks crave a degree of convenience, casseroles can seem like a charming anachronism. They bring to mind perfect 1950s moms wearing aprons and pearl earrings. Yet there is irresistible comfort in a heartwarming casserole, and the entire enterprise can be brought up to date with contemporary ingredients and fresh produce.

For instance, creamy risotto is transformed into an even more homey baked dish; hearty pot pie and shepherd's pie are here in vegetarian and vegan options (and you'll find a vegan version of another classic casserole, Mom's "Tuna"-Noodle Casserole on page 114). Though casseroles require little or no more hands-on time than most skillet dishes, you do need to allow for time in the oven. During that time you can work on the rest of the meal, make a dessert, or put your feet up and relax.

Vegetable Upside-Down Casserole

DAIRY / VEGAN OPTION

4 to 6 servings

Everyone likes fruity upside-down cakes; why not try the same approach with vegetables? This casserole, which is fun to make and even more fun to eat, has quickly become a family favorite. It's a great way to use up small amounts of fresh or frozen vegetables; you can keep it simple or come up with more sophisticated combinations, as tastes dictate.

3 to 4 cups cut-up vegetables of your choice (see Variations)
2 tablespoons light olive oil
1 cup whole-wheat pastry flour
¼ cup wheat germ
½ teaspoon baking powder
½ teaspoon baking soda
1 teaspoon salt
¾ cup low-fat yogurt or soy yogurt
¾ cup low-fat milk, rice milk, or soy milk
1 tablespoon vegetable oil
½ cup grated cheese or nondairy cheese of your choice, optional

1 Sauté the vegetables in olive oil until just tender. Set aside.

2 Preheat the oven to 375° F. Lightly oil a shallow round 2-quart casserole or a 9- by 13-inch baking pan.

3 Combine the flour, wheat germ, baking powder, baking soda, and salt in a mixing bowl. Make a well in the center and add the yogurt, milk, and vegetable oil. Stir together until well mixed.

4 Pour the vegetables into the prepared pan. Sprinkle with the cheese, if using, then pour the batter evenly over the vegetables, gently smoothing it out with a spatula.

5 Bake for 30 to 35 minutes, or until the top is golden and firm. Let stand for about 10 minutes, then cut into wedges or squares to serve.

Broccoli-onion option (using 1 tablespoon oil):

Dairy	Vegan option
Calories: 197	Calories: 195
Total fat: 5 g	Total fat: 5 g
Protein: 10 g	Protein: 7 g
Fiber: 5.9 g.	Fiber: 6.2 g
Carbohydrates: 31 g	Carbohydrates: 34 g
Cholesterol: 4 g	Cholesterol: 0 g
Sodium: 648 mg	Sodium: 628 mg

Variations

Here are some combinations my family likes. Use your own mix or keep it simple and use just one vegetable. As a rule of thumb, use 3 to 4 cups of vegetables (with the exception of tiny veggies like corn and peas, which have more density) and sauté in a wide skillet until just tender. If using onions, sauté until golden before adding other vegetables.

(continued)

- **Corn, tomato, and scallion:** Sauté 2 to 2½ cups cooked fresh corn or frozen corn kernels, thawed; 2 medium tomatoes, diced; and 1 to 2 scallions, sliced thinly, in a little olive oil, just until the tomato has softened slightly. If you'd like, add one 4-ounce can chopped mild green chilies.
- **Broccoli and onion:** Sauté 1 medium-large onion, quartered and sliced thinly, in a small amount of olive oil until golden. Add 4 cups bite-size broccoli florets and a bit of water. Cover and cook, stirring occasionally, until the broccoli is just beyond tender-crisp. Drain off any liquid.
- **Squash and spinach:** Sauté 1 medium zucchini or yellow summer squash, cut lengthwise and sliced thinly into half circles, and 1 or 2 garlic cloves, minced (optional), in a little olive oil until just tender. Add 8 to 10 ounces chopped fresh spinach leaves. Cover and cook just until the spinach wilts, about 1 minute. If desired, add a small quantity of chopped fresh herbs.

Other sautéed vegetables that work well are mushrooms, carrots, peas, and cauliflower. See what's in the vegetable drawer of your refrigerator and have fun!

EMBELLISH IT: It's easy to make an "adult half" to this casserole, though this is entirely optional. Simply divide the sautéed vegetables into two small baking pans. Add embellishments to one batch, such as minced garlic, chopped herbs, sliced sun-dried tomatoes, or green chilies. Divide the batter between the pans and bake as directed.

MAKE IT A MEAL: This needs only a hearty soup or substantial salad to make a satisfying meal. Tomato-based soups such as Dilled Vegetable-Barley Soup (page 50) and Streamlined Minestrone (page 40) complement this recipe well. Or, to keep the meal simple, serve a bountiful tossed salad with some chickpeas or pinto beans tossed in, plus baked or microwaved sweet potatoes.

FOR PICKY EATERS: I can't guarantee it, but presenting this dish as an "upside-down cake" might be sufficient to entice young eaters to try it. It helps to use vegetables you know your children enjoy. Serve with baby carrots and anything from the salad your children might like; add a ranch dressing or Easy Dill Dip (page 256).

DAIRY / VEGAN OPTION

6 to 8 servings

1½ tablespoons light or extra-virgin olive oil

1 cup chopped onion

1 medium green bell pepper, diced

One 28-ounce can crushed or puréed tomatoes

2 teaspoons chili powder

1 teaspoon dried oregano

½ teaspoon ground cumin

One 16- to 20-ounce can black beans or 2½ cups cooked black beans (from about 1 cup dried)

1 medium zucchini, quartered lengthwise and thinly sliced

1 small fresh hot chile pepper, seeded and minced, or one 4-ounce can chopped mild green chilies

Twelve 6-inch corn tortillas, torn or cut into several pieces

8 ounces grated Cheddar cheese or Cheddar-style nondairy cheese

Black Bean and Zucchini Chilaquiles

Chilaquiles is a classic Southwestern casserole made from crumbled tortillas, tomato sauce, and cheese. Here, its savory flavors are augmented with black beans and zucchini.

1 Preheat the oven to 400° F. Lightly oil a 9- by 13-inch baking pan or 2-quart round casserole.

2 Heat the oil in a large saucepan. Sauté the onion until translucent. Add the bell pepper and continue to sauté until it has softened and the onions are golden. Stir in the tomatoes, seasonings, beans, zucchini, and chile pepper. Bring to a simmer, then simmer gently for 5 minutes.

3 Layer as follows in the prepared pan. Half the tortillas, half the tomato-black bean mixture, and half the cheese. Repeat. Bake for 15 to 20 minutes, or until the cheese is bubbly. Let stand for 5 to 10 minutes, then cut into squares or wedges to serve.

MAKE IT A MEAL: This is delicious with Mexican Green Rice (page 230), or any simply prepared cooked grain (see pages 234–35). Instead of grain, Golden Potato Salad (page 73) or Sautéed Skillet Potatoes (page 200) are good with this, too. With any of these options, a simple salad of greens, tomatoes, and avocado completes the meal.

Dairy	Vegan option
Calories: 411	Calories: 361
Total fat: 16 g	Total fat: 11 g
Protein: 20 g	Protein: 19 g
Fiber: 12.2 g	Fiber: 12.2 g
Carbohydrates: 49 g	Carbohydrates: 50 g
Cholesterol: 34 g	Cholesterol: 0 g
Sodium: 465 mg	Sodium: 550 mg

Southwestern Baked Rice Casserole

In this Southwestern casserole, chiles and cilantro add a vivid flavor to rice. This is a great dish to serve hungry teens as part of a hearty meal.

1 Preheat the oven to 350° F. Oil a 1½-quart casserole.

2 Heat the oil in a small skillet. Add the onion and sauté over medium-low heat until lightly browned.

3 In a mixing bowl, combine the onion with all the remaining ingredients. Stir together thoroughly. Pat the mixture into the prepared pan. Bake for 35 minutes, or until the top is golden brown and bubbly.

Note
Substitute any mild white cheese or nondairy cheese you'd like.

MAKE IT A MEAL: Serve with stone-ground tortilla chips and Nearly Instant Bean Dip (page 256). For a heartier meal, try pairing this with Black Bean Sofrito (page 188) and serving stone-ground tortilla chips or warm flour tortillas on the side. A bountiful green salad that includes diced avocado, corn, and tomatoes rounds out either option.

DAIRY / VEGAN OPTION

4 to 6 servings

1 tablespoon light olive oil

1 medium onion, chopped

4 cups cooked brown rice (about 1⅓ cups raw)

8 ounces (2 cups) grated Monterey Jack, or Jack-style nondairy cheese (see Note)

½ cup low-fat yogurt or soy yogurt

½ cup low-fat milk, rice milk, or soy milk

1 cup good-quality bottled salsa, mild or medium-hot

¼ cup minced fresh cilantro

⅓ teaspoon chili powder

Salt and freshly ground pepper, to taste

Dairy	Vegan option
Calories: 426	Calories: 355
Total fat: 20 g	Total fat: 13 g
Protein: 18 g	Protein: 15 g
Fiber: 3.4 g	Fiber: 3.6 g
Carbohydrates: 44 g	Carbohydrates: 47 g
Cholesterol: 50 g	Cholesterol: 0 g
Sodium: 495 mg	Sodium: 601 mg

Creamy Enchilada Casserole

Now you can have "the whole enchilada" without having to fill and roll individual tortillas.

DAIRY / VEGAN OPTION

6 servings

Filling

1 tablespoon light or extra-virgin olive oil

1 small onion, chopped

1 garlic clove, minced

One 16-ounce can vegetarian refried beans

¹⁄₂ cup mild or medium-hot bottled salsa or one 4-ounce can mild green chilies

2 tablespoons minced fresh cilantro, optional

¹⁄₂ teaspoon dried oregano

Sauce:

1¹⁄₄ cups low-fat milk, rice milk, or soy milk

2 tablespoons unbleached white flour

1¹⁄₂ cups grated Monterey Jack or Jack-style nondairy cheese (see Note)

Eight to ten 6-inch corn tortillas, cut into halves

1 scallion, thinly sliced

Salsa for topping, optional

1 Preheat the oven to 400° F. Lightly oil a shallow round 2-quart casserole or 9- by 13-inch baking pan.

2 To make the filling, heat the oil in a medium skillet. Add the onion and sauté over medium heat until translucent. Add the garlic and continue to sauté until the onion is golden. Stir in the remaining filling ingredients and continue to cook until everything is well heated through.

3 To make the sauce, heat 1 cup of the milk in a small saucepan. Dissolve the flour in the remaining milk. Whisk it into the saucepan, then sprinkle in 1 cup of the cheese. Bring the sauce to a gentle simmer, stirring frequently, and cook until thickened.

4 Line the prepared pan with a single layer of tortillas. Pour in the filling and spread evenly over the tortillas. Cover with the remaining tortilla halves.

5 Pour the cheese sauce evenly over the tortillas, then sprinkle with the remaining cheese. Sprinkle the scallions over the top. Bake for 15 minutes, or until the cheese is bubbly. Serve at once, passing around some salsa for topping, if desired.

Note

Substitute any mild white cheese or nondairy cheese you'd like.

MAKE IT A MEAL: With the oven running at 400° F, consider roasting a few vegetables at the same time (see pages 201–2), and complete the meal with a green salad or a Simple Slaw (page 68). This casserole is also nicely complemented by Southwest Summer Succotash (page 218). See "Make it a meal" on page 157 for more ideas.

Dairy	Vegan option
Calories: 352	Calories: 315
Total fat: 14 g	Total fat: 10 g
Protein: 17 g	Protein: 14 g
Fiber: 7.1 g	Fiber: 7.1 g
Carbohydrates: 39 g	Carbohydrates: 43 g
Cholesterol: 32 g	Cholesterol: 0 g
Sodium: 580 mg	Sodium: 648 mg

4 large or 6 medium russet or other all-
    purpose white potatoes, peeled and
    diced
1 tablespoon nonhydrogenated
    margarine
½ cup low-fat milk, rice milk, or soy milk
1 tablespoon light olive oil
1 medium onion, finely chopped
2 medium carrots, peeled and sliced
½ medium head cauliflower, finely
    chopped
1 cup frozen peas, thawed
1 cup cooked fresh corn kernels or
    frozen corn kernels, thawed
2 tablespoons minced fresh parsley
1 tablespoon minced fresh dill, optional
Seasoned salt and freshly ground pepper,
    to taste
Wheat germ

Dairy	Vegan option
Calories: 212	Calories: 214
Total fat: 4 g	Total fat: 4 g
Protein: 6 g	Protein: 6 g
Fiber: 6 g	Fiber: 6 g
Carbohydrates: 39 g	Carbohydrates: 41 g
Cholesterol: 1 g	Cholesterol: 0 g
Sodium: 52 mg	Sodium: 49 mg

Shepherd's Pie

This delicious classic requires 30 to 40 minutes of hands-on time, plus about an equal amount of baking. So, while it may not qualify as a quick dish to make when you come home from work, it's a comforting weekend meal. It's substantial and filling, though my family rarely leaves leftovers.

1 Preheat the oven to 400° F. Lightly oil a shallow, round 2-quart casserole or 9- by 13-inch baking pan.

2 Place the potatoes in a saucepan with enough water to cover. Bring to a simmer, then cover and simmer until tender, about 20 minutes. Drain and transfer to a small mixing bowl.

3 Stir the margarine into the potatoes until melted, then add the milk and mash until fluffy. Set aside.

4 While the potatoes are cooking, heat the oil in a skillet. Add the onion and carrots and sauté over medium heat until the onion is golden. Add the cauliflower and ¼ cup water. Cover and cook until the cauliflower is just tender, about 5 minutes.

5 Add the peas, corn, parsley, and dill, if using. Cook until the mixture is well heated through, then stir in ½ cup of the mashed potatoes. Season with seasoned salt and pepper.

6 Sprinkle the bottom of the prepared pan with a generous layer of wheat germ, then pour in the vegetable mixture and pat in evenly. Spread the mashed potatoes over the top and pat down lightly.

7 Bake for 30 to 35 minutes, or until the potatoes begin to turn golden and slightly crusty. Let stand for 5 minutes, then cut into squares or wedges to serve.

Variations

- To make this dish even more substantial, add 8 ounces of well-drained, finely diced tofu (or baked tofu) or 1 cup cooked or canned beans of your choice.
- Other vegetables can be substituted for the ones listed. Try broccoli instead of cauliflower; zucchini or green beans in place of the corn and/or peas; ½ cup or so of sliced mushrooms is a welcome addition if your family likes them.

MAKE IT A MEAL: I like to contrast this "mild-mannered" casserole with an interesting salad such as Italian Bread-and-Tomato Salad (page 80) or Green Salad with Avocado, Apples, and Baked Tofu (page 75). Beets are a nice addition to this meal in any form. You can roast them simultaneously in the oven (see pages 201–2), or see other ideas on page 217.

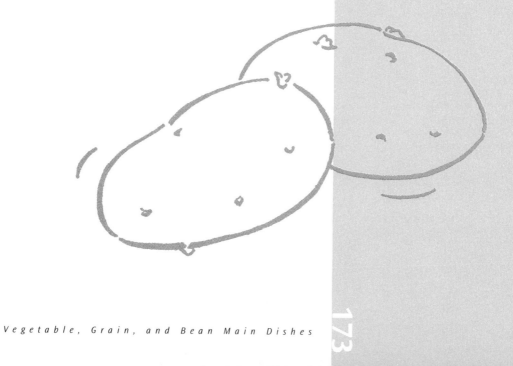

**4 slices whole-grain bread, torn into
small pieces**

¾ cup low-fat milk, rice milk, or soy milk

2 tablespoons olive oil

1 medium to large onion, finely chopped

**4 cups finely chopped vegetables of your
choice (see Variations)**

**1 to 1½ cups grated mild white cheese
or nondairy cheese**

¼ cup soy mayonnaise

**1 tablespoon minced fresh dill or
½ teaspoon dried dill**

½ teaspoon paprika

¼ teaspoon dried thyme

Salt and freshly ground pepper, to taste

Wheat germ, for topping

Dairy	Vegan option
Calories: 233	Calories: 208
Total fat: 15 g	Total fat: 13 g
Protein: 10 g	Protein: 8 g
Fiber: 3.5 g	Fiber: 3.5 g
Carbohydrates: 14 g	Carbohydrates: 17 g
Cholesterol: 22 g	Cholesterol: 0 g
Sodium: 301 mg	Sodium: 323 mg

Vegetable Bread Pudding

I've long enjoyed making and serving bread puddings, which offer a great way to use up the last few pieces of bread in a loaf and vegetables that are getting a bit tired. This is sort of a cheesy cousin to baked stuffings, but with more emphasis on the vegetables than the bread.

1 Preheat the oven to 350° F.

2 Place the bread in a mixing bowl and pour ½ cup of the milk over it. Stir to moisten the bread, then set aside.

3 Heat the oil in a large skillet. Add the onion and sauté over medium-low heat until golden and just beginning to turn brown.

4 Add the vegetables and just enough water to keep the skillet moist; cover and steam until just tender, 5 to 8 minutes.

5 Combine the vegetable mixture with the bread and stir in the remaining ingredients, including the remaining ¼ cup milk. Mix well, then transfer to a shallow 2-quart baking dish. Sprinkle a generous layer of wheat germ over the top.

6 Bake for 35 to 40 minutes, or until the top is golden and just beginning to turn crusty. Let stand for 5 to 10 minutes, then cut into squares or wedges to serve.

Variations

You can use a single vegetable or a combination of two or three. You'll need a total of 4 cups raw vegetables, prepared as instructed below:

- Broccoli, finely chopped and steamed
- Cauliflower, finely chopped and steamed
- Small zucchini, thinly sliced
- Peeled and diced eggplant, steamed
- Firm, ripe tomatoes, diced
- Corn kernels, cooked, fresh or frozen, thawed
- Mushrooms, sliced

MAKE IT A MEAL: To keep it simple, serve this with baked or microwaved sweet potatoes or Sautéed Skillet Potatoes (page 200) and a salad of greens and tomatoes. This is also delicious served with Skillet Baked Beans (page 189) or with a simple soup. Cream of Baby Carrot Soup (page 32), for example, can be made while the casserole bakes. Complete the latter two options with a salad or a platter of raw vegetables and Easy Dill Dip (page 256).

VEGAN

6 servings

1 medium sweet potato

5 medium potatoes, preferably red-skinned or Yukon Gold

1½ cups low-sodium prepared vegetable broth or 1½ cups hot water and 1 vegetable bouillon cube

4 large or 6 average slices whole-grain bread, torn into small pieces

2 tablespoons light olive oil

1 cup chopped onion

1 cup diced celery

¼ cup finely chopped fresh parsley, optional

2 teaspoons salt-free all-purpose seasoning (see page xxvi)

Salt and freshly ground pepper, to taste

Calories: 224

Total fat: 6 g

Protein: 5 g

Fiber: 5.1 g

Carbohydrates: 38 g

Cholesterol: 0 g

Sodium: 161 mg

Two-Potato Bread Pudding

You need not wait until Thanksgiving to enjoy this hearty casserole, which resembles a baked stuffing.

1 Bake or microwave the sweet potato and the white potatoes separately in their skins until done. When cool enough to handle, peel and place in a large mixing bowl. Add half of the broth and coarsely mash.

2 Preheat the oven to 375° F. Generously oil a 2-quart baking dish.

3 Place the bread in a small mixing bowl and pour in the remaining broth. Let soak for several minutes, until the broth is absorbed.

4 Meanwhile, heat the oil in a medium skillet. Add the onion and celery and sauté over medium-low heat until the onion is lightly browned and the celery is tender.

5 Add the onion and celery mixture to the mashed potatoes. Stir in the soaked bread, parsley, if using, and salt-free seasoning. Season with salt and pepper.

6 Pour the mixture into the prepared dish. Bake for 45 minutes, or until the top is a crusty golden brown.

MAKE IT A MEAL: Roast some broccoli and cauliflower florets while this is in the oven (see pages 201–2), and serve with a bountiful tossed salad that includes some chickpeas or black beans.

Veggie Pot Pie

DAIRY / VEGAN OPTION

6 servings

Using a prepared whole-grain crust makes it easy to enjoy this comforting classic. A one-wedge serving of this wonderful pie may not satisfy larger appetites, so double the recipe to ensure second helpings and, with any luck, some leftovers.

1 Cook or microwave the potatoes in their skins until done. When cool enough to handle, peel. Dice two and mash the other two. Set aside.

2 Preheat the oven to 350° F.

3 Heat 1 tablespoon of the oil in a large skillet. Add the onion and carrot and sauté over medium heat until golden.

4 Add the broccoli along with a small amount of water. Cover and cook until the broccoli is tender but not overdone, 3 to 4 minutes.

5 Sprinkle the flour into the skillet, then pour in the milk, stirring constantly. Cook until the liquid thickens a bit, 1 to 2 minutes. Stir in the diced and mashed potatoes. Heat through gently. Stir in the parsley, if using, and season with salt and pepper. Pour the mixture into the pie crust and pat in.

6 Place the bread crumbs in a small mixing bowl. Drizzle with the remaining oil and stir until the crumbs are evenly moistened. Sprinkle evenly over the pie. Bake for 35 to 40 minutes, or until the crust is golden. Let the pie stand for about 10 minutes, then cut into wedges and serve.

MAKE IT A MEAL: For a hearty meal, serve with a substantial salad such as Green Salad with Avocado, Apples, and Baked Tofu (page 75) or Mixed Greens with Green Beans, Beets, and Feta or Goat Cheese (page 81). Scalloped Corn (page 207) can be baked at the same time. Other side dish options are fresh corn on the cob and Simple Glazed Butternut Squash (page 215).

4 medium potatoes, preferably russet

1 tablespoon plus 1 teaspoon light olive oil

1 medium onion, quartered and thinly sliced

1 medium carrot, peeled and thinly sliced

1 cup finely chopped broccoli

2 tablespoons unbleached white flour

½ cup low-fat milk, rice milk, or soy milk

2 tablespoons minced fresh parsley, optional

Salt and freshly ground pepper, to taste

9-inch prepared good-quality pie crust, preferably whole grain

½ cup whole-grain bread crumbs (see Note, page 206)

Dairy	Vegan option
Calories: 301	Calories: 303
Total fat: 14 g	Total fat: 13 g
Protein: 6 g	Protein: 5 g
Fiber: 3.4 g	Fiber: 3.4 g
Carbohydrates: 40 g	Carbohydrates: 42 g
Cholesterol: 1 g	Cholesterol: 0 g
Sodium: 226 mg	Sodium: 223 mg

4 to 6 servings

1½ cups Arborio rice

4 cups prepared vegetable broth,
two 15-ounce cans reduced-sodium
vegetable broth, or two vegetable
bouillon cubes dissolved in 4 cups
hot water

2 garlic cloves, very finely minced

Calories: 198
Total fat: 0 g
Protein: 4 g
Fiber: 0.5 g
Carbohydrates: 43 g
Cholesterol: 0 g
Sodium: 59 mg

Baked Risotto

Risotto, a creamy rice dish made with Arborio rice (available in well-stocked supermarkets and Italian groceries) is a classic Italian comfort food. Traditionally, it's made by cooking the rice on the stovetop, ladling in hot broth, and stirring almost constantly. An easier route to this wonderful dish is simply to combine the basic ingredients in a deep casserole dish and bake, giving it a good stir every 15 minutes until done (the entire process takes 1 hour). During that time, you're free to work on another part of the meal or do something else altogether!

1   Preheat the oven to 375° F.

2   Combine the rice with the stock, 1 cup water, and the garlic in a 2-quart casserole dish. Cover and bake for 1 hour, stirring every 15 minutes. At the third stirring, add 1 more cup of water. When done, the rice should have a tender and creamy texture.

3   Let the risotto stand for 5 minutes before serving.

Variations

Here are some wonderful ways to dress up individual portions of risotto.
Normally, additions are stirred into the risotto, but you can also use them
as toppings, as I do. This way, kids are more likely to enjoy the meal, while
allowing adults and older kids to savor more complex flavors. I also reserve
a portion of whatever vegetable I am planning to add, to serve on the side
for the children's portions.

- Wilted spinach or Swiss chard and corn kernels or goat cheese
- Sautéed zucchini, red pepper, and herbs
- Finely diced baked winter squash, sautéed red onion, and toasted
  walnuts
- Sautéed leeks and chopped imported black olives
- Roasted eggplant and Italian-style stewed tomatoes
- Steamed asparagus and wilted spinach
- Grated fresh Parmesan or Parmesan-style soy cheese
- Grated mozzarella or mozzarella-style nondairy cheese

MAKE IT A MEAL: My favorite salads to serve with this are Cabbage, Apple,
and Raisin Slaw (page 69) and Tri-Color Coleslaw (page 71). Complete the
meal with steamed broccoli or green beans. For an impressive company
meal, serve Creamy Butternut Squash and Apple Soup (page 46) as a first
course.

Curried Potatoes with Peas, Raisins, and Cashews

4 to 6 servings

This dish is a good way to introduce curried flavors to older kids and teens, with raisins and peas lending a subtle sweetness. Once you've got the potatoes ready, the rest of the dish comes together in no time.

6 large red-skinned or Yukon Gold
    potatoes
1½ tablespoons light olive oil
1 large onion, chopped
1 small hot chile pepper, seeded and
    minced, or one 4-ounce can chopped
    mild green chilies
1 to 2 teaspoons good-quality curry
    powder
½ teaspoon ground cumin
1½ cups steamed fresh green peas or
    frozen green peas, thawed
⅓ cup dark raisins
1 tablespoon freshly squeezed lemon or
    lime juice
Salt to taste
¼ to ½ cup chopped toasted cashews,
    for topping
Minced fresh cilantro, for topping

1 Bake or microwave the potatoes in their skins until done but still firm. When cool enough to handle, peel and cut into approximately 1-inch chunks.

2 Heat the oil in an extra-large skillet. Add the onion and sauté over medium heat until golden. Add the chile and sauté, stirring for 1 or 2 minutes.

3 Add ½ cup of water to the skillet. Stir in the curry powder and cumin, followed by the potatoes, peas, raisins, and lemon juice. Cook over medium heat, stirring frequently, until well heated through, 5 to 8 minutes. The dish should be moist (but not soupy), so add a bit of additional water if needed.

4 Season with salt. Scatter the cashews and cilantro over the top of the dish before serving, if desired, or pass to top individual portions. Serve at once.

EMBELLISH IT: Pass a spicy chutney to top individual portions.

MAKE IT A MEAL: For an enticing meal, serve with Tomatoes and Cucumbers in Yogurt (page 79) and Fruited Couscous (page 227).

FOR PICKY EATERS: This dish is an easy one to take apart for young eaters. Bake or microwave an extra potato or two. Split open and top with a bit of nonhydrogenated margarine and a sprinkling of grated cheese or soy cheese. Cook some extra peas to serve plain, and add a few raisins to the plate.

Calories: 256
Total fat: 5 g
Protein: 6 g
Fiber: 6.6 g
Carbohydrates: 50 g
Cholesterol: 0 g
Sodium: 13 mg

Potato and Tempeh Hash

A hearty vegetarian spin on a meaty classic, this is as good served as a quick dinner as it is as an offbeat and hearty breakfast.

1 Bake or microwave the potatoes until done. When cool enough to handle, peel and finely dice.

2 Heat the oil in a large skillet. Add the onion and sauté over medium heat until translucent. Add the bell pepper and continue to sauté until the onion is golden.

3 Add the remaining ingredients, except the salt and pepper. Sauté, stirring frequently, until the mixture is hot and golden brown. If it seems dry, add a small amount of water. Season with salt and pepper and serve.

MAKE IT A MEAL: For a quick dinner, serve with an abundant, colorful tossed salad, whole-grain bread, and orange slices. In warmer months, if desired, add fresh corn on the cob; in cooler months try this with Simple Glazed Butternut Squash (page 215).

VEGAN

4 servings

5 medium-large potatoes
1½ tablespoons light olive oil
1 medium onion, finely chopped
1 medium green bell pepper, finely diced
4 slices tempeh "bacon," cut into small bits
½ teaspoon all-purpose salt-free seasoning (see page xxvi)
1 teaspoon paprika
1 to 2 tablespoons nutritional yeast, optional
Salt and freshly ground pepper, to taste

Calories: 269
Total fat: 8 g
Protein: 9 g
Fiber: 5.7 g
Carbohydrates: 44 g
Cholesterol: 0 g
Sodium: 18 mg

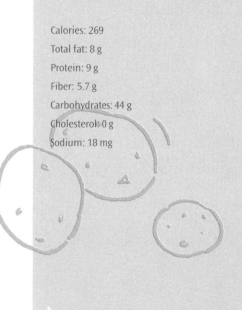

VEGAN / DAIRY OPTION

4 to 6 servings

2 cups coarse yellow cornmeal
1 teaspoon salt, or to taste
2 tablespoons nonhydrogenated
   margarine

Calories: 206
Total fat: 5 g
Protein: 4 g
Fiber: 3.5 g
Carbohydrates: 37 g
Cholesterol: 0 g
Sodium: 479 mg

Polenta

Polenta is the Italian name for a basic cornmeal mush. My sons discovered it when we ate at a favorite vegetarian restaurant in the Hudson Valley. Since then, it has been one of their most beloved quick dinners.

1 Combine the cornmeal with 2 cups of water in a large, deep saucepan and whisk until smooth. Place on medium heat and bring to a simmer, whisking frequently. Stir in 5 cups water, 1 cup at a time, whisking thoroughly after each addition.

2 Make sure that all lumps are whisked out, then cover and simmer, whisking occasionally, until smooth and thick, 15 minutes. If you'd like a thinner polenta, add 1 cup more water, whisk in, and cook 2 to 3 minutes longer.

3 When done, stir in the margarine until melted. Serve in bowls and top as desired.

Variations

Here are a few simple suggestions for topping polenta:

- A sprinkling of grated fresh Parmesan or Parmesan-style soy cheese
- A sprinkling of your favorite grated cheese or nondairy cheese
- Crumbled goat cheese and thinly sliced basil leaves
- Lightly cooked diced tomatoes and thinly sliced basil leaves
- Brown mushrooms, lightly sautéed in olive oil, and dried tomatoes
- Sautéed garlic and wilted greens
- Cooked fresh corn kernels and thinly sliced scallions
- Sautéed onions and bell peppers

MAKE IT A MEAL: Few meals could make my sons happier than a big bowl (or two) of polenta with grated soy cheese, a big serving of steamed broccoli, and a platter of raw veggies. For something a little livelier, precede with a colorful salad like Mixed Greens with Green Beans, Beets, and Feta or Goat Cheese (page 81) or a bountiful green salad. Serve polenta with the desired toppings, plus Sautéed Broccoli, Baby Carrots, and Yellow Squash (page 210) on the side.

Cooking Beans: The Basics

Since this is a book geared toward busy families, I usually call for canned beans, or at least the option is always there. But if you want to cook your own beans, so much the better. Doing so is more economical and allows you to control the salt level. The high salt content of canned beans is, in fact, their major drawback. Otherwise, they are a boon to the busy cook and are great to have in the summer when the long cooking required for beans is less than desirable. I recommend buying canned beans with no additives and rinsing the salty broth away before use. Good-quality canned or jarred organic beans are available in natural foods stores and many major supermarkets.

Raw beans generally swell to about $2\frac{1}{2}$ times their raw volume when cooked. So if you need 2 cups of cooked beans, you'd start with $\frac{3}{4}$ cup dried. But as long as you are going through the effort, it's worthwhile to cook more than you need for just one recipe; freeze the extra beans for later use. I'm not a huge fan of freezing, but beans are, to my mind, one of the foods that freeze most successfully.

Pressure cookers and, on the other end of the spectrum, slow cookers are other good vehicles for cooking beans. Consult manufacturer's instructions for specifics.

1. Rinse the beans in a colander and sort carefully to remove grit and small stones.

2. Combine the beans in a large pot with three to four times their volume of water. Cover and soak overnight. Or bring to a boil and let stand off the heat, covered, for 1 to 2 hours for a quicker soaking method.

3. Drain the soaking water. Though some vitamins may be lost, draining the soaking water also eliminates some of the complex sugars that many people have trouble digesting. Fill the pot with fresh water, about double the volume of the beans. Don't worry about an exact amount, just give the beans plenty of room to simmer.

4. Bring the water to a boil, then lower the heat to a gentle simmer. Partially cover (leave the lid slightly ajar to prevent foaming) and cook slowly and thoroughly to let the beans develop flavor, to prevent the skins from bursting, and to ensure better digestibility. A bean that presses easily between the thumb and forefinger is done. Most beans take about 1½ hours to cook.

5. Add salt only when the beans are done. Salt tends to harden the skins, prolonging the cooking time.

Skillet Black Beans with Potatoes and Tortillas

VEGAN

4 to 6 servings

Here's a hearty bean dish for families that enjoy lively south-of-the-border flavors.

4 medium-large potatoes

1½ tablespoons light or extra-virgin olive oil

1 medium-large onion, chopped

2 to 3 garlic cloves, minced

1 medium green bell pepper, diced

One 4-ounce can mild diced green chilies

One 16-ounce can diced tomatoes

One 16-ounce can black beans, drained and rinsed

2 teaspoons ground cumin

Juice of 1 lime

6 6-inch corn tortillas, cut into short, narrow strips

1 Microwave the potatoes until done but still firm. When cool enough to handle, peel and cut into ½-inch dice. Set aside.

2 Heat the oil in an extra-large skillet. Add the onion and sauté over medium heat until translucent. Add the garlic and bell pepper and sauté until the onion is golden.

3 Add the chiles, tomatoes, beans, and cumin. Bring to a simmer, then cover and simmer gently for 10 minutes.

4 Stir in the lime juice, tortillas, and potatoes and cook briefly, just until heated through. Serve at once.

Calories: 321

Total fat: 6 g

Protein: 11 g

Fiber: 11.7 g

Carbohydrates: 58 g

Cholesterol: 0 g

Sodium: 200 mg

The Vegetarian Family Cookbook

EMBELLISH IT: If your whole family would enjoy a spicier kick, use 1 to 2 fresh hot chilies, seeded and minced, in place of the canned mild chilies. You can also pass some grated Cheddar or Cheddar-style soy cheese and/or minced fresh cilantro for topping.

MAKE IT A MEAL: Complete the meal with a Simple Slaw (page 68) or a simple tossed salad. Add some sautéed zucchini and/or summer squash or steamed broccoli. To make this dish even heartier, serve over hot cooked brown rice or other grain.

4 to 6 servings

1 tablespoon light or extra-virgin olive
oil
1 medium onion, finely chopped
3 to 4 garlic cloves, minced
½ medium green bell pepper, finely
diced
½ medium red bell pepper, finely diced
4 cups cooked black beans (from 1⅓
cups dried) or two 16-ounce cans,
drained and rinsed
1 large firm, ripe tomato, finely diced
1 teaspoon ground cumin
½ teaspoon dried oregano
Juice of ½ lemon or lime
Salt and freshly ground pepper, to taste
¼ cup chopped fresh cilantro or parsley,
optional
Hot cooked brown rice

Calories: 231
Total fat: 4 g
Protein: 13 g
Fiber: 132 g
Carbohydrates: 39 g
Cholesterol: 0 g
Sodium: 5 mg

Black Bean Sofrito

This classic Latin American dish is a good choice for kids and teens who have
acquired a taste for beans.

1 Heat the oil in a large skillet. Add the onion and sauté over medium heat
until translucent. Add the garlic and the bell peppers and continue to sauté
until softened and the onion is golden.

2 Add the beans, tomato, cumin, oregano, and lemon juice along with ⅓
cup water. Bring to a simmer.

3 Mash a small amount of the black beans with the back of a wooden
spoon, just enough to make a thick sauce. Cover and simmer gently over
low heat for 10 minutes.

4 Season to taste with salt and pepper, then stir in the cilantro, if using.
Serve over the hot rice.

MAKE IT A MEAL: Omit the rice and serve with
Expandable Potato Salad (page
72) or Golden Potato Salad
(page 73) on the side. Or
sauté a couple of
yellow summer
squashes, or serve
Simple Glazed
Butternut Squash
(page 215) to add
color to the plate. See
also "Make it a meal" on
page 169.

Skillet Baked Beans

VEGAN

6 servings

If you like the kind of vegetarian baked beans that come in a can, you're sure to love this yummy, quick homemade version.

1 Heat the oil in a large skillet. Add the onion and sauté over medium-low heat until translucent. Add the garlic and continue to sauté until the onion is golden.

2 Add the remaining ingredients plus 3 tablespoons water, stir together, and continue to cook over low heat, stirring occasionally, 10 to 15 minutes. Serve at once.

MAKE IT A MEAL: Serve with baked or microwaved sweet potatoes and a simple cooked grain—brown rice is good, or see Beyond Brown Rice (pages 234–35) for other ideas. Then add a high-nutrient steamed green vegetable (green beans, spinach, Brussels sprouts, or broccoli). A simple slaw (page 68) complements this dish nicely. Quick Three-Grain Brown Bread (page 280) is a delicious accompaniment, if time allows.

1½ tablespoons light olive oil

1 medium-large onion, quartered and thinly sliced

2 garlic cloves, minced

Three 16-ounce cans navy beans, drained and rinsed, or 5 to 5½ cups cooked (about 2 cups dried)

⅓ cup good-quality ketchup

3 tablespoons maple syrup

1 tablespoon molasses or barley malt syrup

1½ teaspoons yellow or Dijon mustard

1 teaspoon paprika

¼ teaspoon ground ginger

Calories: 314

Total fat: 4 g

Protein: 14 g

Fiber: 9

Carbohydrates: 56 g

Cholesterol: 0 g

Sodium: 168 mg

6 to 8 servings

1 tablespoon light olive oil

1 large onion, finely chopped

3 garlic cloves, minced

3 cups cooked brown rice, or one
    6-serving portion cooked
    quick-cooking brown rice

Two 16-ounce cans small red beans,
    drained and rinsed

One 15-ounce can light coconut milk

½ teaspoon dried thyme

Salt and freshly ground pepper, to taste

Calories: 212

Total fat: 6 g

Protein: 6 g

Fiber: 5.3 g

Carbohydrates: 34 g

Cholesterol: 0 g

Sodium: 22 mg

Quick Jamaican Red Beans and Rice

This is a shortcut version of a traditional Jamaican favorite, simply called "rice and peas" (though the "peas" are actually small red beans). I first learned to make this the authentic way from a Jamaican friend—cooking the beans from scratch and cracking open and grating a whole coconut. She told me that each Sunday, families all over the island make a big pot of this dish. While it was a fun project, it *was* rather time-consuming. Busy families may enjoy this quicker route to a satisfying dinner.

1 Heat the oil in a soup pot. Add the onion and sauté over medium-low heat until translucent. Add the garlic and continue to sauté until the onion is golden.

2 Add the rice, beans, coconut milk, and thyme. Bring to a simmer, then cover and cook over low heat until most of the coconut milk is absorbed, about 15 minutes. The mixture should be moist but not liquidy. Season with salt and pepper and serve.

MAKE IT A MEAL: This dish is traditionally served with sautéed plantains, a starchy, banana-like fruit. Try them if you're feeling adventurous. You can also serve Banana Fritters (page 10), an adaptation of another traditional Jamaican recipe. Otherwise, Simple Glazed Butternut Squash (page 215) or Sautéed Broccoli, Baby Carrots, and Yellow Squash (page 210) brighten the plate. A simple salad of greens and tomatoes completes any of these options.

Baked Chickpea Burgers

VEGAN

Makes 8

A number of nourishing ingredients mingle in this baked burger. Though it's tasty enough to be eaten plain as a side dish, it makes a great sandwich as well.

1 Preheat the oven to 350° F. Oil a nonstick baking sheet.

2 Heat the oil in a medium skillet. Add the onion and sauté over medium heat until translucent. Add the carrot and celery and sauté until tender and golden.

3 Combine the vegetable mixture with the remaining ingredients in a food processor. Pulse on and off until the mixture is evenly and finely chopped, but don't purée.

4 Drop by heaping ¼ cupfuls onto the prepared sheet and flatten gently. Bake for 30 minutes, flipping after 20 minutes. Serve at once.

EMBELLISH IT: Serve with Quick Tartar Sauce (page 145) or Tangy Tahini Dressing (page 97) on English muffins or in pita with shredded lettuce or sprouts. Or serve simply with mustard or soy mayonnaise, lettuce, and sliced tomatoes on whole-grain rolls or English muffins.

MAKE IT A MEAL: This is a good accompaniment to many types of dishes—soups, pastas, hearty salads, and grain and potato dishes. Try it with Angel Hair with Zucchini and Bread Crumbs (page 122) and a simple green salad.

1 tablespoon light olive oil
1 medium onion, minced
1 medium carrot, peeled and thinly sliced
1 large celery stalk, diced
One 16-ounce can chickpeas, drained and rinsed
¼ cup wheat germ
2 tablespoons whole-wheat or other whole-grain flour
1 teaspoon salt-free all-purpose seasoning (see page xxvi)
¼ cup soy mayonnaise
Juice of ½ lemon
Salt and freshly ground pepper, to taste

Calories: 115
Total fat: 4 g
Protein: 4 g
Fiber: 3.2 g
Carbohydrates: 15 g
Cholesterol: 0 g
Sodium: 68 mg

Makes 12

Burgers

⅓ cup quick-cooking oats

One 16-ounce can beans, drained and
**   rinsed, or 2 cups well-cooked beans**
**   (from about ⅔ cups dried)**

½ green bell pepper, minced

2 scallions, minced

2 tablespoons soy sauce

½ cup wheat germ

1 to 2 teaspoons salt-free all-purpose
**   seasoning (see page xxvi)**

Light olive oil

Dressing

¾ cup low-fat yogurt or soy yogurt

2 tablespoons Dijon mustard

1 tablespoon minced fresh dill or
**   1 teaspoon dried dill**

1 tablespoon tahini, optional

Dairy	Vegan option
Calories: 78	Calories: 76
Total fat: 1 g	Total fat: 1 g
Protein: 5 g	Protein: 4 g
Fiber: 3.4 g	Fiber: 3.6 g
Carbohydrates: 13 g	Carbohydrates: 13 g
Cholesterol: 1 g	Cholesterol: 0 g
Sodium: 205 mg	Sodium: 199 mg

Savory Bean Burgers with Yogurt-Mustard Dressing

For this perfect pita bread filler, you can use almost any type of well-cooked bean. Pink, pinto, and red beans work particularly well.

1 Combine the oatmeal and ⅔ cup boiling water in a cup. Let stand for 5 minutes.

2 Mash the beans well in a mixing bowl. Add the oatmeal and the remaining burger ingredients, except the oil, and stir until thoroughly mixed.

3 Heat just enough oil to coat the bottom of a large nonstick skillet. When sizzling hot, drop the burger mixture onto the skillet in ¼ cupfuls and flatten lightly to 3- to 4-inch rounds. Cook on both sides over medium heat until nicely browned.

4 Combine all the dressing ingredients in a small bowl and stir until completely blended. Serve with the warm patties.

MAKE IT A MEAL: Serve with a simple coleslaw (page 68) and baked or microwaved sweet potatoes. Another easy option is to serve a bountiful tossed salad and Sautéed Skillet Potatoes (page 200).

Vegetable Sushi

VEGAN

Makes 8 rolls

When it comes to feeding kids, sushi is not usually the first food that springs to mind, yet I've found that more kids than not love sushi. I've watched several of my sons' friends polish off large platters of it in a matter of minutes. I have given sushi lessons to several friends now. It's really helpful the first time to see how it's done, but since I can't come to each of your homes individually, I'll try my best to describe (and draw) the process as clearly as possible.

One personal little innovation is combining sushi rice with short grain brown rice. I tried one batch with only the brown rice and it didn't hold together. But using the two kinds in tandem works perfectly—the brown rice lends a nuttier flavor and more nutrition, and the sticky rice holds everything together. This recipe provides one roll each for 8 people. It's easy to halve the recipe for those times when you want to make a smaller portion.

Vinegared rice:
1 cup short-grain brown rice
1 cup white sushi rice
⅓ cup rice vinegar
2 tablespoons natural granulated sugar (page 283)
½ teaspoon salt

½ medium cucumber, peeled, seeded, and quartered lengthwise
1 medium carrot
1 medium avocado
8 sheets nori (use pretoasted sushi nori)

Pickled ginger
Wasabi paste, optional (see Note)
Reduced-sodium soy sauce

1 Bring 4 cups water to a simmer in a large saucepan. Add the brown rice and simmer, covered, for 10 minutes. Stir in the white rice and continue to simmer until the water is absorbed, about 20 minutes.

2 Transfer the rice to a large bowl. Stir in the vinegar, sugar, and salt. Cover the rice mixture with a clean tea towel and set aside, but don't refrigerate. Plan to begin rolling the sushi once the rice is at room temperature.

3 Cut the cucumber and carrot into very narrow, long pieces, approximately the width of a sheet of nori (but don't worry if they are not the same length. Your first few attempts at cutting the vegetables will not turn out as beautifully as those of an expert sushi chef. I've never mastered this task, but my sushi still tastes and looks good). If you'd like, simply peel off long strips of carrot with a vegetable peeler.

4 Cut narrow strips of avocado lengthwise. It doesn't matter as much how long they are.

Per roll, with a little of each vegetable
Calories: 202
Total fat: 5 g
Protein: 5 g
Fiber: 4.2 g
Carbohydrates: 36 g
Cholesterol: 0 g
Sodium: 148 mg

(continued)

5 Place a sheet of nori, shiny side down, on a bamboo sushi mat (see Tip, below). Spread about ¾ cup of the rice over the surface of the nori with dampened hands, leaving a ½-inch border on the end nearest you and a 2-inch border on the end farthest away.

6 About 1½ inches from the side closest to you, lay 6 or so strips of vegetables close together. You may use one type of vegetable in each roll or combine two or all three.

7 Lift the side of the mat closest to you and roll it over so the nori is tightly rolled over the section with the vegetables. Press down a bit to ensure a snug roll. Wet the far end of the nori and continue rolling, making a snugly closed roll. Set aside and repeat with the remaining sheets of nori.

8 A very sharp, serrated knife is a must for cutting the rolls. Keep a glass of water handy for wetting the knife before cutting each roll. Cut each roll into ½- to ¾-inch sections, and arrange them on a large platter as you go, cut side up.

9 On the serving platter, arrange a small amount of pickled ginger and a small spoonful of wasabi. Or you can arrange the condiments separately on another small plate.

10 Put soy sauce in tiny bowls for individuals or to share, and serve the sushi with chopsticks.

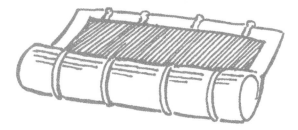

The Vegetarian Family Cookbook

Variation

In place of or in addition to the vegetables suggested, you can try fresh or pickled daikon radish, pickled squash (available in Asian groceries), zucchini, or thinly sliced cooked shiitake mushrooms.

Tip

Using a bamboo mat made for rolling sushi (called a *sudare*) makes the task easier. You'll find this inexpensive item in Asian groceries or most any place where sushi ingredients are sold.

Note

Wasabi, a traditional accompaniment to sushi, is one of the hottest condiments you will ever encounter, so younger kids should be discouraged from taking it.

MAKE IT A MEAL: For a memorable Japanese-style meal, start with Simple Miso Tofu Soup (page 44), then serve the sushi with Cold Soba and Cucumber Salad (page 66), plus cooked edamame (see page 220), Asian Succotash (page 219), or steamed broccoli.

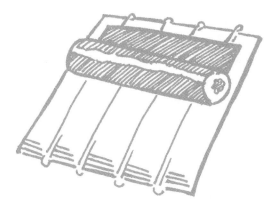

Presenting simple grain dishes in edible containers makes both the grains and the vegetables more exciting. This is an especially nice presentation for fall meals, when "stuffable" vegetables are plentiful and the palate is primed for hearty food. Here's a rundown on how to prepare a few common vegetables for stuffing, followed by suggestions for what to stuff into them:

Winter squashes (butternut, acorn, small sugar pumpkin, and carnival): Halve the squashes lengthwise with a sharp knife. Scoop out the seeds and fibers. Place halves, cut side up, in foil-lined shallow baking dishes and cover tightly with foil. Bake at 375° F, 40 to 50 minutes, or until easily pierced with a knife but still firm. When cool enough to handle, scoop out the pulp, leaving a sturdy ½-inch-thick shell all around. Incorporate the squash pulp into the stuffing or save for another use. Fill the shells with the desired stuffing. Bake 15 to 20 minutes, until well heated through.

Eggplant: Cut off the stem ends and cut in half lengthwise. With a sharp knife, carefully cut away the pulp in small chunks, leaving a sturdy shell about ½ inch thick all around. Chop the eggplant pulp finely, steam until tender, and incorporate into stuffing or save for another use. Fill the shells with the desired stuffing and arrange in foil-lined shallow baking dishes. Cover loosely with foil, and bake at 375° F for 30 minutes. Uncover and bake 10 to 15 minutes, until the shell can be easily pierced with a fork but has not yet collapsed.

Bell peppers: Recipes often call for stuffed bell peppers to be cooked or blanched before stuffing, but I find this step unnecessary. Carefully cut away the stem from each pepper, pulling out many of the seeds with it. Rinse the inside of each pepper to remove the remaining seeds. You can cut the peppers in half lengthwise, in which case they will lie easily on a baking dish; however, some of the stuffing tends to escape from the stem end. Otherwise, leave them whole, cutting a sliver off their bottoms so they will stand more steadily in a baking dish. In either case, prop the peppers securely against one another. Fill the shells with the desired stuffing and arrange in foil-lined baking dishes (deep dishes are desirable if the peppers are left whole). Cover loosely with foil and bake at 375° F for 25 minutes. Uncover and bake 10 to 15 minutes, until done to your liking.

Tomatoes: Large, firm, yet flavorful tomatoes are best for stuffing. Cut each tomato in half crosswise. Carefully scoop out the pulp using a sharp knife to loosen it and a spoon to scoop it out. Leave a sturdy shell about ¼ inch thick all around. Incorporate the tomato pulp into the stuffing if desired or reserve for another use. Fill the shells with the desired stuffing and arrange in foil-lined baking dishes. Bake, uncovered, at 350° F for 25 to 30 minutes, until done to your liking.

Zucchini: Use medium zucchinis for stuffing. Remove the stem ends. A grapefruit spoon is ideal for removing the seeds and creating a cavity, but if you don't have one, use a small, sharp knife to carefully remove enough pulp to result in a ¼-inch-thick shell. If most of what you've scooped out consists of seeds, discard; otherwise, chop the pulp and steam it; if desired, incorporate it into the stuffing or save for another use. Fill the shells with the desired stuffing and arrange in foil-lined baking dishes. Cover loosely with foil and bake at 375° F for 20 to 25 minutes. Uncover and bake for 10 to 15 minutes, or until done but still firm.

Some of the simple grain dishes in Chapter 7 are perfect for stuffing into vegetables. Here are some possibilities:

- **Asian Succotash** (page 219) is good in tomatoes, peppers, and small winter squashes.
- **Quick Couscous and Black Bean Pilaf** (page 233) goes well in any vegetable.
- **Fruited Couscous** (page 227) is good in any vegetable except tomatoes.
- **Seashells in the Sand** (page 228) is good in any vegetable except zucchini.
- **Bulgur with Fine Noodles** (page 229) is especially good in eggplant and bell peppers.
- **Mexican Green Rice** (page 220) is good in any vegetable.
- **Simple Quinoa and Wild Rice Pilaf** (page 232) is good in any vegetable.

CHAPTER SEVEN

Vegetable and Grain Side Dishes

NOT JUST A WAY to fill an empty little portion of the dinner plate, side dishes can be a delicious way to infuse meals with a dazzling array of nutrients. Vegetables, grains, and beans are at the heart of the healthy vegetarian diet, for every stage of life. I've long believed that if there are always plenty of vegetables at the table, even the most finicky of eaters will eventually develop a taste for them. Yes, even vegetarian children can be finicky, but not, in my observation, as much as children raised on the standard American diet. In this chapter you'll encounter an array of easy recipes and techniques for making veggies appealing, including roasting, baking, stir-frying, and more. Consult the guides on pages xviii–xx for information on which vegetables are best purchased in organic form. Given the choice, opt for organic whenever possible.

Also in this chapter, you'll find several simple whole-grain side dishes. Whole grains are among the most unadulterated forms of plant protein. As with vegetables, it's not always easy to get children, vegetarian or not, to appreciate grains, but here you will find a range of ways to ease the entire family into the habit of eating more of these essential foods. And, of course, vegetable, grain, and bean recipes are found throughout this book.

Five Simple Ways to Serve Potatoes

OVEN FRIES: Use 1 large or 2 medium potatoes per person (preferably red-skinned, Yukon Gold, or other firm-fleshed variety). Peel the potatoes and cut them into long, ½-inch-thick strips. Combine them in a large mixing bowl with a modest amount of light olive oil and toss well to coat. Sprinkle with a little salt. Transfer to a nonstick baking sheet. Bake at 425° F, stirring gently every 10 minutes, for 20 to 30 minutes, until crisp and lightly browned. Serve at once. Note that this is also an excellent way to serve sweet potatoes.

SAUTÉED SKILLET POTATOES: For 4 servings, use 4 large or 6 medium potatoes (red-skinned, Yukon gold, or other firm-fleshed variety). Microwave the potatoes until they can be just pierced. When the potatoes are cool enough to handle (In a hurry? Plunge the potatoes into a bowl of ice water), peel and cut into thick, wedge-shaped chunks. Heat just enough light olive oil to coat the bottom of a large nonstick skillet or griddle. Cook the potatoes over medium-high heat in a single layer (do this in batches, if needed), turning frequently, until all sides are golden brown and crisp. If cooking in batches, keep the first batch warm in a covered casserole dish while cooking the second. Sprinkle with salt and serve.

SAUCY POTATOES: For 4 servings, microwave 4 large or 6 medium potatoes (any variety) until done but firm. When cool enough to handle, peel and cut into large dice. Cook over medium-high heat in a skillet with ⅔ cup natural barbecue sauce or Thai peanut sauce, stirring frequently until piping hot, 4 to 5 minutes. Top with sliced scallions or sauté a large onion until golden before adding the potatoes and sauce to the skillet.

CHEESY SMASHED POTATOES: For 4 servings, microwave 4 large or 6 medium baking potatoes (preferably russet) to a medium texture—not too soft, not too firm. When cool enough to handle, peel and cut into large chunks. Place in a shallow microwave-safe casserole dish. Add 1 tablespoon nonhydrogenated margarine and ¼ cup low-fat milk, rice milk, or soy milk, and mash the potatoes coarsely, leaving plenty of chunks. Add a little salt to taste, stir, then sprinkle in about 1 cup mild cheese or nondairy cheese. Microwave on high for 2 to 3 minutes, until the mixture is nicely warmed and the cheese is melted. Or bake at 375° F for 5 to 8 minutes. Try replacing 1 large potato or 2 medium potatoes with 1 sweet potato.

PIZZA POTATOES: Use 1 large potato, any variety, per serving. Bake or microwave the potatoes until done. When cool enough to handle, cut each in half lengthwise. Fluff the inside of each potato half with a fork. Spread about 2 tablespoons of pizza sauce on each half, followed by 2 to 3 tablespoons grated mozzarella cheese or mozzarella-style nondairy cheese. Bake at 400° F for 10 minutes, until the cheese is bubbly. Serve at once. Serve steamed broccoli and a large tossed salad (with chickpeas tossed in) for adults and older kids and raw veggies and dip with some chickpeas on the side for young eaters.

Know Your Spuds

It's surprising that many recipes in books and articles (including my own, mea culpa!) merely state the size of the potatoes (such as "4 medium potatoes") instead of specifying the variety. While potatoes are fairly interchangeable, different varieties yield different results. For example, russets, an oval, brown-skin variety, are best for baking or stuffing, as they have a soft, mealy flesh. They also work well in soups in which it's desirable for the potato to break down and thicken the stock.

Red-skinned potatoes (such as Red Bliss) and yellow-fleshed potatoes (Yukon Gold and Finnish Yellow) have firmer flesh, sometimes referred to as "waxy." These are good for sautéing, for potato salads, and for making oven fries, because they hold their shape well. This isn't to say that they'd be unwelcome in soups; and if you want to use them as a baking or stuffing potato, you just need to be sure they are thoroughly cooked.

White all-purpose potatoes such as White Rose have a very thin skin and flesh that is between mealy and waxy. You can truly use these for any purpose, though they sometimes tend to be very bland. Then there are specialty potatoes, which are best to use as simple side dishes. These include new potatoes (tiny white or red potatoes), fingerlings, and the relatively new blue-fleshed potatoes. The latter don't really taste much different from an ordinary, waxy variety, but they add a bit of drama to the dinner plate.

Roasted Vegetables

Roasting vegetables in a hot oven brings their natural sugars to the surface and maintains nutrients. For kids who aren't keen on steamed or raw veggies, you may find that roasting might spark some interest. Root vegetables are ideal for roasting due to their natural sugars, but lots of other vegetables fare well with this technique. I've found 425° F to be the ideal temperature for my oven, but 400° F works as well. If I have anything else in the oven at either of those temperatures, I try to toss in some vegetables to roast at the same time. Once vegetables are roasted, they're good warm or at room temperature. Leftover roasted vegetables can be used to make wraps or to top pizza.

Here is a brief asparagus-to-zucchini guide to the best common vegetables to roast. Try the following vegetables individually or, when baking time is compatible, in combinations, using the following steps:

1. Toss the prepared vegetables with 1 or 2 tablespoons of olive oil, just enough to coat the surfaces lightly.
2. Scatter onto a lightly oiled roasting pan or baking sheet in a single layer.
3. Bake at 400 to 425° F, stirring every 10 minutes until slightly crisp and touched with brown on the outside and tender on the inside.

Asparagus: Use slender or medium-thick asparagus. Trim about ½ inch off the bottoms. Roast for 8 to 10 minutes, or until they are just tender when pierced with a fork.

Beets: This is a good vegetable to roast individually, unless you don't mind magenta-stained vegetables. To minimize mess, peel beets over a trash or compost container, and slice ¼ inch thick on a cutting board covered with wax paper. Roast in a foil-lined baking dish for 20 to 30 minutes, or until tender.

Broccoli: Cut broccoli stalks into fairly large bite-size pieces and florets. Roast for 20 to 25 minutes.

Carrots or baby carrots: Peel carrots and cut them into medium-thick sticks, about 3 inches long. Baby carrots can be roasted just as they are, making them the simplest veggie that can be tossed into the oven. Roast for 20 to 25 minutes.

Cauliflower: Cut one medium or large cauliflower into bite-size florets and pieces. Roast for 20 to 25 minutes.

Green beans: Trim the ends off green beans and roast them whole for 15 to 20 minutes.

Mushrooms: Clean and stem mushrooms. If small or medium, leave the caps whole. If large, cut in half. When tossing with oil, add a dash or two of soy sauce for extra flavor. Roast for 20 minutes.

Potatoes: See Oven Fries (page 190). You can also cut potatoes into thick slices or wedge shapes before roasting.

Sweet potatoes: Peel and cut in half lengthwise and then into ½-inch-thick slices or cut into thick fry shapes. Roast for 20 to 30 minutes. Sprinkle lightly with dried rosemary before putting in the oven for delicious added flavor.

Turnips, parsnips, and rutabagas: Peel and slice or cut into fry shapes. Roast for 20 to 25 minutes. Roasting makes roots shine. See also Roasted Root Vegetable Medley (page 205).

Zucchini and yellow summer squash: These are nice roasted in tandem. Cut into ½-inch-thick slices or quarter lengthwise and cut into spears. Roast for 15 to 20 minutes, until touched with golden brown spots.

Roasted Sweet Potatoes and Apples

VEGAN

4 to 6 servings

Here's a dish that's as welcome for winter holiday meals as it is for everyday fare. Serve with sandwiches and wraps, veggie burgers, or as a side dish for bean-based main dishes and vegetable casseroles. Serve it with Baked Tofu Nuggets (page 144).

3 large sweet potatoes, peeled, cut in half lengthwise, and sliced ¼ inch thick crosswise
1 tablespoon light vegetable oil
4 medium crisp apples, peeled, cored, and cut into eighths (see Note)
¼ cup maple syrup
Ground cinnamon, to taste
Ground nutmeg, to taste
Salt, to taste

1 Preheat the oven to 425° F. Lightly oil a large nonstick roasting pan.

2 Combine the sweet potatoes with the oil in a mixing bowl and toss to coat.

3 Transfer to the prepared pan. Bake for 15 minutes, stirring after the first 10 minutes.

4 Add the apples and drizzle the mixture evenly with maple syrup. Sprinkle with a small amount of cinnamon, nutmeg, and salt, and carefully stir the mixture together.

5 Bake, stirring occasionally, for another 15 minutes, or until the potatoes and apples are fork-tender and lightly browned here and there on the outside. Serve at once.

Calories: 202
Total fat: 3 g
Protein: 1 g
Fiber: 5 g
Carbohydrates: 44 g
Cholesterol: 0 g
Sodium: 8 mg

Note
Try tart apples, if you'd like.

EMBELLISH IT: If you think your family would enjoy it, stir in ½ cup chopped pitted prunes or mission figs into the mixture once it's out of the oven.

The bright flesh of sweet potatoes hints at their nutrient-rich content—they're a good source of vitamin C, beta-carotene, and several minerals. Sometimes sweet potatoes are labeled "yams," but this is a misnomer. Yams are starchy tubers native to Africa and Asia that are rarely sold in this country. If you come across Garnet yams, for example, grab them, as these smaller sweet potatoes are truly delectable.

The sweet potatoes with widest appeal are the more common, orange-fleshed variety. Quite often in this book, I recommend baking or microwaving them to serve as a simple side dish. My family recently discovered (thanks to a friend who is a living foods enthusiast) that the common sweet potato is quite good raw! Peeled and thinly sliced, it tastes like a very sweet, slightly creamy carrot.

A cousin to the orange-fleshed sweet potato is a yellow-fleshed variety. I've bought it inadvertently a few times, as it is sometimes hard to distinguish from the other kind and is rarely labeled. The yellow potatoes are longer, narrower, and have a slightly redder skin than orange ones. Yellow-fleshed sweet potatoes are drier and mealier and not as sweet. They're good in soups or served mashed as a change of pace from white potatoes, but if you're expecting the brilliant color and sweetness of the orange-fleshed kind, they may disappoint.

Roasted Root Vegetable Medley

Late fall and early winter harvests offer an abundance of hardy root vegetables. They're perfect candidates for oven roasting, which brings out their natural sweetness. This is a good side dish for wraps, sandwiches, and bean dishes. Try it with Baked Tofu Nuggets (page 144).

1 Preheat the oven to 425° F. Lightly oil a large roasting pan or line it with foil.

2 Place the vegetables in a large mixing bowl and toss with the oil and salt.

3 Transfer the mixture to the prepared pan. Bake for 20 to 25 minutes, stirring every 5 to 10 minutes, or until fork-tender and lightly browned on the outside. Serve at once.

Variations

Use a combination of parsnips and turnips. Substitute rutabaga or kohlrabi, cut similarly to the other vegetables, for all or some of the beets.

VEGAN

6 or more servings

1 large sweet potato, peeled, cut in half lengthwise, and sliced ¼ inch thick crosswise

2 large carrots, peeled and sliced ¼ inch thick or into narrow sticks, or 1½ cups baby carrots

2 medium-large turnips, peeled, cut in half, and sliced ¼ inch thick, or 2 medium parsnips, peeled and sliced ¼ inch thick

2 large or 3 medium beets, peeled and sliced ¼ inch thick

2 tablespoons light olive oil

¼ teaspoon salt

Calories: 86

Total fat: 5 g

Protein: 1 g

Fiber: 2.4 g

Carbohydrates: 11 g

Cholesterol: 0 g

Sodium: 135 mg

DAIRY / VEGAN OPTION

4 to 6 servings

1 large head cauliflower or 3 good-size
   broccoli crowns, or half of each, cut
   into bite-size pieces
2 tablespoons nonhydrogenated
   margarine
½ cup soft bread crumbs (see Note)
2 tablespoons wheat germ
½ cup grated Cheddar or Cheddar-style
   nondairy cheese, optional
2 scallions, sliced, optional

Calories: 65
Total fat: 4 g
Protein: 2 g
Fiber: 2 g
Carbohydrates: 6 g
Cholesterol: 0 g
Sodium: 70 mg

Scalloped Cauliflower or Broccoli

Here's a nice way to introduce kids to a gently embellished vegetable dish. My sons enjoy cauliflower and broccoli any way they're served, so when I make this dish, my husband and I are lucky if we get to enjoy a few morsels. This goes well with many types of meals, including pastas, grains, and bean dishes. I also like to make this with casseroles baking simultaneously in the oven, for example, Mom's "Tuna"-Noodle Casserole (page 114).

1 Preheat the oven to 350° F.

2 Place the cauliflower in a large saucepan or a microwave-safe container and steam or microwave until just tender. Drain and transfer to a large, shallow casserole.

3 Melt the margarine in a small skillet. Drizzle half of it over the cauliflower and toss to mix.

4 Add the bread crumbs and wheat germ to the remaining margarine in the skillet and toss to coat. Remove from the heat.

5 Sprinkle the cheese, if using, over the cauliflower, then sprinkle the bread crumb mixture evenly over the top. Sprinkle on the scallions, if desired. Bake for 25 minutes, or until the bread crumbs look crisp and golden. Serve.

Note
To make ½ cup fresh bread crumbs, place 2 slices soft whole-wheat bread, torn into pieces, in a food processor and whirl until they are crumbs.

Scalloped Corn

DAIRY / VEGAN OPTION

4 to 6 servings

Though this is perfectly acceptable to make with frozen corn, it's especially good with just-done, fresh corn kernels. This is a sturdy side dish that goes well with bean dishes as well as casseroles; try Eggless Tofu Quiche (page 136) or Veggie Pot Pie (page 177).

2 tablespoons light olive oil
1 medium onion, chopped
1 small zucchini, thinly sliced
2 medium firm, ripe tomatoes, diced
2 tablespoons unbleached white flour
1 cup low-fat milk, rice milk, or soy milk
3 cups cooked fresh corn kernels or
**   frozen corn kernels, thawed**
¼ teaspoon dried thyme or basil
Salt and freshly ground pepper, to taste
1 cup whole-grain bread crumbs (from 4
**   average slices whole-grain bread)**
**   (see Note, page 206)**

1 Preheat the oven to 350° F.

2 Heat 1½ tablespoons of the oil in a large skillet. Add the onion and sauté until golden. Add the zucchini and tomatoes, and cook briefly, just until softened slightly.

3 Sprinkle in the flour and stir in until evenly distributed. Slowly pour in the milk, stirring constantly.

4 Add the corn and thyme. Cook over medium heat until the liquid has thickened. Season with salt and pepper, then transfer to a 9- by 13-inch or a large, round casserole dish.

5 Mix the bread crumbs with the remaining oil until well coated. Sprinkle the crumbs over the corn mixture. Bake for 20 to 25 minutes, or until the bread crumbs look golden and crisp. Serve.

Dairy	Vegan option
Calories: 269	Calories: 275
Total fat: 7 g	Total fat: 7 g
Protein: 9 g	Protein: 7 g
Fiber: 4.8 g	Fiber: 4.8 g
Carbohydrates: 46 g	Carbohydrates: 49 g
Cholesterol: 2 g	Cholesterol: 0 g
Sodium: 222 mg	Sodium: 215 mg

Serves 4 to 6

1 tablespoon light olive oil
½ teaspoon dark sesame oil
One 15-ounce can baby corn, drained,
  liquid reserved
One 16-ounce package fresh baby carrots
2 thin slices fresh ginger
½ cup frozen green peas, thawed
Pinch of salt

Calories: 92
Total fat: 3 g
Protein: 2 g
Fiber: 4.8 g
Carbohydrates: 14 g
Cholesterol: 0 g
Sodium: 39 mg

Baby Carrot and Baby Corn Stir-Fry

This quick side dish makes a colorful companion to many types of Asian main dishes, including tofu, seitan, and noodle dishes.

1 Heat the oils and ¼ cup liquid from the baby corn together in a stir-fry pan. Add the carrots and ginger and stir-fry until the carrots are tender-crisp.

2 Add the baby corn, peas, and salt. Stir-fry until everything is heated through, then remove the ginger slices and serve.

Variation
Substitute a good handful of torn spinach leaves for the peas. Add them when you would add the peas, and stir-fry until the spinach leaves are wilted but still bright green.

Stir-Fried Broccoli

VEGAN

4 servings

I may never master the art of Chinese-style broccoli, though this recipe is the closest I've come. It combines a quick, hot steaming followed by a brief stir-fry. A good side dish for Asian-style noodle or tofu dishes that don't themselves contain broccoli, such as Vegetable Lo Mein (page 104).

1   Combine the stock, soy sauce, and cornstarch in a small bowl and stir until dissolved. Set aside.

2   Heat the oil plus ¼ cup water in a stir-fry pan. Add the broccoli, garlic, and ginger, if using, and stir together. Cover and cook over high heat, stirring once or twice, 3 to 4 minutes.

3   Uncover and add just a bit more water if the pan is dry. Stir-fry over high heat until the broccoli is done to your liking, then stir in the stock mixture. Continue cooking briefly, just until the liquid thickens, then serve.

Variation

Add a can of drained, cut baby corn to this dish during the final step of stir-frying. Use the liquid from the baby corn in place of the water in the stock mixture.

½ cup vegetable stock or water
2 tablespoons reduced-sodium soy sauce
2 teaspoons cornstarch or arrowroot
1 tablespoon light olive oil
2 large or 3 medium broccoli crowns, cut into bite-size pieces
1 to 2 garlic cloves, minced
½ teaspoon grated fresh ginger, optional

Calories: 62
Total fat: 4 g
Protein: 3 g
Fiber: 2 g
Carbohydrates: 5 g
Cholesterol: 0 g
Sodium: 366 mg

Sautéed Broccoli, Baby Carrots, and Yellow Squash

4 to 6 servings

1 tablespoon light olive oil

2 large broccoli crowns, cut into bite-size
  pieces

1 cup baby carrots

1 medium yellow summer squash

2 scallions, thinly sliced, optional

2 teaspoons nonhydrogenated margarine

Salt and freshly ground pepper, to taste

Calories: 58

Total fat: 4 g

Protein: 2 g

Fiber: 2.2 g

Carbohydrates: 5 g

Cholesterol: 0 g

Sodium: 32 mg

I make this colorful trio of sautéed vegetables often, as it complements many different kinds of main dishes, including pastas, potatoes, and grains. It also adds vivid color to the plate when you are serving something creamy and pale, like Pasta with Enlightened Alfredo Sauce (page 124) or Baked Risotto (page 178).

1   Heat the oil in a wide skillet. Add the broccoli, carrots, and ¼ cup water. Cover and cook over medium-high heat until the broccoli just turns bright green.

2   Meanwhile, cut the narrow part of the squash into ¼-inch-thick circles. Cut the wider part of the squash in half lengthwise and then into ¼-inch-thick half circles.

3   Add the squash and scallions, if using, to the skillet and sauté over medium heat, stirring frequently, until the vegetables are tender-crisp or to your liking.

4   Stir in the margarine, season with salt and pepper, and serve.

GREAT-NORTHERN SEED CO.

Cutting away the tough outer skin of broccoli stems reveals a crisp, tasty part of the vegetable. Trim a ¼-inch slice off the bottom of the stem, then stand it up. With a sharp knife, slice downward on all sides to remove the tough outer layer. What you'll be left with is a squared-off spear, which you can then cut into smaller sticks. I often serve these just as they are, mixed with carrot sticks. They're great for dipping, too. Broccoli stems can also be sliced crosswise and used in salads or sautéed in a bit of olive oil.

Don't Throw Away Those Broccoli Stems!

Sesame Stir-Fried Green Beans

VEGAN

4 servings

Made with fresh, in-season green beans, this is positively addictive. We've never had leftovers of this dish! As you can imagine, this adds spark to many types of Asian-style tofu, seitan, or noodle dishes, but it jazzes up other types of recipes as well, such as Stewed Tofu with Corn and Tomatoes (page 139).

1 tablespoon light olive oil

2 teaspoons dark sesame oil

1 tablespoon reduced-sodium soy sauce

1 teaspoon natural granulated sugar (see page 283)

1 pound fresh green beans, trimmed

2 garlic cloves, minced

1 tablespoon sesame seeds

1 Heat the oils, soy sauce, and sugar slowly in a wide skillet. Add the green beans and stir to coat. Cover and cook over medium heat for 5 minutes.

2 Uncover and add ¼ cup water. Increase the heat to medium-high, then stir-fry until the green beans are done to your liking and slightly seared in spots. If needed, add small amounts of water, just enough to keep the skillet slightly moist but not so much as to prevent the beans from browning. Cooking time depends on the tenderness and thickness of the green beans.

3 Transfer to a serving container and toss with the sesame seeds. Serve warm or at room temperature.

Calories: 108

Total fat: 7 g

Protein: 3 g

Fiber: 4.2 g

Carbohydrates: 10 g

Cholesterol: 0 g

Sodium: 182 mg

Wilted Sesame Spinach or Swiss Chard

VEGAN

4 servings

The time it takes to stem and wash a big bunch of organic spinach or Swiss chard will be worthwhile to anyone who loves fresh greens. This side dish brightens the plate when served with Asian noodle or tofu dishes.

1 Place the greens in a stir-fry pan. For the spinach, cover and steam using just the water clinging to the leaves, until just lightly wilted, 2 to 3 minutes. For the Swiss chard, add about ½ cup water, enough to keep the bottom of the pan moist, cover, and steam until just tender, 4 to 5 minutes. Drain well in a colander.

2 Heat the soy sauce and oil in the stir-fry pan. Add the greens and stir-fry until heated through, 1 or 2 minutes. Season with pepper and toss in the sesame seeds. Serve at once.

Note
If using spinach, remove the stems. If using Swiss chard, remove the thick mid-ribs as well.

12 to 16 ounces fresh spinach or Swiss chard, coarsely chopped (see Note)
1 tablespoon reduced-sodium soy sauce
2 teaspoons dark sesame oil
Freshly ground pepper, to taste
1 tablespoon toasted sesame seeds

Calories: 59
Total fat: 4 g
Protein: 4 g
Fiber: 3 g
Carbohydrates: 4 g
Cholesterol: 0 g
Sodium: 253 mg

Sweet Cinnamon-Maple Glazed Baby Carrots

VEGAN

4 servings

Baby carrots are so handy when you want an easy, nutritious side dish. This makes a sweet counterpoint to hearty pastas, bean dishes, and vegetable casseroles.

1 tablespoon nonhydrogenated
    margarine
2 tablespoons pure maple syrup
¼ cup apple or freshly squeezed orange
    juice
½ teaspoon ground cinnamon, or to
    taste
Dash of ground nutmeg
One 16-ounce bag baby carrots

1 Heat the margarine, syrup, and juice in a wide skillet. Sprinkle in the cinnamon and nutmeg, then stir in the carrots. Cover and cook until the carrots are tender-crisp, 10 to 15 minutes.

2 Uncover and cook over medium-high heat to allow the liquid to thicken and glaze the carrots, 3 to 4 minutes.

EMBELLISH IT: If older kids and teens are open to it, stir in ½ cup sliced prunes, mission figs, or dried apricots once the carrots are done.

Calories: 102
Total fat: 3 g
Protein: 1 g
Fiber: 3.4 g
Carbohydrates: 20 g
Cholesterol: 0 g
Sodium: 64 mg

Simple Glazed Butternut Squash

In spite of the wide variety of winter squashes available, butternut is still my favorite. It's the sweetest and smoothest in my opinion, and my top choice for stuffing, soups, sweet pies, and especially served simply, as in this recipe. During cooler months, this is a good side dish with stews, chilies, and hearty casseroles.

1   Cut the squash in half lengthwise. Place cut side up in a baking dish and cover each half tightly with foil. To the pan, add about $\frac{1}{2}$ inch of water. Bake about 40 minutes until easily pierced with a knife but still firm.

2   When the squash is cool enough to handle, scoop out and discard the seeds. Cut into $\frac{3}{4}$-inch-thick sections, then peel and cut into $\frac{3}{4}$-inch chunks.

3   Combine the remaining ingredients in an extra-wide skillet or stir-fry pan and heat gently, stirring together. Add the squash and turn up the heat to medium-high. Cook, stirring, until the liquid reduces and the squash is nicely glazed, about 10 minutes. Serve at once.

VEGAN

6 servings

1 large butternut squash
2 tablespoons nonhydrogenated margarine
$\frac{1}{4}$ cup apple juice
1 tablespoon maple syrup
Pinch of ground nutmeg
Pinch of salt

Calories: 95
Total fat: 3 g
Protein: 1 g
Fiber: 4 g
Carbohydrates: 18 g
Cholesterol: 0 g
Sodium: 36 mg

4 to 6 servings

6 medium cooked beets (page 217)
2 teaspoons cornstarch or arrowroot
⅔ cup freshly squeezed orange juice
1 tablespoon maple syrup, or to taste
**1 tablespoon freshly squeezed lemon
 juice, or to taste**

Calories: 56
Total fat: 0 g
Protein: 1 g
Fiber: 1.1 g
Carbohydrates: 13 g
Cholesterol: 0 g
Sodium: 47 mg

Orange and Maple-Glazed Beets

My family likes beets so much that we're often happy to eat them plain. Fresh organic beets are incomparable. But when I want to embellish just a little, I turn to this recipe. It goes well with just about any kind of main dish, especially when you want to add some dazzling color to the plate.

1 When cool enough to handle, peel and cut the beets into ½-inch dice and place in a saucepan.

2 In a small container, combine the cornstarch with just enough water to dissolve. Add to the beets along with the remaining ingredients. Heat slowly, stirring frequently, until everything is well heated through and the liquid has thickened, about 5 minutes.

3 Add more syrup or lemon juice to achieve a sweet/tart balance to your liking. Transfer to a serving container and allow to cool until just warm or room temperature, then serve.

I had long thought of beets as somewhat of a nuisance to prepare until a friend shared her simple technique. Leaving 1 inch of the stem on them, simply microwave whole beets in about 1 inch of water in a deep covered container. Before this, I'd experimented with different ways of cooking beets, all of which left a mess everywhere. This way, the only things that get stained are the casserole dish, which can be tossed immediately in the dishwasher, and your fingers, which eventually return to their normal color.

I find that microwaving on high for 2 to 4 minutes per beet is just right (2 minutes for small beets, 4 for medium-large—this, of course, depends on your particular microwave. Start with less time and check for doneness. If the beets aren't done, turn them over and give them some additional time.

Once the beets are cool enough to handle, peel them over the trash or compost container, then dice or slice as desired right on the plate on which they will be served.

Naturally sweet and often quite appealing to kids of all ages, beets are worth serving frequently. Here are some simple ideas:

- Fresh cooked beets are so flavorful that I like to serve plain slices on the plate or tossed into green salads.
- Dress warm sliced beets with a little lemon juice and honey or maple syrup.
- Drizzle natural honey-mustard dressing or a mild vinaigrette over warm beets.
- Roasted beets are delicious; see page 202.
- Raw or partially cooked beets are wonderful grated and tossed into salads or used in slaws.

6 or more servings

Southwestern Summer Succotash

This is a delicious side dish to make when summer vegetables are at their peak and is a good companion for bean and tortilla dishes. Try it with Creamy Enchilada Casserole (page 170) or any of the Easy Quesadillas or Soft Tacos (page 242) that don't contain the same vegetables.

8 ounces green beans, trimmed and cut into 1-inch pieces

2 tablespoons extra-virgin olive oil

1 medium onion, quartered and thinly sliced

2 garlic cloves, minced, optional

3 cups fresh raw corn kernels (from 3 large or 4 medium ears)

1 heaping cup chopped ripe tomatoes

2 small yellow summer squashes, diced

1 fresh mild or hot green chile, seeded and minced, optional

1 tablespoon apple cider vinegar

Salt and freshly ground pepper, to taste

1 Steam the green beans until tender-crisp, about 8 to 10 minutes. Refresh under cold water until they stop steaming and set aside.

2 Heat the oil in a deep saucepan or stir-fry pan. Add the onion and garlic, if using, and sauté over low heat until the onion is golden. Add ½ cup water and the remaining ingredients, except the beans, and stir together. Cover and cook over low heat, stirring occasionally, until the corn and squash are just done, 15 to 20 minutes.

3 Add the beans and cook until heated through, 3 to 5 minutes. Adjust the seasonings and serve.

Calories: 140

Total fat: 5 g

Protein: 4 g

Fiber: 4.5 g

Carbohydrates: 24 g

Cholesterol: 0 g

Sodium: 11 mg

Asian Succotash

VEGAN

4 to 6 servings

In this simple take on traditional succotash, edamame (fresh green soybeans) stand in for the usual baby lima beans, making it not only tastier but more nourishing as well. You can serve this substantial side dish to bolster many kinds of light main dishes, Asian or not.

Combine the corn and edamame in a large saucepan. Add the remaining ingredients and heat gently until heated through. Serve at once.

2 to 3 cups cooked fresh corn kernels or frozen corn kernels, thawed

1 cup cooked edamame, shelled (see page 220)

1 tablespoon nonhydrogenated margarine

1 to 2 scallions, white and green parts, thinly sliced, optional

Salt and freshly ground pepper, to taste

Calories: 133

Total fat: 4 g

Protein: 7 g

Fiber: 3.5 g

Carbohydrates: 21 g

Cholesterol: 0 g

Sodium: 27 mg

Seven Offbeat Vegetables Worth a Try

In my experience, I've found that kids (and adults, for that matter) who like vegetables are particularly fond of the tried-and-true varieties. Broccoli, carrots, peas, potatoes, sweet potatoes, and corn occupy the top rung; "second-string" vegetables include cauliflower, green beans, beets, greens, squashes, and such. If your children, young or older, are open to new vegetable adventures, here are a few that you may not think of buying regularly but that might add fun and variety to the everyday repertoire.

Brussels sprouts: Okay, so these aren't exactly "offbeat" and may actually be one of the vegetables you hated as a child. I list them here, though, because I think they are maligned and underused. I used to tease my sons that they weren't real children, because they've always loved Brussels sprouts. Steam them in a small amount of water until just beyond the bright green stage, and these tiny cabbages can be delightful. Once they become overcooked, I can see where the prejudice may set it. Serve them to your children with a look of excitement on your face. It may be contagious!

Edamame: Fresh green soybeans have become widely available in the West in the past few years. Resembling baby lima beans but less mealy and more flavorful, edamame (eda-MA-may) are a popular appetizer in Japanese restaurants. In midsummer, I get fresh edamame from my local farm markets. They are cooked in their shells for about 10 minutes, then popped open and eaten at room temperature, much like green peas. Edamame are quite easy to find in frozen form in natural foods stores. Package directions call for edamame to be cooked in rapidly simmering water for 5 minutes, whether in or out of the shell.

Jerusalem artichokes: Also marketed as "sunchokes," these knobby roots have no connection with Jerusalem nor do they bear any resemblance to the more common leafy artichokes. They are related in some way to the sunflower plant, however. With a texture that is a cross between a water chestnut and a white potato, and a flavor that is pleasant but hard to describe, Jerusalem artichokes can be scrubbed, sliced, and eaten raw alone or in salads, or quickly sautéed in a little olive oil.

Jicama: Another offbeat root, jicama (HICK-a-mah) is native to the American Southwest, and until the last decade or so was not easy to find outside that realm. Now you will find it in well-stocked supermarkets and produce stores from West to East. Sweet, crunchy, and a bit more watery than other roots, jicama is good sliced and eaten raw or used in salads. You can also sauté it.

Kohlrabi: A round, green vegetable with curious leaf shoots emerging from nearly all its surface, kohlrabi causes great consternation when it is distributed at my Community Supported Agriculture farm. Really, this veggie is quite humble and simple. Once peeled, it can be sliced or cut into sticks and eaten raw; it tastes like a perfect cross between white turnip and raw broccoli stem. Or, it can be quickly sautéed in olive oil or roasted with other root vegetables.

Leeks: A member of the onion family, leeks resemble oversize scallions. Only the white and lightest green parts are edible; the dark green leaves may be washed well, chopped, and used to flavor homemade vegetable stock, or you can simply discard or compost them. Chop leeks and rinse very well before using. Sautéed leeks are wonderful in soups and paired with potatoes or cabbage. You can always substitute them for ordinary onions; and in fact, because their flavor and texture are gentler than white onions, they may be more palatable to younger children.

(continued)

Spaghetti squash: Winter squashes are not often great favorites of children, unless puréed into soups or otherwise disguised, but spaghetti squash may be the exception to this rule. Once baked, the flesh comes out in spaghetti-like strands, and children can get great enjoyment from "combing out" those strands with a fork (provided, of course, that the squash is cool enough to handle). To prepare spaghetti squash: Cut it in half lengthwise; remove the stems and seeds. Place cut side up in a casserole dish with ½ inch of water. Cover tightly with foil and bake at 375° F until easily pierced with a fork, about 40 to 45 minutes. When the squash is cool enough to handle, scrape lengthwise with a fork to release the strands. I like to serve spaghetti squash in its most rudimentary form, sautéed in a little olive oil or nonhydrogenated margarine and seasoned with salt and pepper. Some people like it with marinara sauce, truly as a low-carb substitute for pasta, with or without a little Parmesan cheese.

Mashed Sweet Potatoes with Leeks, Peas, and Walnuts

Simple mashed sweet potatoes are a nourishing side dish in their own right and a nice alternative to mashed white potatoes. For older kids with developing taste buds as well as adults, the tasty topping makes this side dish even more appealing. Serve this to dress up simple meals of veggie burgers, sandwiches, or wraps. This is also an excellent side dish for bean burgers (page 192)

1 Bake or microwave the sweet potatoes until tender. When the sweet potatoes are cool enough to handle, peel and cut into large chunks and place them in a serving bowl.

2 Mash well, then stir in the margarine and milk (heat briefly in the microwave if the potatoes are no longer hot enough to melt the margarine). Add the nutmeg and season with salt and pepper. Cover and set aside.

3 Heat the oil in a skillet. Add the leeks, then cover and cook over medium heat, stirring occasionally, until tender, about 7 minutes. Stir in the peas, ginger, and walnuts. Continue to sauté just until everything is well heated through. Remove from the heat and transfer to a serving container.

4 Serve the sweet potatoes plain to anyone who wants them that way, and pass the leek mixture as a topping to embellish individual portions.

DAIRY / VEGAN OPTION

6 servings

4 large sweet potatoes
1 tablespoon nonhydrogenated margarine
½ cup low-fat milk, rice milk, or soy milk
Pinch of ground nutmeg
Salt and freshly ground pepper, to taste
1½ tablespoons light olive oil
2 large or 3 medium leeks, white part only, chopped and well-rinsed
1 cup frozen green peas, thawed
½ teaspoon grated fresh ginger or ¼ teaspoon ground ginger
½ cup chopped toasted walnuts

Dairy (with topping)	Vegan option (with topping)
Calories: 246	Calories: 245
Total fat: 12 g	Total fat: 11 g
Protein: 6 g	Protein: 5 g
Fiber: 5 g	Fiber: 5.5 g
Carbohydrates: 32 g	Carbohydrates: 33 g
Cholesterol: 1 g	Cholesterol: 0 g
Sodium: 46 mg	Sodium: 43 mg

Batter-Dipped Vegetable Fritters

4 to 6 servings

⅔ cup whole-wheat pastry flour

½ teaspoon salt

1 egg, beaten, or 2 tablespoons ground
flaxseeds, optional

6 cups prepared vegetables (see
Variations)

2 tablespoons light olive oil, or as
needed

Calories: 137

Total fat: 6 g

Protein: 4 g

Fiber: 5.3 g

Carbohydrates: 20 g

Cholesterol: 0 g

Sodium: 239 mg

This preparation is similar to tempura, except that the batter-dipped vegetables are sautéed in a small amount of oil rather than deep-fried. I can make a huge batch of any vegetable with this method and I can almost guarantee there will be no leftovers. This simple but special side dish goes well with just about any type of meal. I like serving it with grain dishes. It's also good with Sweet Potato and Silken Tofu Bisque (page 39).

1 Combine the flour in a mixing bowl with the salt. Add ¾ cup water and whisk together until completely smooth. Stir in the beaten egg and/or flaxseeds, if using, along with 2 tablespoons additional water.

2 Stir the vegetables into the batter until evenly coated.

3 Heat just enough oil to coat the bottom of a wide skillet. When hot, arrange the coated vegetable pieces in the skillet in a single layer (you may need to cook them in batches). Cook over medium-high heat, turning frequently until the pieces are golden brown and crisp.

4 Keep each batch warm in a covered container while preparing the next.

Variations

Here are some vegetables suitable for fritters. Disappointingly, broccoli just doesn't work well. The porous florets absorb too much batter, resulting in a fritter that's soggy rather than crisp. My family especially enjoys cauliflower, zucchini, and carrots when made this way. Choose one of the following vegetables or try a combination of two or three:

Vegetables that need to be lightly steamed before dipped in batter:

- **Cauliflower:** Cut into bite-size florets and steamed until just tender-crisp
- **Green beans:** Trim ends and steam just until tender-crisp

Vegetables that can be raw when dipped in batter:

- **Zucchini and yellow summer squash:** Cut into ½-inch-thick rounds
- **Carrots:** Cut into ¼-inch-thick slices on a long diagonal
- **Japanese eggplant:** Cut into ¼-inch-thick rounds
- **Whole small to medium mushrooms**

Grains Are Grand

The food group considered "the staff of life" often suffers from an image problem and goes in and out of favor, depending on the diet trend *du jour*. In particular, these complex carbohydrates are suspect simply because they are carbs. But in their unadulterated, unrefined form, it's hard to see why anyone would disparage these incredibly nourishing staples. Whole grains should not be lumped into the same category as refined carbs and starchy foods. In fact, they are thoroughly versatile, simply delicious, filling, and packed with nutrients.

Beside boasting a wide range of B vitamins, grains are a good source of iron, potassium, and other valuable minerals. They are also one of the best sources of dietary fiber. All the while, grains are blessedly low in fat: 1 cup of cooked grains, which is more than an average serving, contains about 220 calories and usually less than 2 grams of fat.

Refined grains should be the exceptions for special fare, such as for making risotto with Arborio rice. But as a rule, make the most of your family's grain servings and use unrefined grains, which have their bran and germ intact. Served simply and often, they are an unparalleled addition to any family's healthy food repertoire.

Fruited Couscous

VEGAN

6 servings as a side dish

Try this yummy grain dish on kids and teens who are gaining appreciation for more varied flavors and textures. It's also nice for stuffing vegetables (see pages 196–97), and a good addition to meals with curried dishes such as Coconut Curried Vegetable Stew (page 58).

1 Place the couscous in a heatproof container. Pour 2 cups boiling water over it, then cover and let stand for 15 minutes. When done, fluff with a fork.

2 Meanwhile, heat the oil in a large skillet or steep-sided stir-fry pan. Add the onion and sauté until translucent. Add the apple and continue to sauté until the onion is golden.

3 Stir in the couscous, dried fruits, and spices. Add just enough apple juice to moisten. Cook over medium heat until well heated through, 5 to 8 minutes. Stir in the optional walnuts. Season with salt and pepper and serve.

EMBELLISH IT: If your family is enthused about dried fruits, add another ¼ to ½ cup of a more exotic dried fruit (chopped into small bits), such as mango, papaya, or pineapple.

1 cup couscous, preferably whole grain
1 tablespoon light olive oil
1 medium onion, chopped
1 large sweet apple, peeled, cored, and diced
½ cup dark or golden raisins
½ cup chopped dried apricots or mission figs
½ teaspoon good-quality curry powder
½ teaspoon ground cinnamon
½ cup apple or freshly squeezed orange juice
⅓ cup slivered toasted almonds or chopped toasted walnuts, optional
Salt and freshly ground pepper, to taste

Calories: 213
Total fat: 3 g
Protein: 4 g
Fiber: 4.2 g
Carbohydrates: 44 g
Cholesterol: 0 g
Sodium: 10 mg

6 or more servings as a side dish

1 cup whole-grain couscous or bulgur (see Note)
1 cup tiny shell pasta
2 tablespoons nonhydrogenated margarine
Salt or seasoned salt and freshly ground pepper, to taste

Calories: 195
Total fat: 3 g
Protein: 6 g
Fiber: 2 g
Carbohydrates: 34 g
Cholesterol: 0 g
Sodium: 35 mg

Seashells in the Sand

I'm not usually one for "cute" recipe names, but both the name and the presentation worked wonders to tempt my boys to learn to love whole grains (and they still like this simple grain and pasta combo). Adults will enjoy this dish embellished with fresh herbs. Pair this with bean or vegetable dishes.

1 Place the couscous in a heatproof container and add 2 cups boiling water. Cover and let stand 10 minutes.

2 Meanwhile, cook the pasta until al dente, then drain.

3 Combine the cooked grain and pasta in a serving container. Stir in the margarine until melted, then season with salt and pepper.

Note
If using bulgur, let stand 30 minutes in step 1 or simmer, covered, with 2 cups water for 15 minutes.

EMBELLISH IT: For adult portions, stir in chopped scallions and parsley, dill, or any combination of fresh herbs. This is also delicious topped with a sprinkling of toasted almonds or pine nuts.

Bulgur with Fine Noodles

Combining noodles with a grain is fairly common in eastern European cookery. Here's one such pilaf, which makes for a simple and substantial side dish for beans or vegetables. It's a good way to stuff vegetables, too (see pages 196–97).

1   Bring the stock to a simmer in a medium saucepan. Stir in the bulgur. Either simmer it gently, covered, until the liquid is absorbed, about 15 minutes, or cover and leave it off the heat for 30 minutes.

2   Shortly before the grain is done, bring a generous amount of water to a simmer in another saucepan. Break the pasta in half, then in half again. Cook it in rapidly boiling water until al dente, then drain.

3   Combine the bulgur and pasta in a large serving bowl. Add the margarine and toss to melt. Stir in the scallions, half of the chopped parsley, and the paprika. Season with salt and pepper. Sprinkle the top with the remaining parsley and a little additional paprika. Serve at once.

VEGAN

6 or more servings as a side dish

2 cups prepared vegetable broth, or 2 cups water with 1 vegetable bouillon cube
1 cup bulgur
4 ounces spaghetti or vermicelli
2 tablespoons nonhydrogenated margarine
4 to 5 scallions, white and green parts, thinly sliced
¼ cup chopped fresh parsley, or to taste
½ teaspoon paprika
Salt and freshly ground pepper, to taste

Calories: 175
Total fat: 4 g
Protein: 5 g
Fiber: 4.7 g
Carbohydrates: 31 g
Cholesterol: 0 g
Sodium: 86 mg

4 to 6 servings as a side dish

1 tablespoon light olive oil

1 medium onion, finely chopped

3 garlic cloves, minced

1 small hot green chile, minced, or one
**   4-ounce can chopped mild green**
**   chilies**

1 cup long-grain brown rice

1 teaspoon ground cumin

½ teaspoon dried oregano

Juice of ½ lime

¼ cup chopped fresh cilantro

Salt to taste

Calories: 158

Total fat: 4 g

Protein: 4 g

Fiber: 2.8 g

Carbohydrates: 29 g

Cholesterol: 0 g

Sodium: 8 mg

Mexican Green Rice

Called *arroz verde* in its native language, this is a good side dish to serve with burritos and other Southwestern or Mexican specialties. It's a great grain dish for families with older kids and teens who enjoy a bit of spice. Try it with Black Bean and Zucchini Chilaquiles (page 168).

1   Heat the oil in a large saucepan. Add the onion, garlic, and chile, if using, and sauté over medium heat until golden.

2   Add the rice and 2½ cups water. Stir in the cumin and oregano and bring to a simmer, then cover and simmer gently until the water is absorbed, 30 to 35 minutes. Taste, and if you'd like a more tender texture to the rice, add another ½ cup water and simmer until absorbed.

3   Stir in the lime juice and cilantro, then season with salt. Serve at once.

Stir-Fried Rice with Baby Corn and Peas

Here's an easy and tasty side dish to serve with stir-fries and tofu dishes, and one that I've recommended to round out several dishes, including Orange-Glazed Tofu and Broccoli (page 146).

Heat the oil in a stir-fry pan or large skillet. Add all the ingredients and stir-fry over medium-high heat until the rice is touched with golden spots, 8 to 10 minutes. Serve at once.

Variation
Substitute 1 cup cooked edamame (see page 220) for the green peas.

VEGAN

6 servings

2 tablespoons light olive oil
1 teaspoon dark sesame oil
3 cups cooked brown rice
One 15-ounce can cut baby corn, drained, or 1½ cups cooked fresh corn kernels or frozen corn kernels, thawed
1 cup frozen green peas, thawed
2 to 3 scallions, thinly sliced
2 tablespoons reduced-sodium soy sauce, or to taste
Freshly ground pepper, to taste

Calories: 193
Total fat: 6 g
Protein: 5 g
Fiber: 4.2 g
Carbohydrates: 29 g
Cholesterol: 0 g
Sodium: 245 mg

Simple Quinoa and Wild Rice Pilaf

VEGAN

6 or more servings

½ cup wild rice

1 cup quinoa

1 vegetable bouillon cube

2 tablespoons nonhydrogenated
   margarine

2 scallions, thinly sliced

Salt and freshly ground pepper, to taste

Calories: 153

Total fat: 4 g

Protein: 5 g

Fiber: 3.1 g

Carbohydrates: 24 g

Cholesterol: 0 g

Sodium: 34 mg

Two nourishing grains mingle compatibly in one tasty side dish. See information on these great grains, page 235. It's a great boost to a meal of bean burgers (Chapter 6), sandwiches, and wraps and is especially compatible served with (or stuffed into) fall harvest vegetables (pages 196–97).

1 Combine the rice with 1¼ cups water in a medium saucepan and bring to a simmer. Cover and simmer gently for 30 minutes.

2 Add the quinoa, bouillon cube, and 2 cups water. Cover and simmer gently until the water is absorbed, 15 minutes.

3 Stir in the margarine and scallions. Season with salt and pepper, and serve.

EMBELLISH IT: Top individual servings with minced fresh parsley and/or toasted pumpkin seeds.

Quick Couscous and Black Bean Pilaf

VEGAN

4 to 6 servings as a side dish

Here's a side dish with substance. Use it to embellish vegetable-based main dishes or to pair with main-dish salads like Middle Eastern Pita Bread Salad (page 82).

1 Combine 1½ cups water with the bouillon cube in a medium saucepan and bring to a simmer. When the bouillon cube has dissolved, stir in the couscous, cover, and remove from the heat. Let stand until the water is absorbed, 5 to 10 minutes, then fluff with a fork.

2 Stir in the remaining ingredients and return to medium-low heat, stirring frequently, until heated through. Cover and let stand until needed or serve at once.

Variation

This is also good made with quinoa. See cooking tips on page 235.

EMBELLISH IT: Adults can top their portions with minced fresh herbs such as parsley, dill, cilantro, or oregano. You can also spice it up with one 4-ounce can of chopped mild or hot green chilies or a small amount of minced fresh hot chile.

---

1 vegetable bouillon cube
¼ cup couscous, preferably whole grain
One 16-ounce can black beans, drained and rinsed
½ teaspoon ground cumin
1 tablespoon light olive oil
2 scallions, green parts only, thinly sliced

Calories: 167
Total fat: 3 g
Protein: 7 g
Fiber: 5.5 g
Carbohydrates: 2.7 g
Cholesterol: 0 g
Sodium: 63 mg

When you need a grain to cushion stews and stir-fries, to stuff into vegetables, or to power pilafs, chances are you reach for rice. And while there's nothing wrong with rice—particularly if you've made the switch to brown—exploring a variety of whole grains can expand your culinary horizons and add even greater nourishment to your family meals.

Apart from adding character to meals, whole grains are superb sources of fiber and protein. Because the bran and germ are left intact, they are also fine sources of B vitamins, vitamin E, and an array of minerals.

It's certainly possible to be health conscious and never eat bulgur or quinoa. But why miss out on one of the richest sources of nourishment available?

PEARL OR POT BARLEY: The pearl variety of barley is tasty and versatile, but you may want to try pot barley for greater nutritional impact. Pearl barley loses half its vitamin and mineral content and much of its fiber when its bran and germ are removed. Pot barley undergoes just enough "pearling" to remove the tough hull. It's a chewy, mild-tasting grain that's every bit as versatile as in its more refined form. Use in pilafs, casseroles, and soups and serve hot or cold in marinated grain salads. *Cooking:* Combine 3 parts water for 1 part pearl barley or $3\frac{1}{2}$ parts water for 1 part pot barley in a saucepan and bring to a simmer. Cover and simmer gently and steadily until the water has been absorbed, 40 to 50 minutes. Then, if you'd like the grain less chewy, add another $\frac{1}{2}$ cup water and cook until absorbed.

MILLET: This small round yellow seed is nourishing and versatile, with a mild flavor and a slightly mushy texture. While it is most welcome on the dinner table, you might also consider it a good choice as a hot cooked cereal embellished with honey, chopped nuts, dried fruit, and soy milk—especially if you cook it the night before. Because of its cohesive texture, millet works well in casseroles and as a stuffing for vegetables. *Cooking:* Experiment with different water-to-grain ratios to vary the texture. Use $2\frac{1}{2}$ to $3\frac{1}{2}$ parts water to 1 part grain. The less water used, the drier the result; more water will yield a porridgelike consistency. Bring water to a simmer in a saucepan, then stir in the grain. Cover and simmer, gently but steadily, until the water has been absorbed and the grains have burst, 35 to 45 minutes. Millet's flavor is enhanced by toasting the grains in a dry or lightly oiled skillet for 4 to 5 minutes before cooking.

QUINOA: Quinoa (pronounced (KEEN-wah) is a rediscovered superfood that was once a staple crop of the South American Incas. The nutritional profile of this small, sand-colored grain makes quinoa a standout, with exceptionally high-quality protein and a wide range of minerals. Quinoa is also a culinary delight, cooking to a fluffy texture in just 15 minutes, with a light yet unique flavor. Use it as a bed of grains for bean and vegetable dishes, in pilafs, and in grain salads. *Cooking:* Use 2 parts water to 1 part grain. Bring the water to a simmer in a saucepan. Stir in the grain, then cover and simmer gently until the water is absorbed, 15 minutes. Like other grains, the nutty flavor of quinoa is enhanced by toasting it lightly in a dry or lightly oiled skillet for about 5 minutes before cooking.

BULGUR: Made from parboiled dried, cracked wheat berries, bulgur is chewy, hearty, and versatile. Perhaps best known as the base for the tasty grain salad tabouli, bulgur also makes great pilafs and combines well with nuts, dried fruits, beans, and fresh herbs. It may also be used in casseroles and as a replacement for rice in many dishes. *Cooking:* Use 2 parts water to 1 part grain. The traditional way to cook bulgur is to pour boiling water over it in a heatproof container, cover it, and let stand for 30 minutes. If you need it cooked more quickly, bring water to a simmer in a saucepan. Stir in the grain, then cover and simmer gently until the water is absorbed, 15 minutes.

WILD RICE: A true native of North America, wild rice is unrelated to rice. It's technically not a grain but rather the seed of a tall aquatic grass. The distinctive flavor of wild rice goes a long way; it is commonly paired with brown or white rice and used as a base for flavorful pilafs and marinated salads. Great embellishments for wild rice are fresh herbs, celery, nuts, and dried fruits. *Cooking:* Use 2½ to 3 parts water to 1 part grain, depending on how chewy you like it (more water means less chewy). Combine the water and grain in a saucepan and bring to a simmer. Cover and simmer gently and steadily until the water has been absorbed, 35 to 40 minutes.

CHAPTER EIGHT

Sandwiches, Wraps, and School Lunches

WHETHER YOU NEED a quick entrée for dinner, an easy accompaniment for soup or salad, or some inspiration for school lunches and other portable meals, this chapter presents a batch of ideas and a few simple recipes. For many of the sandwich-type suggestions in this chapter, you merely need the inspiration rather than a full-fledged recipe. Some good bread, a sturdy wrap or pita, plus some fresh ingredients are more crucial than exact proportions; with these on hand, emergency meals can be nearly as good as special-occasion fare.

In this chapter, I have also included school lunches, which can often present a quandary for vegetarian/vegan kids and their parents. We'd all love to know that our children can get a nourishing lunch in school, whether they're vegetarian or not, sparing us (at least some of the time) from what can be a daunting early-morning project. But sadly, this isn't the case in most schools, especially now that fast-food franchises have taken over so many school cafeterias.

From my own years of packing lunches, I know that the last thing I have patience for at 6:30 in the morning is to follow recipes, so instead I offer a listing for a number of tried-and-true lunch options as well as some offbeat choices.

Supper Sandwiches and Super Wraps

With these ideas, you can make as many or as few sandwiches as you need. These ideas will benefit adults, teens, and older kids with more adventurous tastes.

- Thinly sliced avocado, sun-dried tomatoes, and cream cheese (organic dairy or nondairy) or hummus on whole-grain bread or in wraps.

- Thinly sliced avocado, tomatoes, and baked tofu with mustard, soy mayonnaise, or chutney (or any combination) in pita breads or wraps.

- Avocado, thinly sliced sautéed seitan, shredded lettuce, thinly sliced tomato—or any kind of slaw (page 68) in place of the lettuce and tomato—and mustard or soy mayonnaise in pita breads.

- Sautéed tempeh strips or thinly sliced baked tofu with any type of slaw (page 68) in pita breads.

- Sautéed thinly sliced onions, bell peppers, and tempeh strips in pita; Ranch Dressing (page 93) or Tangy Tahini Dressing (page 97) are great flavorings for this.

- "TLT" sandwich: sautéed tempeh bacon, lettuce, and thinly sliced tomatoes with soy mayonnaise on whole-grain bread or in wraps.

- Sautéed thinly sliced onions, thinly sliced raw Granny Smith apples, and melted Cheddar or Cheddar-style nondairy cheese on whole-grain English muffins or pumpernickel bread, served open-faced.

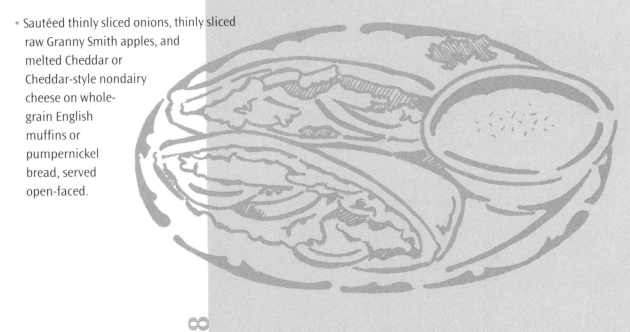

- Goat cheese, arugula, and sun-dried tomatoes on whole-grain mini-hero rolls.

- Cream cheese (organic dairy or nondairy), goat cheese, or sunflower butter with nicely browned, thinly sliced sautéed onion and green cabbage (you can used preshredded coleslaw if you'd like) and sliced black olives (preferably cured) on whole-grain bread, open-faced, if you'd like, or in wraps.

- Sautéed bell pepper strips with spreadable goat cheese, cream cheese (organic dairy or nondairy), or sunflower or pumpkin seed butter on whole-grain mini-hero or other rolls.

- Baby spinach, thinly sliced red bell pepper, finely diced tomatoes, and feta cheese with dressing of your choice in pita breads or wraps.

- Baked sweet potato slices, wilted spinach, and Cheddar cheese or Cheddar-style nondairy cheese in wraps, warmed until melted.

- Cashew butter and Sautéed Apples (page 267) served open-faced on whole-grain bread.

- Mashed chickpea spread (see page 243), thinly shredded lettuce, thinly sliced red bell peppers, and chutney in pita breads or wraps.

- Canned vegetarian refried beans (thinned with a little water if need be), thinly shredded lettuce and sliced tomatoes, and black olives in a wrap. Add grated Cheddar or Cheddar-style nondairy cheese and/or salsa, if desired.

- White bean hummus (page 260), thinly sliced lettuce, tomatoes, green bell peppers, and black olives in pita breads or wraps.

Give in to Tempeh-tation

Tempeh is a soy food whose flavor and texture depart sharply from that of tofu. Its somewhat fermented flavor makes it an acquired taste for some, but those who like it tend to do so in a big way. Significantly, tempeh is one of the few vegan sources of vitamin B_{12} (though *not* a reliable one). Available in 8- to 12-ounce packages, tempeh is ready to use (it can simply be mashed and dressed as described on page 243); its flavor improves, though, by sautéing strips or cubes of it in a little oil and soy sauce. Tempeh strips are a robust and nutritious addition to sandwiches. See some of the suggestions offered in Supper Sandwiches and Super Wraps (pages 238–39).

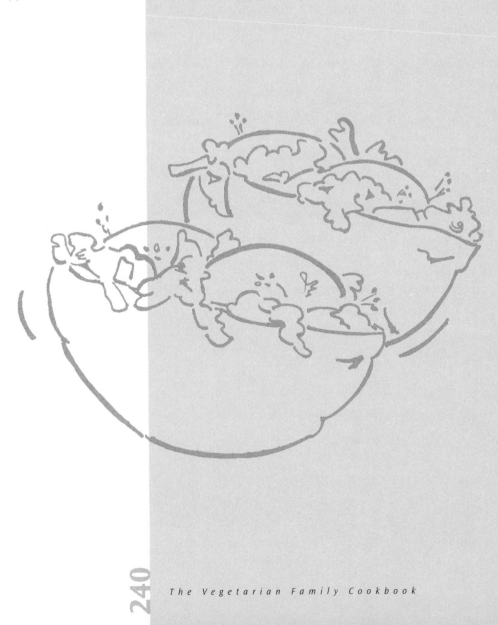

Lively Leftover Wraps and Pitas

Leftovers of the following dishes are wonderful wrapped up or stuffed into pita bread. Salads can be wrapped or stuffed at room temperature or straight from the refrigerator; other dishes can be used at room temperature or lightly warmed:

- Green Salad with Avocado, Apples, and Baked Tofu (page 75)
- Mixed Greens with Green Beans, Beets, and Feta or Goat Cheese (page 81)
- Hearty Seitan Salad (page 83)
- Southwestern Rice and Black Bean Salad (page 86)
- Spring Barley Salad (page 90)
- Black Bean Sofrito (page 188)
- Two Kinds of Tofu in a Sweet and Savory Sauté (page 147)—add shredded lettuce or sprouts and mustard
- Seitan and Broccoli Stir-Fry (page 161)
- Quick Couscous and Black Bean Pilaf (page 233)

Easy Quesadillas or Soft Tacos

Quesadillas and soft tacos are easy, quick accompaniments to serve with soups and salads. They can also be served with heartier dishes such as chilies or Southwestern-style casseroles (such as Southwestern Baked Rice Casserole, page 169) if the appetites in your family run high.

A quesadilla is a sort of Mexican grilled cheese sandwich in a flour tortilla. Soft tacos are also made with flour tortillas and offer a nice departure from the more familiar crisp corn tortilla tacos. Melted cheese (which can be an organic variety of Cheddar or Monterey Jack, or the equivalent of nondairy cheese) is the common denominator of quesadillas, as it helps everything hold together. Cheese is not absolutely necessary in soft tacos, especially if you use refried beans, which also serve to bind the ingredients together. Here are the basics:

Quesadillas: If you're making only one or two quesadillas, you can cook them on a griddle, but if you need several servings, this can become time consuming, defeating the purpose of making this quick dish. Here's a way to make several at a time in the oven: Sprinkle a modest amount of grated cheese over each tortilla (use 8-inch soft flour tortillas). Arrange any other ingredients over the surface. Sprinkle with a little more cheese, and cover with another tortilla. Arrange the quesadillas on a nonstick baking sheet or two, and bake in a preheated 400° F oven for 12 to 15 minutes, until the tortillas turn lightly golden and crisp on both sides. Cut each quesadilla into four equal wedges. Allow two to four wedges per serving, depending on appetite, and eat out of hand.

Soft tacos: Spread desired filling on one half of each tortilla (use 8-inch soft flour tortillas), being careful not to overfill, then sprinkle with cheese if desired. Arrange on individual plates. Heat each serving briefly in the microwave (about 1 minute) or in a preheated 400° F to melt the cheese (about 5 minutes), then fold over. Eat at once with a knife and fork or cut in half and eat out of hand.

Aside from cheese and/or refried beans, here are some suggestions for filling quesadillas or soft tacos. In addition to cheese and beans, two or at most three additional items per quesadilla or soft taco are sufficient:

- Cooked fresh corn kernels or frozen corn kernels, thawed
- Thinly sliced tomato
- Sliced black olives
- Very thinly sliced green or red bell pepper strips
- Green chilies (canned or fresh, seeded and minced)
- Black beans
- Wilted mushrooms
- Wilted spinach or Swiss chard
- Thinly sliced baked sweet potato
- Salsa (red or green)
- Thinly sliced tomatillos

One of the easiest ways to make a family-pleasing sandwich spread is to combine a crumbled high-protein food with soy mayonnaise and finely diced celery. No matter which of the following suggested ingredients you choose, you end up with what might be called a "chicken"-style or "tuna"-style spread. Or we can drop the meaty and fishy analogies altogether and just call the result an incredibly tasty and quick sandwich filling that's good for home, school, or brown-bag lunches as well as light dinners. Choose any one of the following:

- One 12-ounce package of baked tofu (I like to use Soy Boy Tofu Lin for this)
- One 16-ounce container soft tofu, well drained (this becomes faux "egg" salad)
- One 12-ounce package tempeh
- One 16-ounce can chickpeas, drained and rinsed

Crumble any one of these finely in a bowl, then moisten with ½ to ⅔ cup soy mayonnaise, or as needed, and stir in 1 large finely diced celery stalk. If you'd like to embellish this simple formula, you can add a finely minced scallion, a little mustard, and/or ½ teaspoon curry powder. For the faux "egg" salad, a pinch of turmeric contributes an appetizing golden hue. If you don't care for celery, you can substitute finely diced green bell pepper.

These easy high-protein spreads are excellent served on your favorite whole-grain bread or, for portable sandwiches, stuffed into pita. A fun way to serve them to kids is to cut a small whole-grain roll in half and hollow out the center of each, leaving a sturdy, ½-inch shell. Stuff each half with some of the spread and serve open-faced or put the two halves together.

VEGAN

Makes 6

Veggie Deli Heroes with Herb Mayonnaise

This hero is terrific as part of a soup-and-sandwich dinner and is great for brown bag or school lunches.

Dressing:

½ cup soy mayonnaise

1 teaspoon prepared grainy mustard

½ cup minced fresh herbs of your choice (try a combination of basil, dill, and Italian parsley)

1 tablespoon minced chives or scallion, green parts only

6 individual whole-grain hero rolls

One 6-ounce package soy deli slices, any flavor, cut into halves

2 cups finely shredded lettuce

2 to 3 medium firm, ripe tomatoes, thinly sliced

One 4-ounce jar roasted red peppers, drained and thinly sliced

1 Combine the dressing ingredients in a small bowl and stir together.

2 Split the hero rolls lengthwise. Spread each half with some herb mayonnaise. Divide the deli slices among 6 of the roll halves. Divide the lettuce, tomato slices, and red pepper slices among the other 6 roll halves. Put the halves together and serve.

MAKE IT A MEAL: This makes a nice warm-weather meal served with Expandable Potato Salad (page 72) or Family-Friendly Pasta Salad (page 65). Serve the meal with a summery Fruit Smoothie (page 20) or finish the meal with any kind of fruity dessert. This also makes a filling at-home weekend lunch or a good portable lunch for work or school.

FOR PICKY EATERS: Children may prefer these with plain soy mayonnaise rather than the herb mayonnaise. They may also prefer the sandwich without the roasted red peppers.

Calories: 234

Total fat: 9 g

Protein: 9 g

Fiber: 2.3 g

Carbohydrates: 28 g

Cholesterol: 0 g

Sodium: 481 mg

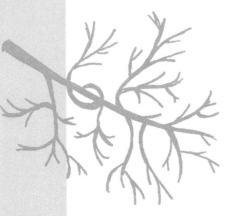

Veggie Cheese Toasts

This is based on the recipe for Welsh rabbit (sometimes called rarebit), a dish of almost pure melted Cheddar cheese (and beer!) served over toast. My version stretches a much smaller quantity of cheese with sweet potato or squash and some finely diced vegetables.

1 Heat the oil in a medium saucepan. Add the zucchini, peas, and tomatoes. Sauté over medium heat until the vegetables are just tender, 4 to 5 minutes. Remove from the heat and transfer the vegetables to a container until needed.

2 Dissolve the flour in about half of the milk, stirring until completely smooth. In the saucepan used for step 1, combine it with the remaining milk, margarine, cheese, mustard, and potato. Heat, whisking often, until the mixture is hot and thickened, about 5 minutes. If you'd like, insert an immersion blender or transfer the sauce to a food processor to make it even more velvety smooth, or use as is.

3 Stir the zucchini mixture into the sauce and cook for about 1 minute. Season with salt.

4 For each serving, place one or two slices of toasted bread on a plate. Pour some of the cheese mixture over the surface of the toast, and serve.

MAKE IT A MEAL: Serve with Oven Fries or Sautéed Skillet Potatoes (page 200) and a bountiful tossed salad or a slaw (page 68). This pairs well with soups, too. Try it with Basic Lentil Soup with Tasty Variations (page 42) or Dilled Vegetable-Barley Soup (page 50). Add carrot and celery sticks or a simple tossed salad to complete the meal.

DAIRY / VEGAN OPTION

8 single-slice or 4 two-slice servings

1 tablespoon light olive oil
1 medium-small zucchini, quartered lengthwise and sliced
½ cup frozen green peas, thawed
2 firm, ripe plum (Roma) tomatoes, diced
2 tablespoons unbleached white flour
1 cup low-fat milk, rice milk, or soy milk
1 tablespoon nonhydrogenated margarine
4 ounces grated Cheddar cheese or Cheddar-style nondairy cheese
1 teaspoon prepared yellow mustard
½ cup well-cooked and mashed sweet potato or butternut squash
Salt to taste
8 slices toasted whole-grain bread

Dairy (per slice)	Vegan option (per slice)
Calories: 183	Calories: 164
Total fat: 10 g	Total fat: 8 g
Protein: 8 g	Protein: 6 g
Fiber: 3.2 g	Fiber: 3.2 g
Carbohydrates: 16 g	Carbohydrates: 19 g
Cholesterol: 16 g	Cholesterol: 0 g
Sodium: 230 mg	Sodium: 263 mg

4 *servings*

4 whole-wheat pita breads (see Tip)
1½ cups part-skim ricotta cheese
¾ cup part-skim mozzarella cheese
Warmed marinara sauce, optional

Calories: 312

Total fat: 12 g

Protein: 23 g

Fiber: 5 g

Carbohydrates: 28 g

Cholesterol: 41 g

Sodium: 524 mg

Pita Cheese Calzones

My kids loved these calzone-type filled pitas when they were younger, especially if made with mini-pitas, which are just the right size for small hands.

1 Preheat the oven or toaster oven to 400° F.

2 Cut along the edge of each pita to create a 4-inch opening.

3 Divide the ricotta and mozzarella among the pitas, stuffing each one carefully.

4 Wrap each pita in foil and bake for 5 to 7 minutes, then serve. If desired, provide a small bowl of warmed marinara sauce to spoon onto individual calzones.

Tip

Substitute two mini-pitas for each regular pita when serving young children.

EMBELLISH IT: Add any one or two of the following ingredients to fill the calzones before baking.

- Steamed finely chopped broccoli florets
- Steamed fresh or frozen green peas
- Steamed zucchini or summer squash slices
- Steamed fresh spinach, well drained
- Cured black olives, sliced
- Sun-dried tomatoes
- Chopped fresh parsley
- Thinly sliced basil leaves

MAKE IT A MEAL: These are a good accompaniment to many soups. Try them with Streamlined Minestrone (page 40) or Navy Bean Soup with Corn and Red Peppers (page 49). For children, serve with Alphabet Vegetable Soup (page 30) to bring smiles. Try them with hearty salads as well. Another nice meal is to team the calzones with Tomatoes with Black Beans or Chickpeas (page 79) and Sautéed Broccoli, Baby Carrots, and Yellow Squash (page 210).

4 servings

8 large slices fresh whole-grain rye bread

Mustard or thousand island dressing
   (natural prepared dressing or
   homemade, page 94), as needed

8 slices soy Canadian bacon slices or
   other deli slices of choice

1 medium avocado, thinly sliced

½ cup well-drained sauerkraut

4 thin slices Swiss cheese or Swiss-style
   nondairy cheese (see Note)

Dairy	Vegan option
Calories: 290	Calories: 312
Total fat: 10 g	Total fat: 14 g
Protein: 22 g	Protein: 21 g
Fiber: 6.4 g	Fiber: 6.4 g
Carbohydrates: 29 g	Carbohydrates: 26 g
Cholesterol: 4 g	Cholesterol: 0 g
Sodium: 1090 mg	Sodium: 985 mg

Avocado Reuben

This classic deli sandwich can be made not only meatless, but dairy-free if desired. It's great for lunch at home or for dinner.

1 Preheat oven to 375° F.

2 Arrange 4 of the bread slices on a baking sheet to create open-faced sandwiches. Spread each with mustard, followed by 2 deli slices, ¼ of the avocado, ¼ of the sauerkraut, and 1 slice cheese per sandwich.

3 Bake for 8 minutes until the cheese melts. Top each sandwich with another slice of bread. Serve at once.

Note

Feel free to substitute any white mild cheese or nondairy cheese you'd like.

MAKE IT A MEAL: Serve with Expandable Potato Salad (page 72) or Golden Potato Salad (page 73) plus a simple lettuce and tomato salad and organic dill pickles.

Mediterranean Salad-Stuffed Bread

VEGAN

4 generous or 8 smaller servings

Inspired by the European *pan bagnat,* this hefty sandwich is an offbeat way to eat an array of seasonal salad ingredients.

1 Cut each bread in half crosswise, then cut each section in half lengthwise. Pull out some of the bread from the center of each, leaving a shell of about ½ inch all around. Reserve the pulled-out bread for another use, such as fresh bread crumbs.

2 Combine the remaining ingredients in a mixing bowl and toss together. Mound some of the salad into each bottom section of the bread shells, then cover with the top section. Gently press together, then wrap each of the four sections snugly in plastic wrap and let stand for 1 hour or so, giving some of the tasty juices a chance to soak into the bread.

3 To serve 8, cut each bread section in half crosswise, otherwise serve the 4 sections as they are.

MAKE IT A MEAL: For a wonderful warm-weather meal or picnic, serve this with Marinated Potato-Tofu Salad (page 74) and a slaw (page 68). For a tasty soup-and-sandwich meal, pair this with Tomato-Tortellini Soup (page 41), Cream of Broccoli Soup (page 29), or Garden Vegetable Soup with Tiny Pasta (page 48).

2 long Italian breads, preferably whole grain
3 firm, ripe plum (Roma) tomatoes, finely diced
6 large dark green lettuce leaves, torn
1 medium red or green bell pepper, cut into very thin short strips
¼ cup chopped black olives (preferably cured)
¼ cup extra-virgin olive oil
Juice of ½ to 1 lemon
¼ cup minced fresh parsley, optional
¼ cup sun-dried tomatoes (oil or dry packed), thinly sliced, optional

Per smaller serving
Calories: 197
Total fat: 9 g
Protein: 4 g
Fiber: 2.3 g
Carbohydrates: 25 g
Cholesterol: 0 g
Sodium: 285 mg

School Lunch Tips and Treats

There are days when the prospect of preparing yet another school lunch, with the clock ticking away, is daunting. I need to maintain lunch preparation diversity not only for the kids' enjoyment and nutritional needs but for my own sanity! While peanut butter (natural-style, of course), and jam (fruit only!) is still a healthy option, being on the making and receiving end of it gets tired after a while.

That's where a list of possibilities comes in handy—one that can be kept in a convenient location in your kitchen (perhaps right with the lunch-making supplies). If possible, too, try to do a little advance planning for the week ahead. Let your kids help with the planning. This will help you avoid the daily morning panic of what to make and ensure that you have the basic ingredients on hand.

Lunch Box Tips

- Keep your lunch-making supplies together in one place to make the process more efficient during the morning rush hour. In a single cabinet, you can store the lunch boxes, sandwich bags, thermoses, plastic spoons and forks, toothpicks, and small plastic storage containers.

- Put flat dry-ice packs in your child's lunch box during warm weather or any time you are sending perishable foods, such as dairy products or egg dishes. These are available wherever lunch boxes or camping supplies are sold.

- Vary the types of bread used for sandwiches. Bagels, rolls, pita pockets, English muffins, raisin bread, and even fresh flour tortillas or wraps can add interest to standard sandwich fare.

- Experiment with thermos foods that work for your children. Some dishes just don't stay warm even in the best of thermoses, and if your children don't have access to microwaves at school, this kind of offering might come home uneaten. However, dishes that taste just as good at room temperature, such as Pineapple Rice Pudding (page 271) or a portion of Mom's "Tuna"-Noodle Casserole (page 114) might be more successful. If your child's school does have a microwave available, your thermos offerings can expand to include macaroni and cheese, soups, and bean and grain dishes.

- If you want your kids to eat the fruit you pack, you may need to resort to some simple tricks. Small chunks of fruit, such as strawberries, grapes, melon, tiny seedless orange sections, and such, served on a small skewer (long cocktail toothpicks are perfect), might appeal more than a whole fruit; similarly, apple slices are more likely to be eaten if you supply a tiny container of dip for them. Try Silken Peanut Spread (page 256) or Sweet Cream Cheese Dip for Fruit (page 268).

- Similarly, raw vegetables become more of a draw when you supply a dip; with carrot sticks (or baby carrots), celery, little broccoli florets, or bell pepper strips, add a tiny container of natural, low-fat ranch or thousand island dressing. See the homemade versions in Chapter 3.

- For very young children—preschoolers, especially—sandwiches become more appealing cut into shapes with cookie cutters.

Lunch Box Main Dish Options

- Wholesome muffins (Chapter 10) have been one of my sons' top choices for lunch for some years, especially Zucchini-Raisin Muffins (page 287) and Apple Muffins (page 291). Muffins are a welcome change of pace from sandwiches. Pack a container of yogurt, plus fresh fruit for a refreshing midday meal.

- Simple tossed salad in pita bread appeals to kids with more adventurous palates. Augment these salads with chickpeas, chunks of baked tofu, or grated cheese or nondairy cheese. Keep pita sandwiches fresh by wrapping first in foil, then in sandwich bags.

- A container of organic yogurt or soy yogurt and fruit salad (don't forget the ice pack!), and a whole-grain roll (with fruit spread, organic dairy or nondairy cream cheese, or nut butter) is a refreshing option. The yogurt and fruit salad can be eaten separately, or your child can mix them together.

- Expand your PB&J horizons by exploring other nut butters (such as cashew and almond) and fruit-only spreads or apple butter.

- Soy-based faux meats can be a boon for expanding lunch box variety. Soy Canadian bacon slices or soy pepperoni on sub rolls might especially appeal to teens. Chicken- and turkey-style soy slices on soft whole-grain bread can suit tastes of any age.

- Cream cheese comes in many guises—organic dairy, soy based, and rice based and is a good starting point for simple sandwiches. You can spread it on whole-grain bagels or rolls, combined with fruit-only spread, apple butter, sliced cucumbers, or chopped olives.

- Likewise, sliced cheeses no longer mean only those fake "cheese food" type. Organic dairy, rice-based, soy-based, and almond-based cheese slices offer a more nutritious, equally convenient option. Layer these types of cheeses with soy deli slices, lettuce, soy mayonnaise and/or mustard for a hearty sandwich with almost certain appeal.

- Pasta salad is a tempting lunch option. Use fun shapes such as wagon wheels, small shells, or tiny tubes. Small shapes pack best into containers. Add your child's favorite veggies—mine like steamed broccoli, black olives, and carrots (see Family-Friendly Pasta Salad, page 65).

- My younger son has long enjoyed Nearly Instant Bean Dip (page 256), packed in a thermos, with stone-ground tortilla chips for dipping on the side. It's filling and tastes good at room temperature.

- See page 231 for a variety of tasty spreads that make high-protein school lunch offerings, especially in pita breads.

- Check out Supper Sandwiches and Super Wraps (pages 238–39), but be aware that some of these tend to be on the moist side, making them more suitable for eating at home than for packing.

Store-Bought Snacks for School Lunches

Sometimes quick snacks are needed for school (or for car trips), and you just don't have time to handcraft them, or you need something in a neatly wrapped package. Many snack products from natural foods stores offer a better alternative to those available in supermarkets. Cookies, cereals, fruit bars, and such are often naturally sweetened. They also tend to be lower in fat, and just as important, most are free of partially hydrogenated fat and high-fructose corn syrup. These two ingredients are commonplace in mass-produced snacks and should be avoided at all costs, both by children and adults.

Chips, cheese puffs, rice crisps, and other crunchy snacks are less salty and fatty than their supermarket counterparts. Many organic options are offered as well. Prices might sometimes (but not always) be a little higher than those of supermarket offerings, but you're getting more value for your money.

Here's a handy list of suggestions for store-bought snacks for school lunch boxes and on the go:

- Natural fruit leathers
- Low-fat fruit and cereal bars
- Granola bars
- Dried fruit, such as apple rings or apricots (look for organic and unsulfured)

- Trail mix (dried fruits mixed with nuts and seeds) or an even simpler combination of raisins and peanuts
- Rice cakes, mini-rice cakes, popped corn cakes, and other whole-grain cakes
- Organic baby carrots
- Organic seedless grapes
- Individual containers of applesauce (don't forget to pack a spoon!)
- Naturally sweetened dry cereals (mix a few varieties together for a crunchy sweet snack for home and for school)
- Natural whole-grain graham crackers
- Veggie sticks, carrot chips, root vegetable chips, and other low-fat, low-salt snacks
- Sesame breadsticks
- Peanut butter or fruit spread sandwiched in whole-grain crackers
- Bagel or pita crisps
- Organic stone-ground tortilla or corn chips

CHAPTER NINE

Healthy Snacks and Fruity Treats

WHEN MY SONS WERE LITTLE, I could more easily lure them and their friends away from play by saying that their "snack" (as opposed to "lunch") was ready. For small children, especially, a snack implies food that is quick, light, and fun. This may seem sneaky, but it worked.

Americans are a snack-crazed culture. And for better or worse, our children seem to be born with this passion for snacking. From the time you become a parent until you pack the kids off for college, snack foods will constitute a sizable portion of your food budget, and the interior of your car will be blanketed with crumbs and wrappers. Providing interesting snacks is also a test of a parent's creative mettle, because what's great one week ("Wow! Fig bars!") will be passé the next ("Fig bars again?").

While it's wise to limit between-meal noshing, our kids seem almost culturally bound to the mid-morning, after-school, and bedtime snack. Rather than giving in to high-fat, high-sugar, wasted calories, better to make the most of this predilection for grazing by serving healthy alternatives to packaged junk foods. Fruit dips, flavored organic popcorn, banana ambrosia, peanut butter and jelly pizza, and lots of ways to make fruit enticing are among many easy offerings in this chapter. In addition to fruits, a surprising number of the ideas you'll find here are based on vegetables, nuts, and whole grains, helping to overthrow the notion that snacks are by definition starchy or sugary.

Like all good things, snacking is best in moderation. If you want your family to snack well, read on to help them do so with style and substance.

Easy, Healthy Snack Ideas

Here are some handy ideas for easy homemade snacks. Most are so simple, they don't require a full-fledged recipe.

NEARLY INSTANT BEAN DIP: Combine ¾ cup fat-free refried beans with ½ cup salsa. Stir together, adding a small amount of water if needed to loosen the consistency. Serve with tortilla chips.

FLAVORED CREAM CHEESE VARIATIONS: Here are some ways to embellish cream cheese (you can use low-fat organic dairy, soy, or rice milk cream cheese). Spread on bagels, crackers, or English muffins for a quick treat.

- **Vegetable:** Place ¼ to ⅓ cup chopped vegetables (any combination of carrots, red or green bell peppers, zucchini, and broccoli stems) in a food processor and pulse on and off until finely chopped. Whirl in ½ cup cream cheese.
- **Pimiento:** Stir ¼ cup finely chopped pimiento-stuffed olives into ½ cup cream cheese.
- **Strawberry or pineapple:** Combine ½ cup finely chopped strawberries or ½ cup well-drained crushed pineapple with ½ cup cream cheese.

EASY DILL DIP: This simple dip can be made in an instant, and makes eating raw vegetables (carrots, celery, cauliflower, broccoli florets, bell peppers) more enticing. In a small serving bowl, combine ½ cup plain low-fat yogurt or soy yogurt with ¼ cup soy mayonnaise and stir together; season to taste with seasoned salt and dried dill. Serve in the center of a platter of raw vegetables.

CINNAMON-RAISIN TOAST: An all-time favorite in our home! Raisin bread makes great cinnamon toast. Simply toast fresh raisin bread, spread lightly with nonhydrogenated margarine, and sprinkle lightly with cinnamon and natural granulated sugar. Look for good-quality raisin bread in natural foods stores.

PB&J PIZZA: Here's a nifty variation on the classic pairing. Use one or two small good-quality pizza crusts and warm them according to package directions. When cool enough to handle, but still warm, spread with a layer of natural style peanut butter, followed by a layer of fruit-only preserves, and/or thinly sliced bananas or strawberries. Cut into 4 or 6 wedges and serve at once.

SILKEN PEANUT SPREAD: Natural-style, peanut-only peanut butter is often too intense for kids, especially younger ones; commercial peanut butters are filled with hydrogenated fats made from unhealthy oils, and high fructose corn syrup. Here's an all-natural, organic, creamy-smooth solution that I wish I had thought of when my children were young: In a food processor, combine ¾ cup natural-style peanut butter with ¾ cup (about half of a 12.3-ounce package) silken tofu, 2 tablespoons maple syrup or honey, and a pinch of salt. Process until velvety smooth. Transfer to an airtight container. Keeps in the refrigerator for up to 2 weeks.

CHOCOLATE-PEANUT BUTTER TRUFFLES: Here's a candylike treat that incorporates healthy elements. Combine ⅓ cup each natural peanut butter or cashew butter, raisins (or soft unsulfured dried apricots), and chocolate chips in a food processor. If desired, add 2 tablespoons ground flaxseeds. Process until completely and smoothly combined. Shape into small balls, not more than 1 inch in diameter, and refrigerate for 30 minutes or so, until firmed up. This makes about 16 trufflelike treats.

CUCUMBER, TOMATO, AND CREAM CHEESE SPIRALS: Spread a thin layer of soft dairy, rice, or soy cream cheese over the entire surface of one or two fresh lavash breads (these soft, rectangular flatbreads are available in supermarket deli sections and natural foods stores). Scatter thinly sliced plum (Roma) tomatoes and peeled cucumber over the surface, then roll up snugly. Cut into ½-inch sections with a sharp knife and arrange on a platter. These are easy to make and a delight to behold!

Sweet Baked Cereal Mix

When you have a little of this and a little of that kind of cereal in mostly empty boxes, this is a clever way to make good use of them. Make sure to use only naturally sweetened cereals.

**8 cups mixed naturally sweetened
   cereals of your choice**
2 tablespoons safflower oil
Ground cinnamon, to taste
1 cup dark or golden raisins
½ cup dried cranberries

Per ½ cup
Calories: 81
Total fat: 2 g
Protein: 1 g
Fiber: 2.4 g
Carbohydrates: 16 g
Cholesterol: 0 g
Sodium: 76 mg

1 Preheat the oven to 275° F. Lightly oil 2 baking pans.

2 Combine the cereals in a large mixing bowl and stir together.

3 Slowly drizzle in the oil and stir to distribute throughout. Sprinkle in cinnamon.

4 Spread the mixture in the prepared pans. Bake for 20 to 25 minutes, stirring once after 10 to 15 minutes of baking. Stir in the raisins and dried fruit.

5 Allow to cool in the baking pans, then store in tightly lidded containers or large jars.

Savory Baked Cereal Mix

This is a good way to use up odds and ends to create a tasty and economical snack.

1 Preheat the oven to 275° F. Lightly oil 2 baking pans.

2 Combine the cereals, pretzels, and nuts, if using, in a large mixing bowl and stir together.

3 Slowly drizzle in the oil and stir to distribute throughout. Add seasoned salt.

4 Spread the mixture in the prepared pans. Bake for 20 to 25 minutes, stirring once after 10 to 15 minutes of baking. Allow to cool in the pans, then store in tightly lidded containers or large jars.

Note
Omit nuts if this mix is to be eaten by younger children.

VEGAN

Makes about 10 cups

4 cups natural unsweetened O-shaped cereal
4 cups natural unsweetened square-shaped cereal
2 cups small pretzels, thin pretzel sticks, or tiny low-fat crackers
½ cup peanuts or cashew pieces, optional (see Note)
2 tablespoons safflower oil
Seasoned salt (such as Spike or Lawry's), to taste

Per ½ cup
Calories: 105
Total fat: 2 g
Protein: 3 g
Fiber: 2.4 g
Carbohydrates: 16 g
Cholesterol: 0 g
Sodium: 61 mg

Makes about 2 cups

**One 16-ounce can Great Northern beans
    or cannellini beans, drained and
    rinsed**
2 tablespoons tahini (sesame paste)
1 garlic clove, optional
Juice of ½ lemon, or to taste
½ teaspoon ground cumin, or to taste
Salt and freshly ground pepper, to taste
Paprika for topping, optional
Fresh pita bread, cut into wedges
Fresh-cut raw vegetables (see Note)

Per ¼ cup hummus

Calories: 62

Total fat: 2 g

Protein: 3 g

Fiber: 2.7 g

Carbohydrates: 8 g

Cholesterol: 0 g

Sodium: 3 mg

White Bean Hummus

I've observed many children (and toddlers, too) enjoying hummus. This variation on the classic Middle Eastern chickpea dip uses white beans and is smoother and milder than most.

1 Combine the beans, tahini, garlic, lemon juice, and cumin plus ¼ cup water in a food processor. Process until smoothly blended. Stop and scrape down the sides, if needed. It should have the consistency of a thick dip, but if it's too thick, add a small amount of additional water.

2 Taste the dip, and while it's still in the processor, season with salt and pepper, then pulse on and off to mix. Transfer to a serving bowl. Sprinkle on a little paprika, if desired.

3 Arrange a platter of pita wedges and fresh vegetables to dip into the hummus.

Note
Try carrot and celery sticks, zucchini or yellow squash slices, and broccoli and cauliflower florets.

Vegetable Pickles

VEGAN

Makes 2 quarts

Since this is not a vacuum-sealed canning project, keep these pickles refrigerated. They'll keep well for 1 week or more. Try mixing three or four different vegetables in your pickle jar.

1 Combine the marinade ingredients with 1 cup water in a saucepan. Heat on medium-high, stirring occasionally, until the salt and sugar are dissolved.

2 Stir the prepared raw vegetables together and place in a clean 1-quart jar. Pour the hot marinade over them. Cover tightly with the lid and refrigerate for about 24 hours before serving.

Marinade:
¹/₂ cup apple cider vinegar
¹/₂ cup apple juice
1 teaspoon salt
**1 tablespoon natural granulated sugar
(see page 283)**
2 garlic cloves, minced, optional
1 teaspoon dill seed, optional

4 cups of vegetables from the following:
Baby carrots
Broccoli florets, cut into bite-size pieces
Cauliflower florets, cut into bite-size pieces
Green beans, cut in half
**Zucchini, sliced into ¹/₄-inch-thick rounds
or into spears**
**Cucumber, cut into spears, and seeded, if
desired (small Kirby's are good for this)**
Turnips, cut into short sticks
Celery, cut into short sticks
Red bell peppers, cut into strips

Per ¹/₂ cup
Calories: 16
Total fat: 0 g
Protein: 0 g
Fiber: 0.6 g
Carbohydrates: 4 g
Cholesterol: 0 g
Sodium: 138 mg

Better Than Store Bought

Here are some snacks commonly sold in both supermarkets and natural foods stores that are easy and economical to make on your own.

Parmesan Pita Chips: Allow 1 small or ½ large pita (preferably whole wheat) per serving. Carefully split the pitas horizontally. Brush the tops of the pitas with a little olive oil. Cut small pitas into 4 wedges and large pitas into 6 or 8 wedges. Arrange on a baking sheet and sprinkle lightly with grated Parmesan cheese or Parmesan-style soy cheese. Bake in a preheated 350° F oven for 10 minutes, or until crisp.

Homemade Bagel Crisps: Store-bought bagel crisps are good, but making them at home is fun, and a good way to use up less-than-perfectly-fresh bagels. Cut bagels (preferably whole grain) in half crosswise (rather than through the thickness), then stand each half on the cut end, and carefully slice very thinly with a sharp knife. Place the slices on a baking sheet and spray them lightly with cooking oil spray. Raisin bagels can be sprinkled with a little cinnamon and natural granulated sugar; sprinkle other types of bagels with seasoned salt, chili powder, or any kind of seasoning you'd like. Bake at 275° F for 20 to 30 minutes, until dry and crisp.

Trail Mix: Sure, you can buy prepared trail mix, but you may enjoy mixing your own, especially if you're already in the habit of keeping several types of nuts and dried fruits in your pantry. Invent your own combinations of nuts (peanuts, cashews, almonds, sunflower or pumpkin seeds, walnuts, pecans, hazelnuts) and dried fruits (raisins, apricots, flour-rolled date pieces, dried cranberries, dried cherries, pineapple, mango, or papaya). For a rich treat, add a small amount of cane-juice sweetened chocolate chips or natural peanut butter chips.

Paper Bag Popcorn: Did you know that all popcorn is microwavable? If you buy your own organic popcorn kernels in bulk, it's not only much more economical, but *you* control how much salt (if any) goes on, and you avoid preservatives and hydrogenated fats. Here's how: Simply put ¼ cup unpopped kernels in a lunch-sized brown paper bag. Fold the top over and secure with a couple pieces of tape. Microwave on high for about 2 minutes, until you no longer hear any popping. Transfer to a large bowl and sprinkle with salt to taste. If you'd like, drizzle a small amount of melted nonhydrogenated margarine on the popcorn and stir well. See also Make Your Own Flavored Popcorn (below).

Make Your Own Flavored Popcorn

Here are some festive flavors to add to the basic Paper Bag Popcorn formula (above):

Chili-Spiced Popcorn: Melt 2 to 3 tablespoons nonhydrogenated margarine in a small saucepan. Stir in 1 teaspoon chili powder, ½ teaspoon paprika, and ½ teaspoon ground cumin. Drizzle over popcorn and toss well.

Popcorn Parmesan: Drizzle 2 to 3 tablespoons nonhydrogenated margarine into the popcorn and toss well. Sprinkle in ¼ cup grated fresh Parmesan or Parmesan-style nondairy cheese and toss again.

Peanut Caramel Corn: Melt 2 to 3 tablespoons nonhydrogenated margarine in a small saucepan. Stir in 2 tablespoons natural granulated sugar until melted. Stir 1 cup peanuts into the popcorn. Drizzle the margarine and sugar mixture over the popcorn and peanuts and toss well. Bake at 275° F for 15 minutes, stirring once after about 10 minutes. Let cool and break apart.

Almond-Maple Popcorn: Melt 2 tablespoons nonhydrogenated margarine in a small saucepan. Remove from the heat and stir in 3 tablespoons maple syrup. Stir 1 cup toasted almonds into the popcorn. Drizzle the margarine and syrup mixture over the popcorn and almonds and toss well. Bake at 275° F for 15 minutes, stirring once after about 10 minutes. Let cool and break apart.

Go Ahead, Have Some Nuts (and Seeds, Too)

Nuts and seeds provide one of the most concentrated sources of protein, B vitamins, vitamin E, and a wide range of minerals, including calcium, for the well-rounded vegetarian diet. Though you want to avoid giving whole nuts to younger children (they are considered a choking hazard), you may begin giving nut butters to toddlers, so long as allergies (particularly to peanuts) are ruled out.

Roasted nuts and seeds are an ideal snack to be eaten straight or mixed with dried fruits, but they can dress up meals and desserts as well. Finely ground nuts make an excellent casserole topping mixed with an equal amount of bread crumbs or wheat germ; whole seeds or chopped nuts add interest when sprinkled on green vegetables, grain or pasta dishes, and breakfast cereals; pumpkin seeds, sunflower seeds, and slivered almonds dress up salads. We keep a jar of toasted, unhulled sesame seeds on the table and sprinkle them on just about everything. Flaxseeds belong in this category, too (see page 290).

Nuts and seeds are composed of 50 to 70 percent fat, but this fat is mainly polyunsaturated and monounsaturated. Surprisingly, the type of fat found in nuts has been shown to lower blood cholesterol levels while maintaining "good" cholesterol. While you may not want to down 1 or 2 cups of nuts at a sitting, a moderate amount—perhaps 1 or 2 ounces a day, can be a marvelous addition to a healthy diet.

I like to store nuts in quart-size mason jars (pint-size jars are good for seeds, which are more compact). Nuts' and seeds' high fat content makes them prone to rancidity, so buy only what you think you can finish within a month or so; if your kitchen stays warm during the summer, it's best to refrigerate nuts and seeds. They freeze well, too.

Consider keeping a variety of nuts and seeds in your pantry for snacking, cooking, and baking:

Almonds	Macadamia nuts	Pumpkin seeds
Brazil nuts	Peanuts	Sunflower seeds
Cashews	Pecans	Sesame seeds
Hazelnuts	Pistachios	Walnuts

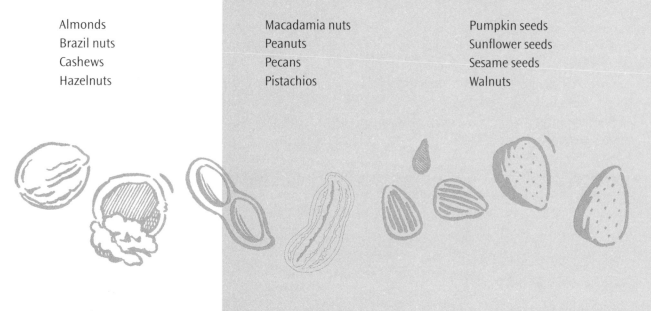

Beyond Peanut Butter

Next time you browse the aisles of a well-stocked natural foods store, make sure to check out the possibilities in the nut butter section. Though peanut butter always rules, you'll also find cashew butter (truly delicious and creamy), almond butter (tasty and nutritious, with a slightly grainy texture), and soy nut butter (made from roasted soy nuts, this provides a good way to obtain soy protein).

Pumpkin butter and sunflower butter are excitingly intense products of these nourishing seeds. Seed butters lack the slight sweetness of nut butters but are savory, almost like a fine pâté. Sesame paste, or tahini, is another contender in this category, though it's used more in sauces and dips (like hummus) and in baking, rather than as a snack or spread.

Most nut and seed butters contain about 15 grams of fat, 180 calories, and 6 grams of protein in a 2-tablespoon serving. They are nutrient-dense, making them a splendid food for growing bodies and a treat for grown-up palates. As with whole nuts, fear not their fat content—used in moderation, nut and seed butters provide necessary and beneficial fats and a plethora of nutrients (see page 263).

Making your own nut butters at home is easy; see page 265.

Homemade Nut Butter

HONEY / VEGAN OPTION

Makes about 1 cup

Making fresh nut butter isn't hard to do, and is a great kitchen project to do with young children, who actually enjoy the process of shelling peanuts. Ideally, use organic nuts. Conventional brands of peanut butter (far and away the most commonly consumed nut butter) almost always contain partially hydrogenated fats and high fructose corn syrup, two unhealthy ingredients. Some brands also contain cottonseed oil, which comes from one of the most heavily sprayed crops on earth. Natural-style nut butters contain the nuts only, and are obviously a better choice, but their flavor and texture are often too intense for younger children.

This homemade version is a perfect compromise, both for flavor and health. For another great peanut butter alternative, see Silken Peanut Spread (page 256).

1 cup shelled roasted peanuts, almonds, or cashews
1 tablespoon vegetable oil
¼ teaspoon salt
1 tablespoon honey, maple syrup, or brown rice syrup

1 Place the nuts in a food processor. Process until the nuts begin to hold together.

2 Add the oil, salt, and honey, and continue to process. Scrape the sides of the container from time to time, and continue to process until the nut butter is at the desired consistency.

3 Transfer the nut butter to a lidded container and keep refrigerated. For easier spreading, microwave for a few seconds before using.

Per tablespoon

Calories: 64

Total fat: 5 g

Protein: 2 g

Fiber: 0.8 g

Carbohydrates: 3 g

Cholesterol: 0 g

Sodium: 35 mg

Tips

- For peanut butter, dry-roasted peanuts from a jar work just fine, but using freshly shelled roasted peanuts results in a more vivid flavor.
- If children other than your own will be partaking of this snack, make sure that none are allergic to peanuts—it's a more common allergy than you'd think and can be quite serious.
- This won't work in a blender—a food processor is a must.

Since we no longer use products containing white sugar, store-bought sweetened cocoa mix is not an option. Now I buy organic cocoa powder in 5-pound bulk quantity; it keeps for a long time and is extremely economical. To make hot cocoa mix, simply combine 1 part cocoa powder with 3 parts natural granulated sugar (i.e., ⅓ cup cocoa plus 1 cup sugar). Use organic natural sugar to make a delicious all-organic cocoa mix. Since our palates have adjusted to less sweetening, we find that 1 rounded teaspoon is sufficient to flavor a good-size mug of hot cocoa. This needs to be dissolved in a small amount of hot liquid; it doesn't dissolve in cold liquid. Here are some contemporary variations on this classic beverage:

Nondairy Hot Cocoa: Sure, you can simply heat chocolate soy milk, but it's not the same. Use plain or vanilla soy milk or almond milk with the cocoa mix. Rice milk with a little added soy creamer also yields wonderful results.

Minty Hot Cocoa: For a delightful cold-weather beverage, dunk a mint tea bag into about ⅓ cup hot water and let steep. Stir in the cocoa mix and whatever type of milk you are using.

Cinnamon-Chili Hot Cocoa: Add a pinch of cinnamon to your hot cocoa; and if you're adventurous like my son Evan, stir in a few grains of chili powder. He got this idea, appropriately enough, from the movie *Chocolat.*

One way to get your family to eat more fruit is to place small bowls of fresh, washed fruit in strategic places, such as in the middle of the kitchen and/or dining room table, in the den, and indeed, anywhere the family tends to hang out. In the summer, stone fruits (peaches, plums, nectarines), berries, and grapes are ideal; in cooler months, apples, pears, bananas, and small seedless oranges are the most sensible if obvious choices. Use ripe, ready-to-eat fruit, and put out only what you expect to be eaten during the day and evening. When the day is over, refrigerate what is left. Or make a fruit salad with what's left and serve it at breakfast.

This strategy works well in some families, but for others, bowls of fruit are nice-looking still lives rather than something to actually eat. If this is the case in your home, you may find, as I always have, that cutting up fruit and arranging it on a platter offers much more assurance that it will be eaten. And if your family needs further nudging, here are a few simple ways to make fruit a greater part of your everyday fare:

Oven-Dried Apples: To dry apples, cut a thin slice off of both stem ends. Cut out the core using a sharp knife, then cut into ¼-inch-thick slices. Arrange in a single layer on baking pans; bake at 200° F for 1½ to 2 hours, or until leathery but still tender. You can also make delicious apple chips, just like the ones you buy in the small bags. Simply slice the apples ⅛ inch thick and bake at 200° F for 1½ to 2 hours, or until just turning crisp. Both dried apples and apple chips are great as snacks.

Apple Slices with Nut Butter Dip: Simply serve small individual bowls of natural-style peanut butter, cashew butter, or Silken Peanut Spread (page 256) with slices of crisp, juicy apples. It's a great combination of flavor and texture!

Sautéed Apples: In addition to being a tasty snack, served alone or with a dollop of vanilla low-fat yogurt or soy yogurt, this makes a nice change-of-pace side dish, especially in the fall and winter. Use firm apples such as Granny Smith, Gala, or Fuji. Peel the apples, then cut into quarters and remove the seeds. Cut each quarter into three or four slices. Heat just enough nonhydrogenated margarine to coat the bottom of a nonstick skillet.

Sauté the apple slices over medium heat until just tender, about 4 to 5 minutes. Sprinkle with ground cinnamon, stir, and serve.

Skewered Fruit: Cut several kinds of fresh seasonal fruit into bite-size chunks and alternate on wooden or bamboo skewers. Kids may enjoy threading the fruit onto the skewers even if they immediately eat it right off! Summer skewers can include strawberries, seedless grapes, cantaloupe, firm watermelon, honeydew, plums, peaches, and apricots. Fall and winter skewers can include pineapple, apple, firm pear, Asian pear, small seedless orange sections, and soft dried fruits such as apricots. Serve plain or with small individual bowls of the cream cheese dip (following).

Sweet Cream Cheese Dip for Fruit: Combine an 8-ounce package or tub of cream cheese (organic dairy, rice, or soy-based) with ⅓ cup undiluted apple juice or orange juice concentrate and a dash of ground cinnamon in a small mixing bowl. Whisk together until smoothly blended. Serve with Skewered Fruit (above) or with crisp apple or pear slices, strawberries, banana chunks (served with cocktail toothpicks), or any other fruit you have on hand for dipping.

Your Own All-Organic Fruity Yogurt: When we switched to organic yogurt, and then to soy yogurt, we found that we just weren't excited by the flavors in the small containers. I continued to buy vanilla low-fat yogurt (then the soy version once we went vegan) for baking and for making smoothies and parfaits, so eventually I hit on the idea of simply stirring a spoonful of organic all-fruit preserves into individual servings of vanilla yogurt. It's not only more economical but the flavor is much more to our liking. Even better, you can also stir homemade fruit sauce (see page 8) into vanilla low-fat yogurt or soy yogurt. Lemon- and banana-flavored yogurts also make excellent backdrops.

Fruit and Yogurt Parfaits: This is one of the easiest, yet most visually appealing ways to dress up fresh fruit. All you need to make a single-serving parfait is about ¾ cup yogurt (organic low-fat or soy) and about ¾ cup fresh fruit. Vanilla-, lemon-, and orange-flavored yogurts all work well. For spring and summer, try sliced strawberries, blueberries, sliced peaches, or nectarines (or any combination of these fruits). In fall and winter, sliced ripe pears, bananas, mangoes, or kiwi (or again, any combination) work nicely. In a parfait glass or balloon wineglass, make two layers each of the fruit and yogurt, then top, if you'd like, with chopped nuts or granola.

Winter Fruit Salads or Platters

With a little resourcefulness, your family can enjoy fruit all winter. It always makes more sense to enjoy fruits that are primarily in season rather than getting summer fruit imported from goodness knows where.

To make an abundant winter fruit bowl, combine your reliable apples and pears with seedless orange sections and/or canned pineapple. Consider adding an Asian pear, a crisp and fragrant cross between apple and pear that's becoming more widely available. Embellish with some dried fruits, such as sliced apricots and cranberries. Tropical fruit is often widely available in winter and can add spark to the limited offerings. Look for mangoes, kiwi, and star fruit, but make sure to buy these in organic form. The same goes for apples and pears, which are hardly exotic but can be pesticide laden when grown commercially.

If platters rather than salads are more appealing to your family, use the same fruits to compose an attractive array. If you'd like, you can provide a dip in a small bowl. Sweet Cream Cheese Dip for Fruit (page 268) is a good choice, or try Silken Peanut Spread (page 256), thinned with a little low-fat milk, rice milk, or soy milk.

Banana-Yogurt Ambrosia

Young children often balk at dishes in which ingredients are "touching." However, I served this often when my sons were younger and had friends visiting. I found that if kids decide for themselves what's touching what, they don't seem to mind a mixed dish. In fact, most kids loved creating patterns in their yogurt with the other items, and often asked for seconds.

1 to 2 medium bananas, sliced

1 cup (about half of one 16-ounce can) unsweetened pineapple tidbits, drained

1 large pear, peeled and diced

½ cup small seedless grapes

½ cup dark or golden raisins or dried cranberries

¼ cup semisweet chocolate chips, optional

1 cup granola, optional

½ cup grated coconut, optional

2 to 3 cups vanilla low-fat yogurt or soy yogurt

1 Place all the ingredients except the yogurt into separate small bowls.

2 Divide the yogurt among 4 to 6 individual serving bowls. Let everyone take a little of whichever ingredients they'd like to dress up their yogurt.

Variations

During warm seasons, use frozen yogurt or nondairy dessert and replace the pineapple with blueberries and/or sliced strawberries.

Dairy	Vegan option
Calories: 234	Calories: 209
Total fat: 2 g	Total fat: 1 g
Protein: 7 g	Protein: 3 g
Fiber: 3 g	Fiber: 4 g
Carbohydrates: 51 g	Carbohydrates: 49 g
Cholesterol: 6 g	Cholesterol: 0 g
Sodium: 85 mg	Sodium: 40 mg

Pineapple Rice Pudding

DAIRY / VEGAN OPTION

4 to 6 servings

Kids of all ages can enjoy this updated comfort food as a snack or dessert, or even as an offbeat lunch box offering, packed in a thermos.

1 Combine the rice with 2½ cups water in a medium saucepan. Bring to a simmer, then cover and simmer gently until the water is absorbed, about 35 minutes. When absorbed, stir in the milk, and simmer until absorbed.

2 Remove from the heat and allow to cool for 5 minutes, then stir in the remaining ingredients.

3 Divide the rice pudding among 4 or 6 serving dishes. Sprinkle each with a little extra cinnamon and serve warm or at room temperature.

¾ cup short-grain brown rice
¾ cup whole milk, or ½ cup soy milk creamer plus ¼ cup rice milk
½ cup dark or golden raisins
¼ cup maple syrup
1 cup well-drained crushed pineapple
1 teaspoon vanilla extract
¼ teaspoon ground cinnamon, plus more for topping
Pinch of ground nutmeg

Dairy	Vegan option
Calories: 226	Calories: 247
Total fat: 2 g	Total fat: 3 g
Protein: 4 g	Protein: 3 g
Fiber: 2.6 g	Fiber: 2.6 g
Carbohydrates: 50 g	Carbohydrates: 53 g
Cholesterol: 5 g	Cholesterol: 0 g
Sodium: 28 mg	Sodium: 29 mg

Dried Fruit

Concentrated sources of natural sweetness and nutrients, dried fruits deserve a prominent place in the family snack pantry. All are excellent sources of dietary fiber and are filled with natural sugars, which, when added to cereals, baked goods, and trail mixes (or just eaten on their own), coax the palate to appreciate natural, rather than refined sweetness. Dried fruits are rich in minerals, notably iron, magnesium, phosphorus, and calcium. They contain varying amounts of vitamins A and C, depending on the fruit.

Many dried fruits available in supermarkets have been treated with sulfur dioxide, a gas that helps the fruits retain their color. Though this preservative is defined as GRAS (generally recognized as safe) by the U.S. Food and Drug Administration, the process is done primarily for cosmetic purposes. Those who would like their dried fruits unsulfured would best purchase them in natural foods stores, where some of the packaged or bulk dried fruits are labeled as such.

Most of us keep raisins in our pantry, but consider other fruits available in dried form, including dates, prunes, apples, peaches, pears, papaya, mango, banana, figs, cranberries, cherries, and pineapple. Please choose organic forms of these fruits as often as possible. Here are a few ways to enjoy dried fruits on a regular basis:

- **As a snack:** It almost goes without saying that most dried fruits are excellent as a naturally sweet snack, eaten out of hand, for children and adults alike.
- **In baked goods:** Raisins, dates, and currants are commonly used in muffins and quick breads; for a change of pace, try using chopped apricots, peaches, pears, or prunes.
- **In trail mixes:** See page 262.
- **In cereals:** Go beyond the commonplace raisins and use other dried fruits, chopped into small bits, to dress up both hot and cold cereals.

- **Stewed dried fruits:** To plump dried fruits, cover them with hot fruit juice. Cover the container and let stand overnight in the refrigerator. Try combining several types to make an interesting winter fruit compote to have for breakfast or dessert, topped with a dollop of low-fat vanilla yogurt or soy yogurt.
- **Fancy fruit salads:** Add any kind of dried fruit (chopped or sliced if large) to fresh fruit salads for variety and texture.
- **Sweet side dishes:** Combine dried fruits with sautéed sweet vegetables (carrots, winter squashes, sweet potatoes, or other root vegetables). Chopped pitted prunes, mission figs, cranberries, and raisins are especially good for this purpose.

In centuries past, when being the "apple of one's eye" was lofty praise, America was so smitten with apples that there were literally hundreds of varieties to choose from. Even the names of nineteenth-century varieties evoke a sense of romance: Yellow Bellflower, Cranberry Pippin, Pumpkin Russet, Maiden Blush.

Today, 2,500 varieties are grown in North America, but only eight varieties make up 80 percent of those sold commercially. We might find half a dozen or so predominant varieties at any given fruit market or supermarket—red and golden Delicious, McIntosh, Granny Smith, Cortland, and Jonathan are among the top choices. New Zealand's fragrant, juicy Braeburns and Fujis from Washington State have caught on, too. A wider search can lead you to spicy Winesap, hybrid Jonagold, and tiny Lady apples.

The preferred way of eating apples is out of hand, yet they're surprisingly versatile in the kitchen. Some simple ways to enjoy them: diced and tossed into salads, sliced and dipped into peanut butter, and baked whole. Lightly cooked diced apples are delicious in grain pilafs and add a delightful nuance to savory soups and stews (see Creamy Butternut Squash and Apple Soup, page 46). Sliced, sautéed, and sprinkled with ground cinnamon, apples make a tasty yogurt topping for a snack or dessert or an uncommon side dish with dinner (see Sautéed Apples, page 267). And of course, apples are always welcome in baked goods—muffins, pies, cakes, cobblers, crumbles, and more.

The number of common varieties may have diminished, but not our enthusiasm—apples are still North America's favorite fruit.

- Whether eating one a day will keep the doctor away is debatable, but apples do score well nutritionally. The average apple contains a respectable 3 to 5 grams of fiber and moderate amounts of vitamin C and potassium.
- Apples are also good teeth cleansers and gum stimulators—good substitutes for a toothbrush when you don't have access to yours.
- Apples store well and retain their juiciness and nutrients for a long period when refrigerated.

- And finally, good news for organic food enthusiasts—organic versions of many apple varieties are becoming increasingly available. Since apples often appear at or near the top of most contaminated fruit lists, it makes sense to use organic apples as much as possible, if not exclusively.

Finally, here's a quick guide to the best uses for the common apple varieties.

- For cooking or baking whole, the best apples are Cortland, Gala, Jonathan, Rome Beauty, and Golden Delicious.
- For eating out of hand, salads, and pilafs, Braeburn, Fuji, Granny Smith (if you like tart apples), Gala, Jonagold, Golden Delicious, McIntosh, Northern Spy, and many of the more unusual or heir-loom varieties are good.
- For pies, cobblers, and crisps, choose Granny Smith (considered by avid bakers the ideal pie apple), Rome Beauty, Jonathan, Winesap, Northern Spy, or McIntosh.
- For applesauce, use Empire, Cortland, Golden Delicious, McIntosh, or Winesap.
- You're probably wondering where the popular Red Delicious apple stands. I can only wonder how this mealy, bland, tough-skinned apple became so commonplace—in my opinion, it's best left in the market bin.

CHAPTER TEN

Wholesome Baked Goods

FEW SENSORY EXPERIENCES offer more pleasure than the wonderful flavors and aromas of homemade baked goods. Baking at home is a good opportunity to create treats that are lower in fat and sugar than those you would buy in a store or bakery. Whole-wheat pastry and other whole flours also make a great way to get whole-grain goodness into kids' growing bodies. Many of the following baked goods contain fresh and dried fruits, vegetables, nuts, seeds, yogurt, and other healthful ingredients, and so are not merely treats but a nice adjunct to healthy vegetarian meals. For those of us who are already grown up, wholesome baked goods are a far wiser choice than high-fat, white-flour pastries.

None of the recipes in this chapter uses eggs (with the exception of the egg option in spoonbread), and all can be made dairy-free. I make ample use of applesauce, low-fat yogurt, and soy yogurt as fat substitutes; these work so well that only a smidgen of oil is needed to make for a tender crumb. This array of healthy baked goods is perfect for vegans, the lactose-intolerant, and anyone who prefers that their treats offer more than empty calories.

In the pages to follow, you'll find recipes for quick breads, muffins, cookies, pies, cobblers, and more. The operative word in this chapter is *easy*; baking doesn't have to be complicated to be an enriching experience on many levels. These are not, I promise, like those "health food" 1960s desserts that resembled (and tasted like) bricks and mortar. Yes, you *can* have your cake (and cookies and muffins) and eat it, too—and now, with just the right touch, minus the fuss and guilt.

Ingredients and Equipment for
Easy Whole-Grain Baking

Since I'd like to encourage nonbakers to try their hand at this gratifying kitchen activity, you can be sure that I'm not going to send you to your nearest restaurant supply shop with a list including springform pans, fancy cake molds, frosting pipers, and the like. Still, there are some basics to stock up on for the kind of simple, homespun baked goods you'll find here. These are easy to find, inexpensive, and, if well chosen, will serve you well for a long time.

* Baking sheets (2)
* 8- by 8-inch or 9- by 9-inch baking pans (having two of this useful size is handy if you bake often)
* 9- by 13-inch baking pan (1)
* Muffin tins, standard-size cups (1)
* 9-inch pie pan (1 or 2; nonstick or tinted glass)

Choose light- to medium-gray bakeware with a durable nonstick finish. Black finishes draw too much heat and cause the bottoms of baked goods to brown too quickly. You need not choose the most expensive, but don't choose the cheapest, either. Make sure the bakeware has heft and solidity. Thin, flimsy baking pans can warp in high heat. They don't last as long, don't conduct heat as well, and don't clean as well as better bakeware. As for other equipment, these recipes require nothing fancier than measuring cups and spoons, oven mitts, and rolling pins. If you suspect your oven isn't completely accurate, you may want to invest in an inexpensive oven thermometer.

Here are some basic ingredients to have on hand:

* **Applesauce** (preferably organic, to use as a fat substitute)
* **Baking powder** (nonaluminum)
* **Baking soda**
* **Chocolate chips** (preferably cane-juice sweetened and ideally also organic; see page 298)
* **Baking spices** (ground cinnamon, nutmeg, and ginger; pumpkin pie spice comes in handy, too)
* **Dried fruits** (dates, apricots, mission figs, and prunes are nice to have on hand)
* **Honey** (vegans may use maple syrup instead)
* **Maple syrup** (pure, of course)
* **Natural granulated sugar** (see page 283; you can buy a brand-name natural sugar, but I prefer organic raw sugar purchased in bulk)
* **Nuts** (walnuts and almonds are most useful in baking)
* **Raisins** (dark and/or golden, preferably organic)

- **Rolled oats and oatmeal**
- **Safflower oil** (good for baking and rich in vitamin E)
- **Whole-wheat pastry flour** (preferably organic; you can buy this in bulk)
- **Yogurt or soy yogurt** (plain and vanilla flavors are both useful; if you use dairy yogurt, choose a low-fat organic brand; soy yogurt is almost always organic)

Optional

- **Nut butters:** Chances are you already have peanut, cashew, and/or almond butter on hand if you are a natural foods enthusiast; these are occasionally useful in baked goods
- **Other organic whole-grain flours:** As you get more involved with whole-grain baking you might like to experiment with adding spelt, kamut, and cornmeal to your baked goods; purchase in modest quantities and keep refrigerated during warm weather; store in the freezer if you don't plan to use up within 2 or 3 months

Makes 1 loaf, about 10 slices

1 cup whole-wheat pastry flour
¾ cup rye flour
½ cup cornmeal
1½ teaspoons baking soda
1 teaspoon salt
1 cup low-fat yogurt or soy yogurt
⅔ cup low-fat milk, rice milk, or soy milk, or as needed
⅓ cup maple syrup, molasses, or barley malt syrup
2 tablespoons safflower oil

Dairy (per slice)	Vegan option (per slice)
Calories: 162	Calories: 160
Total fat: 4 g	Total fat: 4 g
Protein: 5 g	Protein: 4 g
Fiber: 3 g	Fiber: 3.4 g
Carbohydrates: 29 g	Carbohydrates: 29 g
Cholesterol: 2 g	Cholesterol: 0 g
Sodium: 431 mg	Sodium: 417 mg

Quick Three-Grain Brown Bread

Pop this easy bread into the oven while your favorite comforting soup is simmering on the stove.

1 Preheat the oven to 350° F. Lightly oil a 9- by 5- by 3-inch loaf pan.

2 Combine the flours, cornmeal, baking soda, and salt in a large mixing bowl and stir together.

3 Combine the remaining ingredients in another mixing bowl and whisk together until smoothly blended. Make a well in the center of the dry ingredients and pour in the wet mixture, using enough milk to make a smooth, stiff batter. Stir together until completely combined.

4 Pour the batter into the prepared pan. Bake for about 40 minutes, or until the top is golden brown and a knife inserted into the center of the loaf comes out clean. When cool enough to handle, carefully remove the bread from the pan, place it on a rack or platter, and allow it to cool to just warm before slicing.

The recipes in this chapter call for whole-wheat pastry flour. In the past, I've combined whole-wheat pastry flour in equal portions with unbleached white flour, thinking this combination to be lighter and more palatable. However, now that I use 100 percent whole-wheat pastry flour, I simply don't find this is the case; the baked goods may not be as fluffy as white-flour pastries, but they aren't at all heavy. I like the consistency just fine, and have received no complaints from any family members or guests, whether grown-up or pint-size!

Any whole-wheat flour, whether hard-wheat bread flour or soft-wheat pastry flour, is more nutritious because it retains the bran and germ of the whole-wheat berry—fiber, vitamins, and minerals are left intact. Whole-wheat pastry flour is milled from soft winter wheat, which has a lower gluten content than whole-wheat bread flour. Bread flour and pastry flours are really not interchangeable; each does its job in a specific way. Pastry flour has a finer, more powdery texture than bread flour, making it good for cookies, muffins, cakes, and other pastries. It's also wonderful in pancakes, waffles, and savory pies. If you do find that your palate needs to adjust, go ahead and use a mixture of whole-wheat pastry flour and unbleached white flour. After a while, you may find, as I did, that you prefer the whole-wheat pastry flour straight.

Whole-wheat pastry flour—often organic—is easy to obtain in natural foods stores. Purchased in bulk, it's an economical way to do home baking. Bear in mind that whole-wheat pastry and other whole-grain flours are more perishable than refined flours, so if you don't use them up quickly, keep them refrigerated. If you have trouble finding whole-wheat pastry flour, use unbleached white flour, replacing $\frac{1}{4}$ cup of each 1 cup of flour with wheat germ.

The Scoop on Whole-Wheat Pastry Flour

DAIRY / VEGAN OPTION

Makes 1 loaf, about 10 slices

2 cups whole-wheat pastry flour

1½ teaspoons baking powder

1 teaspoon baking soda

1 cup vanilla low-fat yogurt or soy yogurt

⅓ cup maple syrup

2 tablespoons plus 1 teaspoon safflower oil

⅓ cup low-fat milk, rice milk, or soy milk, or as needed

1 cup raisins

1 tablespoon ground cinnamon

2 tablespoons natural granulated sugar (see page 283)

⅓ cup finely chopped walnuts for topping, optional

Dairy	Vegan option
(per slice)	(per slice)
Calories: 207	Calories: 204
Total fat: 4 g	Total fat: 4 g
Protein: 5 g	Protein: 4 g
Fiber: 3.9 g	Fiber: 4.1 g
Carbohydrates: 40 g	Carbohydrates: 41 g
Cholesterol: 2 g	Cholesterol: 0 g
Sodium: 208 mg	Sodium: 196 mg

Quick Cinnamon-Raisin Bread

This cinnamon-scented bread will make any kitchen feel cozy.

1 Preheat the oven to 350° F. Lightly oil a 9- by 5-inch loaf pan.

2 Combine the flour, baking powder, and baking soda in a mixing bowl and stir together.

3 Make a well in the center and pour in the yogurt, maple syrup, 2 tablespoons of the oil, and enough milk to make a smooth, stiff batter. Stir until thoroughly mixed, then stir in the raisins.

4 In a small bowl, combine the cinnamon, sugar, and the remaining 1 teaspoon of oil. Stir until the cinnamon and sugar are evenly moistened. Sprinkle half the mixture into the batter, then gently fold the batter over. Sprinkle in the rest, then fold the batter gently over again.

5 Pour the batter in the prepared pan. Sprinkle the top with walnuts, if desired.

6 Bake for 40 to 45 minutes, or until the top is golden brown and crusty. When cool enough to handle, carefully remove the bread from the pan, place it on a rack or platter, and allow it to cool until just warm before slicing.

In many of the recipes in this chapter (and throughout the book) I recommend using natural granulated sugar as a sweetener. This can be organic sugar bought in bulk or a brand-name natural sugar. And this form of sugar is used quite judiciously, at that. Most of the recipes in this chapter use one half to two thirds less sugar than typical equivalent recipes. Because organic vanilla low-fat yogurt, soy yogurt, or applesauce are used in these baked goods, these act not only as fat substitutes but cut down considerably on the need for granulated sugar.

Into the category of natural granulated sugar fall several varieties, the common denominator being that they are not as refined or bleached as white sugar. Many vegetarians and vegans are not comfortable with the fact that 25 percent of all white sugar is refined using the animal bone-char process. Since white sugar is often sold under generic store-brand labels, it's often impossible to know what you're getting. In addition, the process that turns sugar crystals from their original, lovely tan color to white is not only unnecessary but also quite polluting. Please note that supermarket brands of light and dark brown sugar are actually bleached white sugar with a little molasses added back.

Natural sugar is easy to find in bulk in natural foods stores, where the variations include organic raw sugar (though sugar crystals are not truly raw) and Turbinado sugar. Buying this kind of sugar in bulk is the most economical. My personal favorite is organic raw sugar. I find it yields excellent results in baking. Florida Crystals is a brand name of unbleached sugar; it comes in bags and containers, and you might look for it if your market doesn't sell natural sugar in bulk.

There are also several brands of natural sugar than are even less refined than the fine tan crystals just described. These are excellent, but because they have more of their natural molasses left intact, they have a rather assertive flavor and coarser texture. Sucanat and Rapadura are two well-known brands. Their granules have a deep tawny hue, and they retain more of the nutrients, particularly minerals, found in sugar cane.

As an all-purpose sweetener for baking, cooking, and in hot or cold drinks, use any kind of natural granulated sugar in a 1-to-1 replacement for white sugar.

What Is Natural Granulated Sugar?

1 cup cornmeal

2 tablespoons nonhydrogenated
   margarine

1 teaspoon salt

1 tablespoon natural granulated sugar
   (see page 283)

1 teaspoon baking soda

¾ cup low-fat yogurt or soy yogurt

¼ cup low-fat milk or rice milk

2 eggs, well beaten, or 2 tablespoons
   ground flaxseeds mixed with ¼ cup
   hot water (see Note)

Maple syrup or all-fruit preserves,
   optional

Dairy/egg	Vegan option
Calories: 184	Calories: 94
Total fat: 4 g	Total fat: 3 g
Protein: 4 g	Protein: 2 g
Fiber: 1.0 g	Fiber: 1.6 g
Carbohydrates: 14 g	Carbohydrates: 15 g
Cholesterol: 49 g	Cholesterol: 0 g
Sodium: 433 mg	Sodium: 410 mg

Spoonbread

Spoonbread is a softer, moister version of cornbread. It's nice served with bean soups and makes an offbeat breakfast option when served with maple syrup or all-fruit preserves.

1 Preheat the oven to 375° F.

2 Combine the cornmeal with 1 cup hot water in a mixing bowl and whisk together. Add the margarine, stirring until melted.

3 Stir in the remaining ingredients, except the syrup, and whisk until smooth.

4 Pour into a 9- by 9-inch nonstick baking pan. Bake for 25 to 30 minutes, or until the top is golden. When done, let stand for 5 minutes or so, then cut into squares. Serve topped with maple syrup, if desired.

Note

This doesn't have as much of a soufflélike texture if made with ground flaxseeds instead of eggs, but it still sets up well.

Tip

If we want to have this for breakfast, I make it the night before, especially if there is something else in the oven. Or sometimes leftovers suffice for breakfast. In the morning, this is delicious reheated in a skillet with a small amount of nonhydrogenated margarine.

Leslie's Corn Bread Cake

Truly a cross between a bread and a cake, this delicious vegan cornbread is as welcome with coffee or tea as it is with chili and other bean dishes. This was contributed by my friend Leslie Cerier, an organic caterer and author of *Going Wild in the Kitchen.*

1 Preheat the oven to 350° F. Lightly oil a 9- by 13-inch baking pan.

2 Combine the cornmeal, flour, salt, and baking powder in a large mixing bowl and stir together.

3 Make a well in the center and pour in the remaining ingredients. Whisk together until smooth.

4 Pour the batter into the prepared pan. Bake for 30 minutes, or until golden and a knife inserted in the center tests clean. Cool until just warm, then cut into squares to serve.

VEGAN

Makes about 15 squares

2 cups yellow cornmeal

2 cups whole-wheat pastry flour

$\frac{1}{2}$ teaspoon salt

2 tablespoons baking powder

$\frac{1}{2}$ cup corn oil or other light vegetable oil

$\frac{1}{2}$ cup pure maple syrup

$\frac{1}{2}$ cup vanilla soy or rice milk

$1\frac{1}{2}$ cups apple juice

1 tablespoon vanilla extract

Calories: 94

Total fat: 4 g

Protein: 3 g

Fiber: 1 g

Carbohydrates: 13 g

Cholesterol: 0 g

Sodium: 471 mg

Muffin Mania

The basic muffin recipe on page 288 incorporates my favorite healthy baking technique—using vanilla low-fat yogurt, soy yogurt, or applesauce as a base and fat substitute. It makes the muffins amazingly moist while greatly reducing the need for added fat.

Muffins are best eaten within a day or at most two after they are baked, so if you're not going to be feeding a crowd of hungry muffin fans, I suggest either freezing half of them or halving the recipe.

When young children are involved, I highly recommend making a dozen mini-muffins. They're a perfect size for smaller hands and appetites. There will be enough batter left over to make seven or eight regular-size muffins.

Making muffins is a fun kitchen project to do with children. Even the youngest of bakers will enjoy placing the liners in the muffin tins; older kids can help measure and mix some or all of the ingredients. Dolloping the batter into the muffin tins might get messy if younger children do it, but older kids can do it with a tablespoon (or a teaspoon for mini-muffins) and some patience.

The Vegetarian Family Cookbook

Zucchini-Raisin Muffins

DAIRY / VEGAN OPTION

Makes 12

These moist muffins make a great snack, and a welcome change of pace from sandwiches for school lunches.

1 Preheat the oven to 350° F. Place foil liners in 12 standard-size muffin cups.

2 Combine flour, wheat germ, baking powder, baking soda, cinnamon, and sugar in a mixing bowl and stir together.

3 Make a well in the center and pour in the yogurt, oil, and enough milk to make a smooth, slightly stiff batter. Stir until completely mixed, then stir in the zucchini, raisins, and walnuts, if using.

4 Divide the batter among the muffin cups. Bake 20 to 25 minutes, or until a knife inserted into the center of one tests clean.

5 Transfer to a plate or rack when cool enough to handle, and serve warm or at room temperature.

Variation

Add ½ to ¾ cup semi-sweet chocolate chips to the batter. Yes, zucchini and chocolate are surprisingly compatible!

Tip

This makes a nice quick bread. Pour batter into a lightly oiled 9-by-5-by-3-inch nonstick loaf pan and bake 40 to 45 minutes, or until a knife inserted into the center tests clean. Remove from pan and cool on a rack or platter to just warm before slicing.

1¾ cups whole-wheat pastry flour
¼ cup wheat germ or ground flaxseeds, or half of each
1½ teaspoons baking powder
½ teaspoon baking soda
½ teaspoon ground cinnamon
½ cup natural granulated sugar (see page 283)
1 cup vanilla low-fat yogurt, soy yogurt, or applesauce
2 tablespoons safflower oil
⅓ cup low-fat milk, rice milk, or soy milk, or as needed
1 cup firmly packed grated zucchini
¾ cup raisins, or other chopped dried fruit
⅓ cup chopped walnuts, optional

Dairy	Vegan option
Calories: 168	Calories: 161
Total fat: 3 g	Total fat: 3 g
Protein: 5 g	Protein: 4 g
Fiber: 3.2 g	Fiber: 3.2 g
Carbohydrates: 33 g	Carbohydrates: 32 g
Cholesterol: 1 g	Cholesterol: 0 g
Sodium: 81 mg	Sodium: 73 mg

Basic Muffins, Seven Ways

2 cups whole-wheat pastry flour

2 tablespoons wheat germ or ground flaxseeds

2 teaspoons baking powder

1 teaspoon baking soda

⅓ cup natural granulated sugar (see page 283)

1 cup low-fat vanilla yogurt or soy yogurt, or applesauce

2 tablespoons safflower oil

⅓ cup low-fat milk, rice milk, or soy milk, or as needed

Additional ingredients (see Variations)

1 Preheat the oven to 350° F. Place foil liners in 12 standard-size muffin cups.

2 Combine the flour, wheat germ, baking powder, baking soda, and sugar in a mixing bowl and stir together.

3 Make a well in the center and pour in the yogurt, oil, and enough milk to make a smooth, stiff batter. Stir together until thoroughly combined.

4 Stir in any additional ingredients, then divide the batter among the muffin cups.

5 Bake for 20 to 25 minutes, or until the tops are golden and a knife inserted into the center of one tests clean. When cool enough to handle, transfer the muffins to a plate or rack to cool. Serve warm or at room temperature.

Dairy	Vegan option
Calories: 133	Calories: 126
Total fat: 3 g	Total fat: 3 g
Protein: 4 g	Protein: 3 g
Fiber: 2.6 g	Fiber: 2.8 g
Carbohydrates: 24 g	Carbohydrates: 23 g
Cholesterol: 1 g	Cholesterol: 0 g
Sodium: 183 mg	Sodium: 175 mg

Variations

Here are a few simple suggestions for additions to the basic recipe. Be creative and see what ideas you can come up with!

- **Raisin or Raisin-Nut Muffins:** Add 1 cup raisins or ¾ cup raisins and ¼ to ½ cup finely chopped walnuts. If you'd like, add ½ teaspoon of ground cinnamon.
- **Berry Muffins:** Add 1 cup of fresh or frozen blueberries (small wild blueberries work particularly well in muffins), or 1 cup of very sweet chopped fresh strawberries, or the equivalent of drained, frozen strawberries.
- **Chocolate Chip Muffins:** Add ¾ to 1 cup of semisweet chocolate chips or mini chips.
- **Cocoa Muffins:** Add ¼ cup unsweetened dry cocoa. Add nuts and/or raisins or other dried fruit to these as well.
- **Pear and Golden Raisin or Dried Apricot Muffins:** Add ¼ cup each finely chopped ripe pear and golden raisins or dried apricots.
- **Dried Fruit or Fruit-Nut Muffins:** Add ⅔ cup finely chopped mixed dried fruits, such as apricots, dried apple, dates, mango, and papaya, and ¼ to ½ cup chopped walnuts or pecans.
- **Banana Muffins:** Add 1 medium chopped banana, and any or all of the following: ½ cup semisweet chocolate chips (preferably cane juice sweetened), ½ cup raisins, ⅓ cup chopped walnuts.

Flax Facts

As you glance through the recipes in this chapter, you'll notice that some provide an option for using ground flaxseeds. These tiny seeds are touted as a good egg substitute in baking because they become somewhat gummy when in contact with liquid. While this is true, it's not my primary aim in their use. It's more because baked goods are an ideal vehicle for this valuable source of healthy omega-3 fatty acids, which are otherwise challenging to obtain in vegetarian and vegan diets. Flax is also a good source of a type of soluble fiber that helps maintain ideal cholesterol levels. It provides omega-6 fatty acids and many essential minerals.

Until recently, it has been necessary to buy whole flaxseeds and grind them in a spice or coffee grinder to get their full benefits. Now, preground flaxseeds are available, making them handy to use not only in baked goods but for sprinkling over hot and cold cereals, salads, pasta, etc. Both flaxseeds and flax oil are highly perishable, so keep them refrigerated. Another way to reap flaxseeds' fatty acid benefits is by using the oil in salads or dressings (direct exposure to heat damages the nutrients). Just 1 teaspoon oil or 1½ tablespoons of ground seeds per day provide a good supplement to the healthy vegetarian or vegan diet.

Apple Muffins

DAIRY / VEGAN OPTION

Makes 12

These chewy muffins make a delightful change of pace treat for breakfast, served with yogurt, soy yogurt, or cottage cheese. In addition, if you pack a couple of these per person in lunch boxes, they provide a welcome respite from sandwiches.

1 Preheat the oven to 350° F. Place foil liners in 12 standard-size muffin cups.

2 Combine flour, wheat germ, baking powder, baking soda, sugar, cinnamon, and pumpkin pie spice, if using, in a mixing bowl and stir together.

3 Make a well in the center and add the applesauce, oil, and enough milk to make a smooth and slightly stiff batter. Stir until completely mixed. Stir in the apples, raisins, and walnuts, if using.

4 Divide the batter among the muffin cups. Bake 20 to 25 minutes, or until a knife inserted into the center of one tests clean.

5 Transfer to a plate or rack when cool enough to handle, and serve warm or at room temperature.

Tip
This makes a nice quick bread. Pour batter into a lightly oiled 9-by-5-by-3-inch nonstick loaf pan. Bake 40 to 45 minutes, or until a knife inserted into the center tests clean. Carefully remove bread from the pan, place on a rack or platter, and allow to cool until just warm before slicing.

$1^3/_4$ cups whole-wheat pastry flour
$1/_4$ cup wheat germ or ground flaxseeds, or half of each
2 teaspoons baking powder
$1/_2$ teaspoon baking soda
$1/_3$ cup natural granulated sugar (see page 283)
1 teaspoon ground cinnamon
$1/_2$ teaspoon pumpkin pie spice, optional
1 cup applesauce, vanilla low-fat yogurt, or soy yogurt
2 tablespoons safflower oil
$1/_3$ cup low-fat milk, rice milk, or soy milk
$1^1/_2$ cups finely diced peeled apple (about 2 medium)
$1/_2$ cup dark or golden raisins
$1/_4$ cup finely chopped walnuts, optional

Dairy	Vegan option
Calories: 152	Calories: 153
Total fat: 3 g	Total fat: 3 g
Protein: 3 g	Protein: 3 g
Fiber: 3.7 g	Fiber: 3.7 g
Carbohydrates: 30 g	Carbohydrates: 31 g
Cholesterol: 0 g	Cholesterol: 0 g
Sodium: 120 mg	Sodium: 119 mg

Cranberry-Orange Muffins

DAIRY / VEGAN OPTION

Makes 12

The flavors of orange and cranberry are most companionable in these moist muffins.

1 $\frac{3}{4}$ cups whole-wheat pastry flour
$\frac{1}{4}$ cup wheat germ or ground flaxseeds, or half of each
$\frac{1}{2}$ cup natural granulated sugar (see page 283)
1$\frac{1}{2}$ teaspoons baking powder
1 teaspoon baking soda
$\frac{1}{2}$ teaspoon ground ginger
1 cup orange, lemon, or vanilla low-fat yogurt or soy yogurt
$\frac{1}{4}$ cup undiluted thawed frozen orange juice concentrate
2 tablespoons safflower oil
$\frac{1}{4}$ cup reconstituted or freshly squeezed orange juice, or as needed
1 cup dried cranberries (see Note)
$\frac{1}{4}$ cup sliced almonds for topping

1 Preheat the oven to 350° F. Place foil liners in 12 muffin cups.

2 Combine flour, wheat germ, sugar, baking powder, baking soda, and ginger in a mixing bowl and stir together.

3 In another bowl, combine the yogurt, juice concentrate, oil, and reconstituted juice and whisk together until smooth. Make a well in the center of the dry ingredients and pour in the wet mixture. If the batter is too stiff, add a very small amount of additional orange juice. Stir together until completely mixed, then stir the cranberries into the batter.

4 Divide the batter evenly among the muffin cups. Scatter a few almonds over the top of each muffin. Bake for 20 to 25 minutes, or until the tops are golden and a small knife inserted into the center of one tests clean. Cool on a plate or rack and serve warm or at room temperature.

Note
By all means, use fresh cranberries when they are in season. Coarsely chop 8 ounces cranberries in a food processor, then combine in a bowl with 2 tablespoons natural granulated sugar. Let stand for 10 minutes before stirring into the batter.

Dairy	Vegan option
Calories: 171	Calories: 167
Total fat: 5 g	Total fat: 5 g
Protein: 5 g	Protein: 4 g
Fiber: 3.5 g	Fiber: 3.7 g
Carbohydrates: 29 g	Carbohydrates: 29 g
Cholesterol: 1 g	Cholesterol: 0 g
Sodium: 167 mg	Sodium: 158 mg

Jam-in-the-Middle Banana Muffins

DAIRY / VEGAN OPTION

Makes 12

Concealing a burst of all-fruit preserves in the center, these muffins will delight kids of all ages—including parents, who will appreciate the fact that they contain four different fruits or fruit derivatives. Use any type of all-fruit preserves—I've tried these with strawberry, peach, blueberry, and apricot, and they're all good! I usually make 6 muffins using one type of jam and the rest with another.

1 Preheat the oven to 350° F. Place foil liners in 12 muffin cups.

2 Combine flour, wheat germ, baking powder, baking soda, and sugar in a mixing bowl and stir together.

3 Make a well in the center and pour in the applesauce, oil, and enough milk to make a smooth and slightly stiff batter. Stir together until completely mixed, then stir in the bananas and raisins.

4 Fill muffin cups halfway with batter. Drop about 1 teaspoon all-fruit preserves in the center of each one, then divide the remaining batter to cover each cup.

5 Bake for 20 to 25 minutes, or until the tops are golden and a knife inserted into one tests clean. You'd normally test the center of the muffin, but with these, you'll have to veer off to the side a bit, or you'll hit the jam. When cool enough to handle, transfer to a plate or rack to cool. Serve warm or at room temperature.

2 cups whole-wheat pastry flour

2 tablespoons wheat germ or ground flaxseeds

2 teaspoons baking powder

1 teaspoon baking soda

$\frac{1}{2}$ cup natural granulated sugar (see page 283)

1 cup applesauce

2 tablespoons safflower oil

$\frac{1}{4}$ cup low-fat milk, rice milk, or soy milk, or as needed

1 large or 2 medium-small bananas, quartered lengthwise and sliced

$\frac{1}{2}$ cup golden or dark raisins

$\frac{1}{4}$ cup (approximately) all-fruit preserves

Dairy	Vegan option
Calories: 182	Calories: 182
Total fat: 3 g	Total fat: 3 g
Protein: 4 g	Protein: 3 g
Fiber: 3.5 g	Fiber: 3.5 g
Carbohydrates: 38 g	Carbohydrates: 39 g
Cholesterol: 0 g	Cholesterol: 0 g
Sodium: 172 mg	Sodium: 172 mg

Some Nifty Things About Baking with Kids

Though the recipes in this section aren't necessarily presented as "baking with kids" projects, most have components that can easily be accomplished by young hands. If you'd like to get your children involved and interested in the process of food preparation, I doubt you'll find anything more tempting to lure them to the kitchen than baking. Here are some of the perks of baking with your children:

- Baking can be a live demonstration of math concepts: "Measure three ½ cups of flour, because we need 1½ cups." "Let's divide this cake into nine equal squares." It's a good way to teach young kids to be aware of time: "This has to be in the oven for 20 minutes, so help me remember to take it out when the long hand is on the four." There's also a hint of chemistry to glean from watching wet and dry ingredients coalesce to become something completely new.

- Baking is an excellent way to introduce kids to simple preparation tasks. By the age of three, children can pour measured ingredients into bowls, open packages, sort ingredients, stir and mix with supervision, and place toppings where needed. From ages four and up they can help grease pans, knead and shape dough, slice soft foods like bananas, attempt to measure accurately, learn to use a rolling pin, cut shapes with cookie cutters, and roll dough into small balls.

- For older kids who have the interest, making baked goods on their own yields a great sense of accomplishment. And receiving the praise for the delicious results is the icing on the cake. My younger son was easily able to make many of these recipes on his own by the time he was ten. I stayed nearby to answer questions and to deal with the hot oven.

- Creating homemade baked goods is an instant spirit-lifter for all involved. When kids are involved with the process as well as the product, they get the gratification of working with their hands, and learn patience and perseverance. They gain an appreciation for the effort and artistry that goes into the preparation of food. When that lesson sinks in, they're far more likely to eat—and enjoy—something they've helped make.

Double Chocolate Oatmeal Cookies

VEGAN

Makes about 36

This delectable cookie is a treat for chocolate lovers.

1 Preheat the oven to 350° F. Lightly oil 2 baking sheets.

2 Combine flour, oats, baking powder, baking soda, sugar, cocoa powder, and flaxseeds if using, and stir together.

3 Make a well in the center and add the applesauce and oil. Stir together until the wet and dry ingredients are completely mixed. Add a bit more applesauce if needed to make a smooth and slightly stiff batter.

4 Stir in the chocolate chips and walnuts, if desired. Drop the batter onto the prepared sheets in slightly rounded tablespoonfuls about 1 inch apart. Bake for 10 to 12 minutes, or until the bottoms are just lightly browned. Let stand for 1 to 2 minutes, then carefully remove with a spatula to plates to cool.

Note
I usually make half the batch without walnuts, then add ¼ cup chopped walnuts to the remaining batter.

Variation
Substitute natural peanut butter chips for half of the chocolate chips.

1½ cups whole-wheat pastry flour
½ cup quick-cooking oats
1 teaspoon baking powder
½ teaspoon baking soda
½ cup natural granulated sugar (see page 283)
⅓ cup unsweetened cocoa powder
2 tablespoons ground flaxseeds, optional
1 cup applesauce
2 tablespoons safflower oil
1½ cups semisweet chocolate chips, preferably cane juice sweetened
½ cup chopped walnuts, optional (see Note)

Per cookie
Calories: 80
Total fat: 3 g
Protein: 1 g
Fiber: 1.2 g
Carbohydrates: 13 g
Cholesterol: 0 g
Sodium: 28 mg

Magic Chocolate Chip Cookies, Four Ways

VEGAN

Makes 36

2 cups whole-wheat pastry flour

1 teaspoon baking powder

½ teaspoon baking soda

½ cup natural granulated sugar (see page 283)

2 tablespoons ground flaxseeds, optional

1 cup applesauce

2 tablespoons safflower oil

Additional ingredients (see Variations)

These cookies use only a third of the sugar called for in most conventional cookie recipes, and butter is replaced with applesauce and just a smidgen of oil—that's the magic. From their smooth texture, you'd never think that these cookies are whole grain, made with whole-wheat pastry flour. I now make a batch weekly, as mandated by my sons, who think that store-bought cookies, even natural brands, pale beside these.

1 Preheat the oven to 350° F. Lightly oil 2 baking sheets.

2 Combine flour, baking powder, baking soda, sugar, and flaxseeds, if using, in a mixing bowl and stir together.

3 Make a well in the center and add the applesauce and oil. Stir together until the wet and dry ingredients are completely mixed, adding a bit more applesauce if needed to make a smooth and slightly stiff batter.

4 Stir in the additional ingredients. Drop the batter onto the prepared sheets in slightly rounded tablespoonfuls about 1 inch apart. Bake for 10 to 14 minutes, or until the bottoms are just lightly browned. Let stand for 1 to 2 minutes, then carefully remove with a spatula to a rack or plates to cool.

Variations

Choose one combination. The nutritional data are per 1 cookie.

- **Chocolate chip–walnut:** Add 1½ to 2 cups semisweet chocolate chips (preferably cane juice sweetened) and ½ cup chopped walnuts.

- **Chocolate chip–raisin:** Add 1½ to 2 cups semisweet chocolate chips (preferably cane juice sweetened) and ¾ cup dark raisins.

- **Chocolate chip–trail mix:** Add 1 cup chocolate chips and 1 to 1½ cups of your favorite trail mix (containing nuts, dried fruits, and seeds). This makes a robust cookie that really is great to take out on the hiking trail.

- **Chocolate chip–granola:** Add 1 cup chocolate chips and 1 to 1½ cups of good-quality granola for a crunchy cookie that's sure to delight both old and young hippies alike!

Per Cookie

Chocolate chip–walnut
Calories: 96
Total fat: 4 g
Protein: 2 g
Fiber: 1.1 g
Carbohydrates: 14 g
Cholesterol: 0 g
Sodium: 28 mg

Chocolate chip–raisin
Calories: 94
Total fat: 3 g
Protein: 1 g
Fiber: 1.2 g
Carbohydrates: 26 g
Cholesterol: 0 g
Sodium: 29 mg

Chocolate chip–trail mix
Calories: 93
Total fat: 3 g
Protein: 1 g
Fiber: 1.3 g
Carbohydrates: 16 g
Cholesterol: 0 g
Sodium: 31 mg

Chocolate chip–granola
Calories: 94
Total fat: 3 g
Protein: 2 g
Fiber: 1.4 g
Carbohydrates: 16 g
Cholesterol: 0 g
Sodium: 35 mg

Be Choosy About Chocolate

A few years ago, the food media burst forth with reports of studies claiming that chocolate may actually be good for us. Chocolate's chemical core contains myriad substances that raise the level of serotonins and endorphins (the body's feel-good and falling-in-love hormones); plus, its caffeine-like components contribute to quick energy bursts, perfect for athletic and intellectual effort. These studies even speculated that dark chocolate is good for heart health, and contains cancer-fighting antioxidants!

While these claims are generally accepted, it's still wise to be choosy about what kind you and your family consume. Encourage them to be connoisseurs of pure, fine dark chocolate instead of candy bars (yes, even vegetarians can succumb to the lure of candy bars, especially from those strategically placed machines), which are filled with white sugar and often partially hydrogenated fats. Natural foods stores are a great source for fine organic chocolates, including the brands Green and Black's, Newman's Own, and Rapunzel.

The same wisdom applies when choosing chocolate for baking. Natural foods stores, once again, are your source for more natural, and naturally sweetened, chocolate chips (cane juice instead of white sugar). Tropical Source makes excellent dairy-free baking chocolate. Their semisweet, peanut butter, and espresso chips are superb. Sunspire is one of the only easy-to-find sources of natural organic chocolate chips. The flavor is not the most chocolatey, but they are acceptable, particularly if you are adamant about using only organic ingredients. I often purchase organic chocolate chips in bulk from Jaffe Brothers (www.organicfruitsandnuts.com); they are sporadically unavailable, alas, but are wonderful for baking and for making homemade chocolates.

The brands mentioned here as well as most other organic chocolates are considered Fair Trade, which means that those who import and distribute them adhere to practices that do not force cocoa growers to accept substandard wages and working conditions.

Oatmeal-Raisin Cookies with Carrots or Apple

VEGAN

Makes about 30

A hint of carrot or tiny apple bits sets these soft, chewy cookies apart from the commonplace.

1 Preheat the oven to 350° F. Lightly oil 2 baking sheets.

2 Combine flour, oats, wheat germ, baking powder, baking soda, and sugar in a mixing bowl and stir together.

3 Make a well in the center and add the applesauce and oil. Stir together until the wet and dry ingredients are completely mixed. Add a bit more applesauce if needed, to make a smooth, slightly stiff batter.

4 Stir in the carrot and raisins. Drop the batter onto lightly oiled baking sheets in slightly rounded tablespoonfuls about 1 inch apart. Bake for 10 to 12 minutes, or until the bottoms are just lightly browned. Let stand for 1 or 2 minutes, then carefully remove with a spatula to plates to cool.

1½ cups whole-wheat pastry flour

1 cup quick-cooking oats

2 tablespoons wheat germ or ground flax seeds

1 teaspoon baking powder

½ teaspoon baking soda

⅓ cup natural granulated sugar (see page 283)

1 cup applesauce

2 tablespoons safflower oil

¼ cup firmly packed finely grated carrot, or ½ cup peeled and finely diced apple

1 cup raisins

⅓ cup chopped walnuts, optional

Per cookie

Calories: 67

Total fat: 1 g

Protein: 2 g

Fiber: 1.5 g

Carbohydrates: 13 g

Cholesterol: 0 g

Sodium: 35 mg

Graham Thumbprint Cookies

Though a number of steps are involved, this recipe is not at all difficult, and is in fact fun to make. It's the perfect rainy-day baking project to do with children.

4 graham crackers (regular, cinnamon, or honey flavored)

1½ cups whole-wheat pastry flour

½ cup natural granulated sugar (see page 283)

½ teaspoon baking soda

½ teaspoon baking powder

¼ teaspoon ground ginger

½ teaspoon ground cinnamon

2 tablespoons ground flaxseeds, optional

¾ cup applesauce

2 tablespoons safflower oil

¼ cup all-fruit preserves, or as needed (use one or two different flavors)

Per cookie

Calories: 63

Total fat: 1 g

Protein: 1 g

Fiber: 1.1 g

Carbohydrates: 12 g

Cholesterol: 0 g

Sodium: 42 mg

1   Place the graham crackers in a food processor fitted with the metal blade. Process until the crackers are finely ground crumbs. You need ½ cup of crumbs.

2   Combine the crumbs with the flour, sugar, baking soda, baking powder, ginger, cinnamon, and flaxseeds, if using, and stir together.

3   Make a well in the center and add the applesauce and oil. Stir together until completely mixed into a medium-soft dough. Add a bit more applesauce if needed. If time allows, cover the bowl with a piece of plastic wrap and refrigerate about 30 minutes.

4   Preheat the oven to 350° F. Lightly oil 2 baking sheets.

5   With well-floured hands, pinch off pieces of the dough to form 1-inch balls. Arrange them on the prepared sheets about 1 inch apart. Flatten slightly with your palm.

6 Bake for about 12 minutes, or until the cookies begin to turn golden, and remove from the oven. While the cookies are still warm, but not hot enough to burn, make a thumbprint in the center of each cookie, pushing the thumb down almost, but not quite, to the bottom of the cookie. Fill each hole with about ½ teaspoon of preserves.

7 Return the cookies to the oven for 2 minutes, then allow to cool for 1 or 2 minutes before carefully removing to plates to cool.

Note
Use more than one type of preserves to make a colorful assortment.

VEGAN

Makes 12 squares

¾ cup whole-wheat pastry flour

2 tablespoons wheat germ or flaxseeds

½ teaspoon baking soda

½ teaspoon ground cinnamon

½ cup applesauce

2 tablespoons safflower oil

¾ to 1 cup all-fruit preserves

⅓ cup quick-cooking oats

2 tablespoons finely ground almonds or walnuts

2 tablespoons natural granulated sugar (see page 283)

Calories: 141

Total fat: 3 g

Protein: 2 g

Fiber: 1.6 g

Carbohydrates: 27 g

Cholesterol: 0 g

Sodium: 62 mg

Jam Bars

Richly sweetened with all-fruit preserves, these bars are an enjoyable treat for kids and adults alike.

1 Preheat the oven to 350° F. Lightly oil a 9- by 9-inch baking pan.

2 Combine flour, wheat germ, baking soda, and cinnamon in a mixing bowl and stir together.

3 Make a well in the center and add the applesauce and 1 tablespoon of the oil. Stir together until the wet and dry ingredients are completely mixed. Add a bit more applesauce if needed to make a smooth, slightly stiff dough.

4 Spread the batter into the prepared pan with the help of a baking spatula. Use the spatula to carefully spread the preserves evenly over the batter.

5 Combine oats, nuts, sugar, and remaining oil; stir together well. Sprinkle evenly over the preserves, and pat down gently.

6 Bake for 25 to 30 minutes, or until the topping is golden. Allow to cool in the pan until just warm, then cut into 12 squares.

Soft and Chewy Granola Bars

My attempts to make crisp and chewy granola bars were only marginally successful; they tasted good, but getting them out of the baking pan required a sledgehammer, even when I used baking parchment. Here's the best of both worlds—chewy granola in a soft dough.

1 Preheat the oven to 350° F. Lightly oil a 9- by 9-inch baking pan.

2 Combine the flour, flaxseeds, baking soda, sugar, and salt in a mixing bowl and stir together.

3 Make a well in the center and pour in the applesauce and oil. Stir together until the wet and dry ingredients are completely mixed, then stir in the granola, raisins, and chips, if using. Add a bit more applesauce if needed, to make a smooth, slightly stiff dough.

4 Pour the batter into the prepared pan. Bake for 20 to 25 minutes, or until a knife inserted into the center tests clean. Let cool until just warm, then cut into 8 bars.

VEGAN

Makes 8 bars

¾ cup whole-wheat pastry flour
2 tablespoons ground flaxseeds or wheat germ
½ teaspoon baking soda
2 tablespoons natural granulated sugar (see page 283)
Pinch of salt
½ cup applesauce
1 tablespoon safflower oil
1 cup granola, purchased or homemade (pages 14–16)
½ cup raisins or currants
½ cup natural peanut butter chips or chocolate chips, preferably cane juice sweetened, optional

Calories: 175
Total fat: 6 g
Protein: 4 g
Fiber: 3.5 g
Carbohydrates: 29 g
Cholesterol: 0 g
Sodium: 105 mg

Easy Graham Cracker Crust

VEGAN

*Makes one 9-inch crust,
6 to 8 servings*

10 full-size natural graham crackers
¼ cup maple syrup

Calories: 55
Total fat: 1 g
Protein: 0 g
Fiber: 0.5 g
Carbohydrates: 12 g
Cholesterol: 0 g
Sodium: 42 mg

When it became difficult to find prepared graham cracker crusts made without trans-fats and white sugar, I had to come up with an alternative. This crust takes minutes to prepare and contains no added fat. I like to use whole-grain, organic graham crackers. It's suitable for baked or unbaked pies.

1 Place the graham crackers in a food processor. Process until the mixture resembles fine crumbs.

2 With the processor running, drizzle the maple syrup in through the feed tube and continue to process until the crumbs are lightly moistened.

3 Transfer the mixture to a lightly oiled 9-inch pie plate. Press evenly over the bottom and up the sides. Fill as desired and bake or chill.

Simple Oat Crust

VEGAN

Makes one 9-inch crust,
6 to 8 servings

This crust is as easy as it gets; just mix and press into a pie pan. This crust is suitable for baked pies.

1 Combine the oats and syrup in a mixing bowl. Stir together until the oats are evenly moistened.

2 Transfer the mixture to a lightly oiled 9-inch pie plate. Press evenly over the bottom and up the sides. Fill as desired and bake.

1¼ cups quick-cooking oats
¼ cup maple syrup

Calories: 85
Total fat: 1 g
Protein: 2 g
Fiber: 1.5 g
Carbohydrates: 17 g
Cholesterol: 0 g
Sodium: 2 mg

*Makes one 9-inch pie,
6 to 8 servings*

**2 cups well-baked and mashed butternut
squash or sugar pumpkin (see Notes)**
**¾ cup silken tofu (about half of a
12.3-ounce aseptic package)**
**½ cup natural granulated sugar
(see page 283)**
1 teaspoon ground cinnamon
**½ teaspoon pumpkin pie spice
(or ¼ teaspoon *each* ground nutmeg
and ground ginger)**
**One 9-inch good-quality graham cracker
or whole-grain pie crust, or 1 recipe
Easy Graham Cracker Crust (page 304)**

Calories: 176

Total fat: 2 g

Protein: 4 g

Fiber: 2.8 g

Carbohydrates: 39 g

Cholesterol: 0 g

Sodium: 64 mg

Not-Just-for-Thanksgiving Squash or Pumpkin Pie

I find that the smooth, sweet butternut purée tastes just as good as sugar pumpkin—perhaps even better! Once you've got the vegetable baked, which I do ahead of time, making this nourishing pie is a snap. It contains no eggs or dairy, but no one will notice the difference.

1 Preheat the oven to 350° F.

2 Combine the squash, tofu, sugar, cinnamon, and pumpkin pie spice in a food processor. Process until velvety smooth.

3 Pour the mixture into the crust. Bake for 40 to 45 minutes, or until set and the crust is golden. Let the pie cool to room temperature. Cut into wedges to serve.

Notes

- To bake butternut squash or sugar pumpkin, halve the vegetable (you need a really good knife to do so!) and scoop out the seeds and fibers. Place the halves cut side up in a foil-lined, shallow baking dish and cover tightly with more foil. Bake for 40 to 50 minutes, or until easily pierced with a knife. When cool enough to handle, scoop out the pulp and discard the skin. Use any leftover squash or pumpkin pulp for another purpose.
- If you want to make this in a hurry, you can use a 16-ounce can of puréed pumpkin—but it won't taste as good or as fresh!

VEGAN

Chocolate Tofu Banana "Cream" Pie

Makes one 9-inch pie,
6 to 8 servings

Silken tofu is a great base for pudding—it has just the right consistency, minus the bother of a flour-thickened sauce.

1 recipe Easy Graham Cracker Crust (page 304) or Simple Oat Crust (page 305)
Two 12.3-ounce aseptic packages silken tofu
1 cup semisweet chocolate chips, preferably cane juice sweetened
⅓ cup pure maple syrup, or to taste
2 medium bananas, thinly sliced

1 Preheat the oven to 350° F. Prepare the pie crust.

2 Purée the tofu in a food processor or blender until completely smooth. Transfer to a small saucepan and add the chocolate chips. Cook over medium-low heat, stirring often, until the chocolate chips have melted. Stir in the maple syrup.

3 Pour the mixture into the crust and bake for 25 to 30 minutes, or until the top of the pudding feels fairly firm to the touch. Allow to cool completely, then refrigerate for at least 1 hour, preferably 2 hours.

4 Just before serving, cover the top of the pie with banana slices arranged in concentric, slightly overlapping circles, then cut into wedges to serve.

Calories: 308
Total fat: 10 g
Protein: 9 g
Fiber: 2.5 g
Carbohydrates: 47 g
Cholesterol: 0 g
Sodium: 77 mg

Variation
Forget about the pie—simply follow step 2 to make a delicious chocolate pudding. After cooking, transfer to individual bowls and refrigerate until cooled to your liking.

Guilt-Free Chocolate Brownie Cake

The classic comfort dessert is brought up to date by replacing the butter with vanilla low-fat yogurt and just a little oil. This is my sons' most frequently requested birthday cake, but we don't always wait for special occasions to enjoy it.

1 Preheat the oven to 350° F. Lightly oil a 9- by 9-inch baking pan.

2 Combine the flour, sugar, cocoa powder, baking soda, salt, and flaxseeds, if using, in a mixing bowl and stir together.

3 Make a well in the center and pour in the yogurt, oil, vanilla, and enough milk to make a smooth and slightly stiff batter. Stir until completely mixed, then stir in the chocolate chips.

4 Pour into the prepared pan. Bake for 30 to 35 minutes, or until the sides of the cake begin to pull away from the pan, and a knife inserted in the middle comes out clean (with the exception of the melted chocolate chips). Allow to cool in the pan until just warm, then cut into squares to serve.

DAIRY / VEGAN OPTION

Makes 12 or 16 squares

1$\frac{1}{2}$ cups whole-wheat pastry flour
$\frac{1}{2}$ cup natural granulated sugar (see page 283)
$\frac{1}{3}$ cup unsweetened cocoa powder
$\frac{1}{2}$ teaspoon baking soda
$\frac{1}{4}$ teaspoon salt
2 tablespoons ground flaxseeds, optional
1 cup vanilla low-fat yogurt or soy yogurt
2 tablespoons safflower oil
1 teaspoon vanilla extract
$\frac{1}{4}$ cup low-fat milk, rice milk, or soy milk, or as needed
$\frac{1}{2}$ cup chocolate chips, preferably cane juice sweetened

Dairy	Vegan option
Calories: 141	Calories: 135
Total fat: 4 g	Total fat: 4 g
Protein: 3 g	Protein: 3 g
Fiber: 2.3 g	Fiber: 2.5 g
Carbohydrates: 24 g	Carbohydrates: 23 g
Cholesterol: 1 g	Cholesterol: 0 g
Sodium: 98 mg	Sodium: 91 mg

Chocolate Chip-
Apricot Blondies

Here's a fruity variation on brownies that my family likes just as much as the all-chocolate version.

1½ cups whole-wheat pastry flour

1 teaspoon baking powder

½ teaspoon baking soda

Pinch of ground nutmeg

2 tablespoons ground flaxseeds, optional

¾ cup vanilla low-fat yogurt or soy yogurt

¼ cup maple syrup or rice syrup

2 tablespoons safflower oil

¼ cup low-fat milk, rice milk, or soy milk, or as needed

¾ cup finely diced dried apricots

¾ cup semisweet chocolate chips, preferably cane juice sweetened

¼ cup finely chopped walnuts, optional

1 Preheat the oven to 350° F. Lightly oil a 9- by 9-inch baking pan.

2 In a mixing bowl, combine the flour, baking powder, baking soda, nutmeg, and flaxseeds, if using, and stir together.

3 Make a well in the center and pour in the yogurt, syrup, oil, and enough milk to make a smooth and slightly stiff batter. Stir until completely mixed. Stir in the apricots, chocolate chips, and walnuts, if desired.

4 Transfer the mixture to the prepared pan. Bake for 25 to 30 minutes, or until the top is golden brown and a knife inserted into the center tests clean (with the exception of the melted chocolate chips). Allow to cool in the pan until just warm, then cut into squares to serve.

Dairy	Vegan option
Calories: 159	Calories: 155
Total fat: 5 g	Total fat: 5 g
Protein: 3 g	Protein: 3 g
Fiber: 2.6 g	Fiber: 2.7 g
Carbohydrates: 26 g	Carbohydrates: 25 g
Cholesterol: 1 g	Cholesterol: 0 g
Sodium: 84 mg	Sodium: 78 mg

Fruit Crumbles of All Sorts

Fruit crumbles are a wonderful way to highlight fresh fruit. With an easy-to-prepare oat and wheat germ topping, they are as healthful as they are delicious.

1 Preheat the oven to 350° F. Lightly oil a 9- by 9-inch baking pan or 9-inch pie pan. Prepare the fruit of your choice, set aside.

2 Combine the oats, walnuts, wheat germ, sugar, and cinnamon in a small bowl. Drizzle in the oil and stir until the dry ingredients are evenly moistened.

3 Pour the prepared fruit into the prepared pan and pat in evenly. Sprinkle the topping evenly over the fruit.

4 Bake for 30 to 35 minutes, or until the topping is golden and turning crisp. Allow to cool until just warm, then serve on its own or topped with a dollop of frozen yogurt, if desired.

VEGAN

6 servings

Prepared fruit (see Variations, page 313)
⅓ cup quick-cooking oats
⅓ cup finely chopped or ground walnuts
⅓ cup wheat germ
2 tablespoons natural granulated sugar (see page 283)
Pinch of ground cinnamon
1½ tablespoons safflower oil
Vanilla frozen yogurt or nondairy frozen dessert, optional

Batter only
Calories: 126
Total fat: 8 g
Protein: 3 g
Fiber: 1.6 g
Carbohydrates: 11 g
Cholesterol: 0 g
Sodium: 2 mg

Fruit Cobblers of All Sorts

Using ripe, sweet seasonal fruits, you can create luscious cobblers all year round.

Prepared fruit (see Variations)
1 cup whole-wheat pastry flour
⅓ cup natural granulated sugar (see page 283)
1 teaspoon baking powder
½ teaspoon baking soda
2 tablespoons ground flaxseeds, optional
⅔ cup applesauce, or vanilla low-fat yogurt or soy yogurt
1 tablespoon safflower oil
2 tablespoons low-fat milk, rice milk, or soy milk, or as needed
¼ cup finely chopped walnuts, optional
Vanilla frozen yogurt or nondairy frozen dessert, optional

1 Preheat the oven to 350° F. Lightly oil a 9- by 9-inch baking pan. Prepare the fruit of your choice, set aside.

2 Combine the flour, sugar, baking powder, baking soda, and flaxseeds, if using, and stir together.

3 Make a well in the center and stir in the applesauce, oil, and enough milk to make a smooth and slightly stiff batter. Stir until completely mixed.

4 Pour the prepared fruit into the prepared pan and pat in evenly. Scatter the walnuts over top, if desired. Pour the batter over the fruit and pat in evenly with the help of a baking spatula.

5 Bake for 25 to 30 minutes, or until golden. Allow to cool until just warm, then serve on its own or topped with a dollop of frozen yogurt, if desired.

Batter only
Calories: 143
Total fat: 3 g
Protein: 3 g
Fiber: 2.8 g
Carbohydrates: 29 g
Cholesterol: 0 g
Sodium: 169 mg

Variations

Nutritional data are per serving for fruit filling only.

- **Apples and/or pears:** Combine 4 to 5 cups peeled, thinly sliced apples or pears (or combine the two fruits in one dessert—they are delicious together!) with ¼ cup maple syrup, ¼ teaspoon ground cinnamon, and a pinch of nutmeg.

- **Blueberries or blackberries:** Toss 1 pint (2 to 2½ cups) berries with 1 to 2 tablespoons natural granulated sugar (see page 283).

- **Peaches or nectarines:** Combine 4 to 5 cups thinly sliced peaches or nectarines with 2 tablespoons natural granulated sugar (see page 283) or maple syrup.

Apples and/or pears

Calories: 84

Total fat: 0 g

Protein: 0 g

Fiber: 2.2 g

Carbohydrates: 22 g

Cholesterol: 0 g

Sodium: 1 mg

Blueberries or blackberries

Calories: 46

Total fat: 0 g

Protein: 0 g

Fiber: 1.5 g

Carbohydrates: 12 g

Cholesterol: 0 g

Sodium: 3 mg

Peaches or nectarines

Calories: 47

Total fat: 0 g

Protein: 1 g

Fiber: 1.4 g

Carbohydrates: 12 g

Cholesterol: 0 g

Sodium: 0 mg

Barley Malt Syrup: Dark, sticky, and boldly flavored, barley malt syrup is neither as assertive as blackstrap molasses nor as sweet as honey. Primarily maltose, a complex sugar that enters the bloodstream slowly, barley malt syrup offers trace amounts of B vitamins and several minerals. It's a good addition to squash and pumpkin breads, bran muffins, and hearty rye or pumpernickel breads. Use it to glaze sweet potatoes and to make winter "malteds" combined with bananas and soy milk.

Brown Rice Syrup: A traditional Asian sweetener, brown rice syrup is made from rice starch converted into maltose, a complex sugar. Rice syrup is the mildest-flavored of the liquid sweeteners and contains trace amounts of B vitamins and minerals. Use it interchangeably with honey in cooking and baking, to sweeten hot or cold beverages and cereals, or as a spread for fresh breads.

Honey: Natural foods stores offer ways to explore this venerable sweetener beyond the common clover variety, from mild alfalfa honey, to more complex-flavored wildflower honeys, to strong, dark buckwheat honey. Since honey is primarily glucose, a simple sugar, there's little agreement about whether it's much better for us than sugar. Some say that it's harder on the teeth, and vegans avoid it altogether as an insect-derived product. Honey does contain trace amounts of some B vitamins and many minerals. The darker the honey, the more nutrients it contains. About $\frac{1}{2}$ cup honey equals the sweetness of 1 cup of sugar. Use it as a general-purpose sweetener for hot beverages, in smoothies, and for cooking and baking. In baking, reduce the amount of liquid called for, and lower the oven temperature by 25° F.

Maple Syrup: While this well-loved sweetener is mainly sucrose, a simple sugar, it does contain several trace minerals, including small but measurable amounts of calcium and iron. Avoid imitation maple syrups; look for ones labeled pure and graded Fancy, Grade A, or Grade B. Apart from its favored use as a topping for pancakes, maple syrup adds a delectably mellow sweetness to baked goods and puddings.

Molasses: Long prized in southern American cookery, molasses is arguably the most nutritious of natural sweeteners. Look for organic unsulfured molasses, derived from sugar cane, for optimal quality. Molasses is rich in iron and vitamin B_6 and also provides calcium and potassium. Use molasses in making rye or pumpernickel breads, in sweet potato dishes, and to make robust barbecue sauces. Barbados molasses is a close relative of blackstrap; it is somewhat lighter in color and gentler in flavor.

Appendix:

General Nutritional

Information, Books, and

Web Resources to Explore

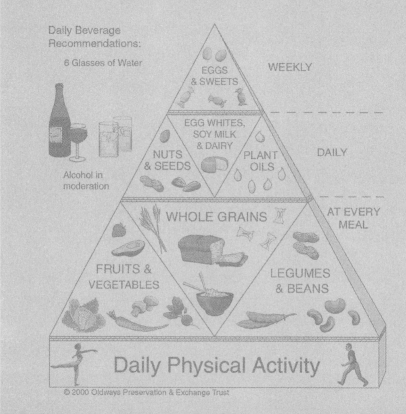

Daily Beverage Recommendations:

6 Glasses of Water

Alcohol in moderation

EGGS & SWEETS — WEEKLY

EGG WHITES, SOY MILK & DAIRY

NUTS & SEEDS

PLANT OILS — DAILY

WHOLE GRAINS — AT EVERY MEAL

FRUITS & VEGETABLES

LEGUMES & BEANS

Daily Physical Activity

© 2000 Oldways Preservation & Exchange Trust

Nutritional Glossary for Vegetarian and Vegan Diets

Amino acids: An amino acid is a building block of protein. There are some 20 amino acids required to make a complete protein. The body can manufacture all but 8; these are referred to as the indispensable (formerly referred to as "essential") amino acids. With a balanced, varied diet, proteins complement themselves during the course of a day; no need to worry over combining just the right amino acids at every meal. Eating a variety of plant proteins ensures that all indispensable amino acid needs are met.

Calories: A calorie is a unit of energy measured in terms of heat. Food contains calories that, when burned (more precisely, metabolized), produce a specific amount of energy. If more calories are taken in than burned off, they are stored as fat, resulting in weight gain.

Carbohydrates: Along with fat and protein, carbohydrates are chemical compounds known as the large nutrients. Carbohydrates are the body's ideal fuel source. Starches, sugars, and fiber are all carbohydrates. Foods referred to as complex carbohydrates contain starch, the main form of carbohydrate energy, and fiber, the parts of plant foods that pass through the body undigested. Complex carbohydrates are important energy sources, since they are broken down and used slowly by the body. Here are some examples of the different types of carbohydrates: *Starches* are best consumed as complex carbohydrates. These include whole grains and cereals (brown rice, barley, and other whole grains, whole-grain breads, and whole-grain pastas), and root vegetables (including sweet and white potatoes). These provide the dual benefit of providing energy as well as dietary fiber. *Sugars* are found in fruit, dairy products, and refined sugar, among other foods. *Refined sugars* are the least desirable, as they provide mainly empty calories and contribute to tooth decay.

Cholesterol: This chemical compound is actually of great importance to several functions of the internal organs and is a part of every cell. The problem lies in that the liver can manufacture all the cholesterol the body needs for its essential functions; when excessive cholesterol is ingested in the form of food, it causes a build up of plaque in the arteries, which is said to lead to heart disease. Foods high in cholesterol are eggs, fatty meats, butter, and full-fat dairy products.

Enriched: When whole grains are refined of their nutritious bran and germ, they are then usually enriched with specific added nutrients as established by federal guidelines. The nutrients added back are iron and some of the B vitamins: thiamin, niacin, riboflavin, and folic acid. Still, enriched white products like bread, rice, and pasta are less beneficial than their whole-grain versions. They are low in fiber and have less magnesium, zinc, vitamin B_2, vitamin E, and chromium than whole-grain products.

Fat: Fat is an organic compound of fatty acids and is one of the three large nutrients, along with carbohydrates and protein. It provides a very concentrated source of stored energy for the body and is necessary for hormonal function and

 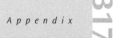

tissue health. The average American's fat intake has until recently been about 40 percent of total calorie intake. Though it is often recommended that this be cut down to 30 percent, some nutritionists feel this amount is still too high.

Fats are composed of fatty acids, like linoleic and linolenic, which can both be derived from plant sources. There are three types of dietary fat—saturated, polyunsaturated, and monounsaturated. Saturated fat, found in meat, butter, and hard cheeses, is considered the least beneficial and, in fact, can lead to heart disease if consumed in large quantities. Polyunsaturated and monounsaturated fats are plentiful in plant sources. Nuts, olives and olive oil, certain vegetable oils, and avocado are good sources of beneficial fats. The good fats are necessary to maintain good health. They help absorb the fat-soluble vitamins (A, D, E, and K) and are beneficial for the skin, hair, cells, and capillaries. Trans-fats, or hydrogenated fats, are laboratory produced and are found in many processed foods. These are completely unhealthy and unnecessary and should be avoided.

Fiber: This is actually a general term for a family of plant substances including pectin, cellulose, lignin, hemicellulose, gums, and mucilage. These are the parts of plants that pass through the body undigested, adding the bulk that is crucial for the regulation of the digestive system. Fiber is concentrated in the bran of grains, skins of certain fruits, filaments found in the flesh of vegetables, and so on. This valuable substance is considered crucial to health, especially that of the digestive system. Fiber fills the stomach and small intestine, absorbing water and slowing down digestion enough to prolong the feeling of fullness. Cultures that traditionally enjoy high-fiber diets rarely suffer from constipation or hemorrhoids and are less likely to develop colon cancer. High-fiber foods include whole grains, legumes, nuts and seeds, fruits and vegetables. Between 25 and 35 grams of fiber a day is considered a diet high in fiber.

Lactose: Lactose is milk sugar, the component of milk that is indigestible to many adults and some children. To digest lactose, the body must be able to produce an enzyme that converts the lactose to glucose and galactose. Products like yogurt contain bacterial cultures that convert most of the lactose to glucose and galactose, making them more digestible (though not always completely appropriate for those who are lactose intolerant).

Minerals: These elemental substances are essential nutrients needed to regulate many bodily functions. Two types of minerals are used: the major minerals and the trace minerals. Both are vital, but the distinction lies in the amounts present in the body. Following are descriptions of some of the most important minerals:

* **Calcium** is best known for its role in the formation and maintenance of bones and teeth. It also assists in muscle contraction, blood clotting, and nerve function. Some good sources are low-fat dairy products (though there is a growing question as to whether dairy calcium is the optimal source of absorbable calcium for the body); tofu (especially if prepared with calcium sulfate); sesame seeds; almonds; dark green leafy vegetables; fortified foods like soy milk and some fruit juices; and some soy, almond, and rice cheeses (check labels).

* **Iron** is important for production of hemoglobin, a blood protein that carries oxygen. Some good sources are tofu, legumes (including peas and lentils), sunflower seeds, pumpkin seeds, some soy-based meat substitutes, enriched

cereals, whole grains, oats, cream of wheat, dried fruits, and blackstrap molasses. Simultaneous intake of vitamin C–rich foods helps with the absorption of iron.

- **Magnesium** is needed for strong bones and teeth, building protein, muscle contraction, and nerve function. Some good sources are nuts, grains, legumes, dark green vegetables, and soy foods.

- **Phosphorus** plays an essential role in cell functions and the activation of enzymes. Some good sources are dairy products, eggs, legumes, nuts, and grains.

- **Potassium** helps maintain fluid balance, is important for cell and nerve function, and supports muscle contraction, including heartbeat. It is a mineral common to many foods; there is little danger of deficiency. Some good sources are dried and fresh fruits, particularly bananas and oranges; and many vegetables, notably potatoes, seeds, and wheat germ.

- **Zinc** is needed for the production of new cells and is important for enzyme functions, taste perception, and wound healing. Some good sources are whole grains, particularly wheat germ, fortified cereals, beans, nuts and seeds, and dairy products.

Protein: Along with carbohydrates and fats, protein is one of the three large nutrients. Protein is an essential factor in the building and maintenance of all bodily tissues and in the formation of enzymes and hormones. It's composed of some 22 amino acids, 9 of which the body cannot manufacture and which must be obtained from food. A persistent myth about vegetarian diets is that they don't provide adequate protein. Nutritional wisdom dictates, however, that if the diet is varied and provides sufficient calories, there is little chance that protein supply could be inadequate. Contrary to popular opinion, protein is not hard to get in a vegetarian or even a vegan diet, since all foods, with the exception of sugars and oils, have at least some protein. Vital as protein is, it has recently been accepted that more protein is not necessarily better. Protein is also not the body's ideal source of energy—it comes in third after carbohydrates and fats. Dairy products and eggs are, of course, high in protein, but some good plant-based protein sources are beans and legumes, grains, nuts and seeds, soy products, and certain vegetables. For more on protein, see pages 321–22.

Vitamins: Vitamins are complex organic compounds, essential in minute quantities to assist the metabolic functions of the body. Here are some of the most common vitamins and what they do for you:

- **Vitamin A** is important to vision, for the maintenance of healthy skin and mucous membranes, and for resistance to infectious diseases. Some good sources are dark green vegetables and deep yellow vegetables and fruits (such as squashes, carrots, apricots, and peaches).
- **B Vitamins** (with the exception of B_{12}) are generally found in plentiful quantity in whole grains and cereals, wheat germ, yeasts, nuts and seeds, beans, and some green vegetables.

Vitamin B$_1$ (thiamin) assists in functions of the nervous system and supports normal appetite. Some good sources are legumes, whole or enriched grain foods, orange juice, peas, seeds, wheat germ, and nutritional yeast.

Vitamin B$_2$ (riboflavin) is important in cell functions, enzyme functions, and to support normal vision and skin health. Some good sources are dairy products, eggs, whole or enriched grain foods, spinach, soybeans, almonds, and wheat germ.

Vitamin B$_3$ (Niacin), aids in metabolism and supports the health of the nervous and digestive systems. Some good sources are legumes, nuts, mushrooms, and whole or enriched grains.

Vitamin B$_6$ (pyridoxine) is also important in metabolism and helps make red blood cells. It also promotes healthy skin. Some good sources are seeds, whole grains, bananas, tomatoes, orange juice, and some sea vegetables.

Vitamin B$_{12}$ is essential for general growth and for the functions of the blood cells and nervous system. Eggs and dairy products are reliable sources. Apart from tempeh and some sea vegetables (which are not considered reliable sources) B$_{12}$ is not found in plant sources, and so vegans are advised to make sure to use fortified soy milk, fortified meat analogs, fortified breakfast cereals, or vegetarian vitamin supplements. Red Star Vegetarian Support Formula nutritional yeast is an additional source.

Folate helps the body produce new cells. Good sources include leafy green vegetables, oranges, cantaloupe, and legumes.

- **Vitamin C** is vital in forming collagen, which binds the body's cells, and is also needed for the health of the tissues. Vitamin C is also thought to be of benefit to wound healing and resistance to infection. Some good sources are citrus fruits, melons, dark green vegetables, tomatoes, bell peppers, strawberries, and papaya.

- **Vitamin D** is needed to absorb calcium and phosphorus, which are crucial to the formation and maintenance of bones and teeth. Some good sources are fortified milk or soy milk and egg yolks. It can be produced by the body following sunlight exposure. If your diet is in short supply of vitamin D foods or sunlight exposure, make sure to supplement.

- **Vitamin E** is important in the functions of the blood cells and muscles. It also protects against oxidative damage (hence the term "antioxidant"). Vitamin E–rich foods include avocado, wheat germ, oats, sweet potato, soybeans, nuts, sunflower seeds, sesame seeds, and vegetable oils.

Protein in a Plant-Based Diet

Not long ago, the word *protein* would likely have conjured an image of a thick steak. But in these fat- and cholesterol-conscious times, informed eaters are learning that protein comes in varied forms, many from the plant world: Aromatic grain and nut pilafs, tofu stir-fries, whole-grain pancakes, and bean enchiladas are just a few examples. The coming-of-age of vegetarian cookery and the proliferation of ethnic cuisines have stretched the definition of protein sources.

As more Americans cut back on their intake of meat and high-fat dairy products, incorporating alternative protein sources into the diet is becoming more commonplace. Even if you have no intention of going vegan, or even vegetarian for that matter, the ideal to strive for is a diet rich in plant-based foods, with those being the primary protein sources. Many nutritionists recommend that at least two thirds of dietary protein be derived from plant-based foods, no matter what diet or lifestyle you follow.

Whole grains, legumes, soy products, and nuts and seeds are primary protein sources in a plant-based diet. And nearly all vegetables contribute to daily protein needs. Dairy products can also be good sources of non-plant-based proteins for those who choose to use them, with the best choices being organic low-fat versions of milk, yogurt, and cottage cheese. Hard cheeses, butter, and other full-fat dairy products pose health risks similar to meats. Those and all animal proteins, including eggs, should be used with care and moderation.

How Much Protein?

All basic tissues of the human body are composed of protein, including the skin, muscles, tendons and cartilage, even hair and nails. New protein is needed to form enzymes, hormones, and antibodies; replace old cells; build new tissues; and transport nutrients in and out of cells.

The body can manufacture all but 8 of the 20 amino acids that make up proteins. These 8 amino acids are referred to as indispensable (formerly known as "essential") amino acids and must be derived from food. That's why getting sufficient good-quality protein is crucial.

Past generations of vegetarians heard much about "protein complementarity." Currently this notion is considered passé. While complementarity is essential to form usable proteins, complementary foods need not necessarily be combined in the same meal. Amino acids that don't form a complete protein survive in the body for 12 hours. Eating a variety of foods throughout the day ensures proteins from plant-based foods will be completed by those in other foods.

The operative word when it comes to protein is *sufficient*. More is not better. Excess protein can't be stored, and its elimination puts a strain on the kidneys. Too-high protein consumption is linked to kidney disease; cancers of the colon, breast, and kidney; and even osteoporosis. The World Health Organization's *Technical Report 797* states: "There are no known advantages from increasing the proportion of energy derived from protein (15 percent of total calories) and high intakes may have harmful effects in promoting excessive losses of body calcium and perhaps in accelerating age-related decline in renal (kidney) function."

How much, then, is just enough? The Recommended Daily Allowance (RDA), established by the National Academy of Sciences, calculates that an adult in good health needs 0.36 gram of protein per pound of body weight. Thus a 160-pound man needs about 58 grams of protein a day, and a 120-pound woman needs about 43 grams. To put this into perspective, here's how a 120-pound woman could fulfill her daily requirement. For breakfast, she has 1 cup of yogurt with fruit and a slice of whole-wheat bread. In her salad at lunch, she includes ½ cup of chickpeas and a sprinkling of sunflower seeds. A between-meal snack is a bagel with hummus or almond butter. Her main dish at dinner is a generous portion of cooked spaghetti tossed with 1 cup broccoli and 4 ounces of tofu.

Some notable exceptions to the RDA guidelines: Pregnant and lactating women need considerably more protein—add 25 grams of protein per day. Infants and children need more total protein per body pound than adults. For toddlers ages one through three years, calculate 0.5 gram per pound of body weight; children four through thirteen years, 0.43 gram per pound, and teens, 0.39 gram per pound.

Exploring a Vegan Diet

According to Brenda Davis, R.D., and Vesanto Melina, M.S., R.D., authors of *Becoming Vegan,* "The vast majority of studies assessing the dietary intakes and nutritional status of vegans reassure us that well-planned vegan diets can supply adequate nutrition . . . It is important to recognize, however, that as with nonvegetarian or lacto-ovo vegetarian diets, vegan diets can be both adequate and inadequate." The most important first step in going vegan is to seek reliable information, read, and learn.

- Good books to start with are *Becoming Vegan: The Complete Guide to Adopting a Healthy Plant-Based Diet* by Brenda David and Vesanto Melina (Book Publishing Company, 2000) and *Simply Vegan* by Debra Wasserman and Reed Mangels (Vegetarian Resource Group, 1999).

- The Vegetarian Resource Group's Web site (www.vrg.org) is one of the Web's premier destinations for all things vegan, including articles on nutritional needs from infancy to adulthood. Request their brochure *Vegan Diets in a Nutshell,* which encapsulates ways to obtain protein, calcium, zinc, iron, and vitamins D and B_{12}. Becoming a member of the group includes a subscription to *Vegetarian Journal,* a quarterly publication of nutrition, ethics, and recipes with a primarily vegan slant.

- For tips on raising vegan children, look for the *Vegetarian Baby and Child* supplement in *VegNews* (for subscription information, go to www.vegnews.com). VegFamily (www.vegfamily.com) is an excellent Web resource dedicated to supporting vegan families, including product reviews, expert Q&As, personal stories, and more. This site is hosted by Erin Pavlina, who is also the author of *Raising Vegan Children in a Non-Vegan World* (VegFamily, 2003).

- Explore large natural foods stores and well-stocked supermarkets to learn about products suited to the vegan diet. The "soy dairy" is often side by side with conventional dairy products and there you'll find soy milk, cheeses, cream cheese, and even coffee creamer. Soy isn't the only way to replace dairy; explore rice- and almond-based milks and cheeses as well. Butter is easily replaced with nonhydrogenated margarine. Try making your favorite recipes using some of these vegan substitutes.

- The best way to go vegan is gradually. If that's your goal, segue gently from a lacto-ovo vegetarian diet. Many people give up eggs first, then milk. Cheese is often the last to go. Eat only plant-based foods once a week at first to see how you—and your palate—react. If it suits you, add another plant-based day per week for a while, then make the complete switch when you feel ready.

Useful Books and Publications

For all the information you need on beginning or maintaining a healthy vegetarian or vegan diet, my favorite sources are *Becoming Vegetarian: The Complete Guide to Adopting a Healthy Vegetarian Diet* by Vesanto Melina, Brenda Davis, and Victoria Harrison (Book Publishing Company, 1995) and *Becoming Vegan: The Complete Guide to Adopting a Healthy Plant-Based Diet* by Brenda Davis and Vesanto Melina (Book Publishing Company, 2000). Here are a few other good resources for the how-to's of raising healthy children.

Raising Vegetarian Children: A Guide to Good Healthy and Family Harmony by Vesanto Melina and Joanne Stepaniak (McGraw-Hill, 2002). The co-author of *Becoming Vegetarian* and *Becoming Vegan* teams up with vegan expert Stepaniak for an up-to-date guide for families.

Healthy Food for Healthy Kids: A Practical and Tasty Guide to Your Child's Nutrition by Bridget Swinney (Meadowbrook Press, 1999). Not entirely vegetarian, but very well done, put forth in a clear and friendly manner.

A Teen's Guide to Going Vegetarian by Judy Krizmanic (Puffin Books, 1994). Though it has been around for a while, this is still the book I recommend first to teens wanting to gain their knowledge firsthand.

The Family Nutrition Book: Everything You Need to Know About Feeding Your Children from Birth Through Adolescence, by William Sears and Martha Sears (Little, Brown, 1999). The Searses obviously love children, their own and others', and give sound, caring information.

Healthy Cooking for Kids: Building Blocks for a Lifetime of Good Nutrition by Shelly Null (St. Martin's Press, 1999). Interesting vegan recipes with a plethora of nutritional information specifically geared toward feeding children.

Raising Vegan Children in a Non-Vegan World: A Complete Guide for Parents by Erin Pavlina (VegFamily, 2003). The first-ever guide on raising vegan children, including plenty of social and ethical information.

Making Your Own Nondairy Cheeses

If you would like to try your hand at making your own cheeselike foods at home, here are two good resources:

The Uncheese Cookbook: Creating Amazing Dairy-Free Cheese Substitutes and Classic "Uncheese" Dishes by Joanne Stepaniak (Book Publishing Company, 1994).

The Wild Vegetarian Cookbook by "Wildman" Steve Brill (Harvard Common Press, 2002).

Web Sites of Interest

Needless to say, Web resources on food and nutrition are vast, and so the following list represents only a sampling of sites that address the issues of food and nutrition for children, teens, and families. Most of those listed are primarily dedicated to vegetarian and vegan diets, though some address the topic of healthy eating for kids and families in a more general venue.

All4Vegan

www.all4vegan.net

This site provides medical, ethical, and environmental facts, plus links to help make being a vegetarian an easy transition for both you and your family.

American Dietetic Association

www.eatright.org

This well-respected organization's site offers a position paper on vegetarian nutrition. Fact sheets on vegetarian and vegan nutrition are available from the Vegetarian Nutrition Dietetic Practice Group (a part of the ADA) at www.vegetariannutrition.net.

CyberParent

www.cyberparent.com

Although not a vegetarian site, it offers a helpful article on how to get your children to eat more vegetables. It may be worth a try if you have a picky eater. It also has tips on how to convert your child to a vegetarian diet and a page on vegetarian teens.

Dole 5 a Day

www.dole5aday.com

Home of the famous 5-a-day campaign, this site helps teach the importance of eating five fruits and vegetables every day and provides recipes and games for kids to try.

Healthwell

www.healthwell.com

Here you'll find information on the nutrients children need, including special information on vegetarian children.

Healthy Habits

www.rileyforkids.org/healthyhabits/nutrition/index.html

This site breaks down the nutritional needs of kids from grade school to teenagers. It also offers nutritional information for parents and professionals.

In a Vegetarian Kitchen

www.vegkitchen.com

My own Web site! You'll find dozens of easy-to-follow recipes, vegetarian tips, seasonal menus, and vegetarian forums. There's a special section of vegetarian and vegan recipes for children called "Kid-Friendly Recipes." Sign up for my free quarterly "Vegetarian Kitchen" newsletter and "Recipe of the Week" newsletter.

New Century Nutrition

www.newcenturynutrition.com/index.html

The goal of this Web site is to create a bridge between traditional and Western health practices, with a particular emphasis on Chinese culture. It has in-depth information about food, nutrition, and health issues.

Nutrition for Kids

http://nutritionforkids.com

Although it's not a vegetarian site, it has many helpful articles on healthy eating.

Physician's Committee for Responsible Medicine

www.pcrm.org

Vocal advocates for plant-based diets, this organization's site contains lots of helpful tips on making the transition.

Planet Veggie

www.planetveggie.com

This site offers a few good articles: "Healthy Foods for Kids," "Raising Healthy Veggie Kids," "A Vegetarian Diet Is Best for Athletes," and "The Difference Between Fruits and Vegetables."

Vegan Society

www.vegansociety.com/html/info/info26.html

A practical guide to veganism during pregnancy and throughout childhood.

Vegetarian Nutrition for Teenagers

http://vegsoc.wellington.net.nz/teen.htm

A good source of information on raising a healthy vegetarian teenager.

Vegetarian Resource Group

www.vrg.org/family/

One of the premier Web resources for vegetarians and vegans of all ages, including kids and teens. Here you'll find articles on raising a vegetarian or vegan family. Many of these have been written by Reed Mangels, Ph.D., R.D., and include "Feeding Vegan Kids," "Vegetarian Nutrition for Teenagers," and "Calcium in the Vegan Diet." You can also peruse articles from the *Vegetarian Journal,* where you'll find scientific studies, recipes, and more.

Vegetarian Society

www.vegsoc.org/info/children1.html

This site has a section on nutritional information for vegetarian kids from preschool to age 12.

Vegetarian Teen

www.vegetarianteen.com

Here's a place where vegetarian teens can enjoy an online community and also contribute personal stories and articles to the site.

VegFamily

www.vegfamily.com

A site dedicated to vegan family life, it addresses a wide range of topics concerning a healthy vegan lifestyle and many articles on being a pregnant vegan. Here you can also find recipes, a veggie kids page, product reviews, and sign up to receive a free newsletter.

Veggie Files

www.veggiefiles.com/dir/what_eat/cooking_tips/

This site has a page called the "Picky Veggiesaurus Rex" that offers parents tips on how to get picky vegetarian eaters to vary their food intake.

Veggie Kids

www.execpc.com/~veggie/tips.html

Tips on getting children to eat more vegetables and fruits, plus practical tips for feeding vegetarian children.

Veggies Unite!

www.vegweb.com

A vast Web resource that includes information on feeding vegan and vegetarian children.

VegsSource

www.vegsource.com

This multiple-award-winning site provides "vegetarian support 25 hours a day, 8 days a week." It has a "Vegetarian Parenting" page with articles and information on raising vegan and vegetarian children.

Viva! Guides

www.viva.org.uk/guides/nutritioninanutshell.htm

At this site, you'll find numerous informative pages ranging from topics on healthy vegetarian pregnancy and feeding your vegetarian child to comparisons between vegetarian and nonvegetarian diets.

Whole Foods Market

www.wholefoodsmarket.com/healthinfo

The large natural foods supermarket chain's Web site offers a plethora of detailed information on healthy foods—how to choose them, when to buy them, and a rundown on varieties of common and uncommon fruits and vegetables.

WholehealthMd

www.wholehealthmd.com

Simply put, a vast resource and treasure trove of information on healthy foods from A to Z.

Community Supported Agriculture

Community Supported Agriculture is a way to support sustainable agriculture while at the same time obtaining weekly shares of just-harvested produce. Look for one whose focus is organic. It's a wonderful way to link farms and families. Here are two resources for locating CSA farms in your area:

Community Supported Agriculture of North America

www.umass.edu/umext/csa/

This site contains information on what CSA is, a resource list, and a link to a searchable database.

Alternative Farming Systems Information Center

www.nal.usda.gov/afsic/csa/

Here you'll find a national, state-by-state database of CSA farms.

Selected Sources, Great Reasons to Go Vegetarian (page xix)

Lower rates of obesity

Appleby, P. N., M. Thorogood, J. I. Mann, and T. J. Key. "The Oxford Vegetarian Study: An Overview." *American Journal of Clinical Nutrition* 70 (1999), 525S–531S.

Key, T., and G. Davey. "Prevalence of Obesity Is Low in People Who Do Not Eat Meat [Letter]." *British Medical Journal* 313 (1996), 816–17.

Vegetarians have higher fruit and vegetable intakes

Haddad, E. H., L. S. Berk, J. D. Kettering, et al. "Dietary Intake and Biochemical, Hematologic, and Immune Status of Vegans Compared with Nonvegetarians." *American Journal of Clinical Nutrition* 70 (1990), 586S–593S.

Lower estrogen levels

Barbosa, J. C., T. D. Schultz, S. J. Filley, and D. C. Nieman. "The Relationship Among Adiposity, Diet, and Hormone Concentrations in Vegetarian and Nonvegetarian Postmenopausal Women." *American Journal of Clinical Nutrition* 51 (1990), 798–803.

Soy's protective effect with regard to breast cancer

Shu, X. O., F. Jin, Q. Dai, et al. "Soyfood Intake During Adolescence and Subsequent Risk of Breast Cancer Among Chinese Women." *Cancer Epidemiology, Biomarkers, and Prevention* 10 (2001), 483–88.

Vegetarian diets may protect against heart disease

Key, T. J., G. E. Fraser, M. Thorogood, et al. "Mortality in Vegetarians and Nonvegetarians: Detailed Findings from a Collaborative Analysis of 5 Prospective Studies." *American Journal of Clinical Nutrition* 70 (1999), 516S–524S.

Studies on Seventh-Day Adventists showing vegetarians live longer

Fraser, G. B., and D. J. Shavlik. "Ten Years of Life. Is It a Matter of Choice?" *Archives of Internal Medicine* 161 (2001), 1645–52.

Index

A

African dish, 54–55
Alfredo Sauce, Enlightened, 124–25
Almond butter, 5, 264, 279
Almond cheese, xxiii
Almond milk, xxiii, 266, 323
Ambrosia, Banana-Yogurt, 270
Apples
  about, 274–75
  Apple Muffins, 291
  Apple Slices with Nut Butter Dip, 267
  Cabbage, Apple, and Raisin Slaw, 69
  Cinnamon-Apple Granola, 15
  Cinnamon Apple or Pear Smoothie, 24
  in cobbler, 313
  Creamy Butternut Squash and Apple
    Soup, 46–47
  Green Salad with Avocado, Apples, and
    Baked Tofu, 75
  Oatmeal-Raisin Cookies with Carrots or
    Apple, 299
  Oven-Dried Apples, 267
  in pancakes, 7
  Roasted Sweet Potatoes and Apples, 203
  Sautéed Apples, 267–68
Applesauce
  apples for, 275
  as fat substitute, 278, 323
Arroz verde, 230
Artichokes, 102, 221
Asian noodles, 101–2
Asian-style recipes. See also Stir-fries
  Asian-Flavored Coleslaw, 70
  Asian Noodles with Stir-Fried Corn and
    Cabbage, 106
  Asian Sesame Salad Dressing, 96
  Asian Succotash, 219
  Basic Chinese Sauce, 152
  Chinese Vegetable and Tofu Soup, 33
  Cold Soba and Cucumber Salad, 66
  Gingery Japanese Noodles with
    Mushrooms and Snow Peas, 107
  Miso Noodle Soup with Crisp Vegetables,
    34

  Orange-Glazed Tofu and Broccoli, 146
  Parsley or Cilantro Sauce, 67
  seitan in, 133, 153
  Simple Miso Tofu Soup, 44
  Teriyaki Tofu Triangles, 148
  Vegetable Chow Mein, 105
  Vegetable Lo Mein, 104
  Vegetable Sushi, 193–95
  Wilted Sesame Spinach or Swiss Chard,
    213
Asparagus
  roasted, 202
  in Spring Barley Salad, 90
Avocado, Apples, and Baked Tofu, Green
  Salad with, 75
Avocado Reuben, 248

B

Baked goods, 276–315
  apples in, 275
  breads (See Breads/toast)
  Chocolate Chip-Apricot Blondies, 310
  cookies (See Cookies/bars)
  dairy-free, 277
  flaxseed in, 290
  Fruit Cobblers of All Sorts, 312–13
  Fruit Crumbles of All Sorts, 311
  Guilt-Free Chocolate Brownie Cake, 309
  Leslie's Corn Bread Cake, 285
  muffins (See Muffins)
  pies (See Pies)
  projects involving kids in, 294, 300
Bananas
  Banana-Blueberry Smoothie, 23
  Banana Fritters, 10
  Banana Muffins, 289
  Banana-Yogurt Ambrosia, 270
  in breakfast sandwich, 5
  Chocolate Tofu Banana "Cream" Pie, 308
  Jam-in-the-Middle Banana Muffins, 293
  Nutty Chocolate-Banana Smoothie, 25
  in pancakes, 7
  Peanut Butter and Banana Roll-ups, 3
  in smoothies, 20

Barley, 234
  Dilled Vegetable-Barley Soup, 50
  Lentil Barley Soup, 42
  Spring Barley Salad, 90
Barley malt syrup, 314
Beans. See also Chickpeas; Lentils
  about, 184–85
  bean dip, 256
  black (See Black beans)
  in cold vegetable platters, 84
  green (See Green beans)
  Navy Bean Soup with Corn and Red
    Peppers, 49
  Pasta Salad with Southwestern Flavors,
    63
  Quick Jamaican Red Beans and Rice,
    190
  Savory Bean Burgers with Yogurt-
    Mustard Dressing, 192
  Skillet Baked Beans, 189
  in vegetarian diet, 199
  White Bean Hummus, 260
Beets
  about, 217
  in cold vegetable platters, 84
  Mixed Greens with Green Beans, Beets,
    and Feta or Goat Cheese, 81
  Orange and Maple-Glazed Beets, 216
  roasted, 202
Bell peppers, 196. See also Peppers
Berries
  Berry Muffins, 289
  in cobbler, 313
  Cream Cheese and Berry Roll-ups, 3
Bifun, 101
Biscuits, Yogurt, 12
Black beans
  Black Bean and Zucchini Chilaquiles,
    168
  Black Bean Sofrito, 188
  Quick Black Bean and Sweet Potato
    Chili, 53
  Quick Couscous and Black Bean Pilaf,
    233

Skillet Black Beans with Potatoes and Tortillas, 186–87
Southwestern Rice and Black Bean Salad, 86–87
Tomatoes with Black Beans or Chickpeas, 79
Blueberries, 8, 289, 313
Blueberry Smoothie, Banana-, 23
Bread Pudding, Two-Potato, 176
Bread Pudding, Vegetable, 174–75
Breads/toast. See also Pita bread; Sandwiches/wraps
  for breakfast, 5
  Cinnamon-Raisin Toast, 256
  corn- (See Cornbread)
  Italian Bread-and-Tomato Salad, 80
  Leslie's Corn Bread Cake, 285
  Little Garlic Toasts, 59
  Mediterranean Salad-Stuffed Bread, 249
  Quick Cinnamon-Raisin Bread, 282
  Quick Three-Grain Brown Bread, 280
  Spoonbread, 284
  Veggie Cheese Toasts, 245
Breakfast, 1–25
  Banana Fritters, 10
  Basic Yogurt Pancakes, 6–7
  Breakfast Burritos, 3
  Breakfast Quesadillas, 3
  cereals (See Cereals)
  Cottage Cheese Salad, 4
  Cream Cheese and Berry Roll-ups, 3
  dried fruit for, 273
  granolas (See Granolas)
  ideas for, 3–4, 11
  Muffin Tin Popovers, 9
  pantry for, 2–3
  Peanut Butter and Banana Roll-ups, 3
  Potato and Tempeh Hash, 181
  sandwiches for, 5
  smoothies (See Smoothies)
  Tofu and Potato Hash Browns, 142
  Tofu Scrambles Galore, 3, 140–41
  waffles, 8
  Yogurt Biscuits, 12
Broccoli
  about, 211

in cold vegetable platters, 84
Cream of Broccoli Soup, 29
Creamy Tofu and Broccoli Skillet, 143
Orange-Glazed Tofu and Broccoli, 146
roasted, 202
Sautéed Broccoli, Baby Carrots, and Yellow Squash, 210
Scalloped Cauliflower or Broccoli, 206
Seitan and Broccoli Stir-Fry, 161
Stir-Fried Broccoli, 209
Tortellini or Ravioli with Broccoli, 119
Brown rice syrup, 314
Brownie-type desserts
  Chocolate Chip-Apricot Blondies, 310
  Guilt-Free Chocolate Brownie Cake, 309
Brussels sprouts, 220
Buckwheat noodles, 101
Bulgur
  about, 235
  Bulgur with Fine Noodles, 229
  Seashells in the Sand, 228
Burgers
  Baked Chickpea Burgers, 191
  Savory Bean Burgers with Yogurt-Mustard Dressing, 192
  Savory Tofu Burgers, 135
Burritos, 3, 141
Butter, xxv, 321
  fruit, 5
  nut (See Nut butters)
  seed, 264

C
Cabbage, Apple, and Raisin Slaw, 69
Cabbage, Asian Noodles with Stir-Fried Corn and, 106
Cake, Guilt-Free Chocolate Brownie, 309
Cake, Leslie's Corn Bread, 285
Calzones, Pita Cheese, 246–47
Candy. See Chocolate-Peanut Butter Truffles
Canola oil, xxiv–xxv
Carrots
  Baby Carrot and Baby Corn Stir-Fry, 208
  Carrot-Orange Mango Smoothie, 22
  in cold vegetable platters, 84
  Cream of Baby Carrot Soup, 32

Oatmeal-Raisin Cookies with Carrots or Apple, 299
roasted, 202
Sautéed Broccoli, Baby Carrots, and Yellow Squash, 210
Sweet Cinnamon-Maple Glazed Baby Carrots, 214
Casein, xxiii–xxiv
Cashew butter, 5, 264, 279
Cashews, Curried Potatoes with Peas, Raisins, and, 180
Casseroles
  about, 164
  Creamy Enchilada Casserole, 170–71
  Mom's "Tuna"-Noodle Casserole, 114–15
  Shepherd's Pie, 172–73
  Vegetable Upside-Down Casserole, 165–66
Cauliflower
  in cold vegetable platters, 84
  Curried Pasta with Cauliflower and Chickpeas, 126
  roasted, 202
  Scalloped Cauliflower or Broccoli, 206
Celery, 84, 240, 243
Cereals
  cold, 4, 272
  hot, 17–19, 272
  Savory Baked Cereal Mix, 259
  Sweet Baked Cereal Mix, 258
Cheese
  making nondairy, 324
  rennetless, xxiii
  substitutes for, xxiii–xxiv, 323
Cheese (dairy or nondairy)
  in breakfast sandwiches, 5
  Cheesy Sweet and White Potato Soup, 38
  in cold vegetable platters, 84
  Grilled Cheese Strips, 59
  for hot cereal, 19
  Mixed Greens with Green Beans, Beets, and Feta or Goat Cheese, 81
  Pita Cheese Calzones, 246–47
  protein in, 321
  Tofu Scrambles Galore, 141
  Tomatoes with Goat Cheese or Feta Cheese and Black Olives, 78

Veggie Cheese Toasts, 245
Chickpeas
    Baked Chickpea Burgers, 191
    in cold vegetable platters, 84
    Curried Pasta with Cauliflower and
        Chickpeas, 126
    in sandwiches, 240, 243
    Tomatoes with Black Beans or
        Chickpeas, 79
Chilaquiles, Black Bean and Zucchini, 168
Chili
    Cincinnati Chili Mac, 113
    Classic Vegetarian Chili, 52
    Quick Black Bean and Sweet Potato
        Chili, 53
Chinese food. See Asian-style recipes
Chocolate
    about, 298
    Chocolate Chip-Apricot Blondies, 310
    Chocolate Chip Muffins, 289
    Chocolate-Peanut Butter Truffles, 257
    Chocolate Tofu Banana "Cream" Pie, 308
    Double Chocolate Oatmeal Cookies, 295
    Guilt-Free Chocolate Brownie Cake, 309
    Magic Chocolate Chip Cookies, Four
        Ways, 296–97
    in whole-grain baking, 278
Chocolate soy milk, 25, 266
Cilantro Sauce, 67
Cocoa
    about, 298
    Cocoa Muffins, 289
    variations on hot, 266
Coconut Curried Vegetable Stew, 58
Coleslaw. See Slaws
Cookies/bars
    Double Chocolate Oatmeal Cookies, 295
    Graham Thumbprint Cookies, 300–301
    Jam Bars, 301
    Magic Chocolate Chip Cookies, Four
        Ways, 296–97
    Oatmeal-Raisin Cookies with Carrots or
        Apple, 299
    Soft and Chewy Granola Bars, 303
Corn
    Asian Noodles with Stir-Fried Corn and
        Cabbage, 106

Asian Succotash, 219
Baby Carrot and Baby Corn Stir-Fry, 208
in cold vegetable platters, 84
Composed Couscous and Corn Salad,
    88–89
Creamy Corn Chowder, 31
Navy Bean Soup with Corn and Red
    Peppers, 49
Scalloped Corn, 207
Southwestern Summer Succotash, 218
Stewed Tofu with Corn and Tomatoes,
    139
Stir-Fried Rice with Baby Corn and Peas,
    231
Tomato and Corn Relish, 78
Corn grits, 17
Corn pasta, 102
Cornbread
    Leslie's Corn Bread Cake, 285
    Spoonbread as version of, 284
Cornmeal, 17, 279. See also Polenta
Cottage cheese, protein in, 321
Cottage cheese salad, 4
Couscous
    Composed Couscous and Corn Salad,
        88–89
    Fruited Couscous, 227
    Quick Couscous and Black Bean Pilaf,
        233
    Seashells in the Sand, 228
Cracked grains, 17
Cranberry-Orange Muffins, 292
Cranberry-Pecan Granola, 16
Cream cheese (dairy and nondairy)
    in breakfast sandwich, 5
    Cream Cheese and Berry Roll-ups, 3
    Cucumber, Tomato, and Cream Cheese
        Spirals, 257
    embellishing, 256
Crisps, apples for, 275
Croutons, Crispy, 59
Cucumbers
    Cold Soba and Cucumber Salad, 66
    in cold vegetable platters, 84
    Cucumber, Tomato, and Cream Cheese
        Spirals, 257
    Tomatoes and Cucumbers in Yogurt, 78

Curried recipes
    Coconut Curried Vegetable Stew, 58
    Curried Pasta with Cauliflower and
        Chickpeas, 126
    Curried Potatoes with Peas, Raisins, and
        Cashews, 180

D
Dairy products, xxii, xxiii, 321, 323
Desserts. See Baked goods; Snacks and
    treats
Dill dip, 256
Dilled Vegetable-Barley Soup, 50
Dips, 13, 61
    bean dip, 256
    for fruit, 267, 268, 269
    Nut Butter Dip, 267
    Sweet Cream Cheese Dip, 268
    White Bean Hummus, 260
Dried fruit, 267, 268, 269, 272
    about, 272–73
    in baked goods, 272, 289
    in cereal, 18, 272
    Dried Fruit or Fruit-Nut Muffins, 289
    in fruit salad, 273
    stewed, 273
    in whole-grain baking, 278

E
Eastern European dish, 229
Edamame, 219, 220
Eggless Tofu Quiche, 136–37
Eggplant, stuffed, 196–97
Eggs, xiv, xxii, 1, 5, 277, 321
Enchilada Casserole, Creamy, 170–71

F
Fajitas, Sizzling Seitan or Tofu, 156–57
Flaxseed, xxvi, 14, 19, 290
Flour
    types of whole-grain, 279
    whole-wheat pastry, xxvi, 279, 281
French Dressing, 95
Fritters, Banana, 10
Fritters, Batter-Dipped Vegetable, 224–25
Fruit
    All-Organic Fruity Yogurt, 268

for breakfast, 4
dried (*See* Dried Fruit)
Fruit and Yogurt Parfaits, 268–69
Fruit Cobblers of All Sorts, 312–13
Fruit Crumbles of All Sorts, 311
Fruited Couscous, 227
in muffins, 289
organic, xix–xxii
in pancakes, 7
platters of, 269
Skewered Fruit, 268
in smoothies, 20–26
Sweet Cream Cheese Dip for, 268
in Trail Mix, 262
for treats, 267–75
tropical, 269
Fruit butter, 5
Fruit cobblers, 275, 312–13
Fruit preserves
in breakfast sandwich, 5
Jam Bars, 302
Jam-in-the-Middle Banana Muffins, 293
Fruit salads, 4, 269, 273
Fruit sauces, 8

G
Grains. *See also* Baked goods; Whole grains
about, 226, 234–35
in edible containers, 196–97
in hot cereals, 17–19
in pancakes, 7
refined, 226
as side dishes (*See* Side dishes)
in vegetarian diet, 199
Granolas
Cinnamon-Apple Granola, 15
Classic Crunchy Granola, 14
in cookies, 297
Cranberry-Pecan Granola, 16
Soft and Chewy Granola Bars, 303
Grape leaves, 84
Greek-style recipe, 84
Green beans
in cold vegetable platters, 84
Mixed Greens with Green Beans, Beets, and Feta or Goat Cheese, 81

roasted, 202
Sesame Stir-Fried Green Beans, 212
Southwestern Summer Succotash, 218
Triple Jade Stir-Fry with Tofu or Seitan, 150–51
Greens with Green Beans, Beets, and Feta or Goat Cheese, Mixed, 81
Grits, 17

H
Hash, Potato and Tempeh, 181
Hash Browns, Tofu and Potato, 142
Herb Mayonnaise, 244
Hominy grits, 17
Honey, 278, 314
Hummus, White Bean, 260

I
Italian Bread-and-Tomato Salad, 80

J
Jamaican recipes, 10, 190
Japanese food. *See* Asian style recipes
Jerusalem artichokes, 221
Jicama, 84, 221

K
Kamut, 279
Kidney beans, 84
Kohlrabi, 84, 221

L
Lacto-vegetarianism, xxiv
Lactose, xxiii, 13, 277, 318
Latin American dish, 188
Leeks, onions vs., 221
Lentils
Basic Lentil Soup with Tasty Variations, 42–43
Lentil "Frankfurter" Soup, 42
Pasta with Hearty Lentil and Spinach Sauce, 127
Lunches, 236–53. *See also* Sandwiches/wraps
quesadillas/tacos for, 242
school, 237–40, 250–53

M
Macaroni
and cheese variations, 109–12
Cincinnati Chili Mac, 113
Macaroni and Cheese with Secret Silken Tofu Sauce, 110
Macaroni Salad with Vegetable Confetti, 64
Ultimate Macaroni and Cheese, 109
Main dishes, 162–97
Baked Chickpea Burgers, 191
Baked Risotto, 178–79
Black Bean and Zucchini Chilaquiles, 168
Black Bean Sofrito, 188
Creamy Enchilada Casserole, 170–71
Curried Potatoes with Peas, Raisins, and Cashews, 180
in edible containers, 196–97
Polenta, 182–83
Potato and Tempeh Hash, 181
Quick Jamaican Red Beans and Rice, 190
Savory Bean Burgers with Yogurt-Mustard Dressing, 192
Shepherd's Pie, 172–73
Skillet Baked Beans, 189
Skillet Black Beans with Potatoes and Tortillas, 186–87
Southwestern Baked Rice Casserole, 169
Two-Potato Bread Pudding, 176
Vegetable Bread Pudding, 174–75
Vegetable Sushi, 193–94
Vegetable Upside-Down Casserole, 165–66
Veggie Pot Pie, 177
Mango fruit sauces, 8
Mango Smoothie, Carrot-Orange, 22
Maple syrup, 278, 315
Margarine, nonhydrogenated, xxv, 19, 323
Marinara Sauce, Sneaky, 120–21
Mayonnaise. *See* Soy mayonnaise
Mediterranean Salad-Stuffed Bread, 249
Mexican dishes. *See* Southwestern/Mexican dishes
Middle Eastern recipes, 82, 260

Milk, xxiii–xxiv, 18, 321, 323
Millet, 234
Minestrone, Streamlined, 40
Miso Noodle Soup with Crisp Vegetables, 45
Miso Tofu Soup, Simple, 44
Molasses, 315
Muffins, 286–93
  Apple Muffins, 291
  Banana Muffins, 289
  Basic Muffins, Seven Ways, 288–89
  Berry Muffins, 289
  Chocolate Chip Muffins, 289
  Cocoa Muffins, 289
  Cranberry-Orange Muffins, 292
  Dried Fruit or Fruit-Nut Muffins, 289
  Jam-in-the-Middle Banana Muffins, 293
  Muffin Tin Popovers, 9
  Pear and Golden Raisin or Dried Apricot Muffins, 289
  Raisin or Raisin-Nut Muffins, 289
  variations of, 289
  Zucchini-Raisin Muffins, 287
Mushrooms
  Gingery Japanese Noodles with Mushrooms and Snow Peas, 107
  Mixed Mushrooms Stroganoff, 128–29
  roasted, 202
  Tofu Scrambles Galore, 141
Mustard Dressing, Yogurt-, 192

N
Navy Bean Soup with Corn and Red Peppers, 49
Nectarines, 8, 313
Noodles. See Pasta/noodles
Nuggets, Baked Tofu, 144
Nut butters, 5, 264, 265, 323
  Nut Butter Dip, 267
  in whole-grain baking, 279
Nut milk products, xxiii
Nut oils, xxiv
Nutritional information, 316–28
Nuts, 18, 278, 289, 321
  about, 263–64
  in Trail Mix, 262

O
Oats/oatmeal, 17–18, 279
  Double Chocolate Oatmeal Cookies, 295
  in granolas, 14–16
  Oatmeal-Raisin Cookies with Carrots or Apple, 299
  Simple Oat Crust, 305
Oils, xxiv–xxv
  olive, xxiv, 78
  partially hydrogenated, xxv
Okra, substitute for, 54–55
Olive oil, xxiv, 78
Onions, leeks vs., 221
Orange and Maple-Glazed Beets, 216
Orange-Glazed Tofu and Broccoli, 146
Orange Mango Smoothie, Carrot-, 22
Orange Muffins, Cranberry-, 292
Organic food, xviii–xxiv, 216, 278–79
  chocolate, 298
  fruit, 269
  yogurt, 13, 268

P
Pan bagnat, version of, 249
Pancakes
  Basic Yogurt, 6–7
  fruit sauces for, 8
  variations on, 7
  into waffles, 8
Pantry, 2–3, 272
Parfaits
  for breakfast, 4
  Fruit and Yogurt Parfaits, 268–69
Parmesan Pita Chips, 262
Parsley Sauce, 67
Parsnips, roasted, 202
Partially hydrogenated oils, xxv
Pasta/noodles, 98–131. See also Macaroni
  about, 99–103
  Alphabet Vegetable Soup, 30
  Angel Hair with Zucchini and Bread Crumbs, 122–23
  Asian noodles, 101–2
  Asian Noodles with Stir-Fried Corn and Cabbage, 106
  for breakfast, 3
  buckwheat, 101 (See also Soba)
  Bulgur with Fine Noodles, 229
  Curried Pasta with Cauliflower and Chickpeas, 126
  durum wheat, 100
  Garden Vegetable Soup with Tiny Pasta, 48
  Gingery Japanese Noodles with Mushrooms and Snow Peas, 107
  Green Noodles, 116–17
  Harvest Medley Pasta, 130–31
  Lentil Soup with Tiny Noodles, 42
  Miso Noodle Soup with Crisp Vegetables, 45
  Mixed Mushrooms Stroganoff, 128–29
  Mock Chicken Noodle Soup, 36–37
  Mom's "Tuna"-Noodle Casserole, 114–15
  Parsley or Cilantro Sauce for, 67
  Pasta with Enlightened Alfredo Sauce, 124–25
  Pasta with Hearty Lentil and Spinach Sauce, 127
  Pasta with Sneaky Marinara Sauce, 120–21
  ramen, 101
  refined, 99, 100
  rice noodles, 101
  Ricotta Pasta with Raisins and Peas, 118
  in salads (See Pasta salads)
  Seashells in the Sand, 228
  Simple Miso Tofu Soup, 44
  Simple Ramen Noodle Soup, 34–35
  Soba with Tofu, Tomatoes, and Basil, 108
  Tomato-Tortellini Soup, 41
  Tortellini or Ravioli with Broccoli, 119
  Vegetable Chow Mein, 105
  Vegetable Lo Mein, 104
  whole-grain, 99, 100, 101, 102–3
Pasta salads, 63–67
  Cold Soba and Cucumber Salad, 66
  Family-Friendly Pasta Salad, 65
  Macaroni Salad with Vegetable Confetti, 64
  Parsley or Cilantro Sauce for, 67
  Pasta Salad with Southwestern Flavors, 63
Peaches, 8, 313

Peanut butter
  Chocolate-Peanut Butter Truffles, 257
  Homemade Nut Butter, 265
  Peanut Butter and Banana Roll-ups, 3
  Silken Peanut Spread vs., 256
  substitutes for, 5
  vs. other nut butters, 264, 265
  in whole-grain baking, 279
Peanut Caramel Corn, 263
Peanut Stew, West African, 54–55
Pears, 8, 313
  Cinnamon Apple or Pear Smoothie, 24
  Pear and Golden Raisin or Dried Apricot
    Muffins, 289
Peas
  Curried Potatoes with Peas, Raisins, and
    Cashews, 180
  Gingery Japanese Noodles with
    Mushrooms and Snow Peas, 107
  Mashed Sweet Potatoes with Leeks,
    Peas, and Walnuts, 223
  Ricotta Pasta with Raisins and Peas, 118
  Stir-Fried Rice with Baby Corn and Peas,
    231
Peppers
  in cold vegetable platters, 84
  Navy Bean Soup with Corn and Red
    Peppers, 49
  stuffed, 196–97
Pickles, Vegetable, 261
Pies
  apples for, 275
  Chocolate Tofu Banana "Cream" Pie, 308
  Easy Graham Cracker Crust for, 304
  Not-Just-for-Thanksgiving Squash or
    Pumpkin Pie, 306–7
  Simple Oat Crust for, 305
Pilaf, Quick Couscous and Black Bean,
  233
Pilaf, Simple Quinoa and Wild Rice, 232
Pineapple Rice Pudding, 271
Pineapple Rice Salad, 85
Pita bread
  fillings for, 192, 241
  Middle Eastern Pita Bread Salad, 82
  Parmesan Pita Chips, 262
  Pita Cheese Calzones, 246–47

Pizza, PB&J, 256
Pizza Potatoes, 201
Polenta
  for breakfast, 17
  as main dish, 182–83
Popcorn variations, 262, 263
Popovers, Muffin Tin, 9
Pot pie, 177
Potassium, 319
Potato salads
  Expandable Potato Salad, 72
  Golden Potato Salad, 73
  Marinated Potato-Tofu Salad, 74
Potatoes (white)
  about, 201
  Cheesy Smashed Potatoes, 200
  Cheesy Sweet and White Potato Soup, 38
  Curried Potatoes with Peas, Raisins, and
    Cashews, 180
  Oven Fried Potatoes, 200
  Pizza Potatoes, 201
  Potato and Tempeh Hash, 181
  roasted, 202
  Saucy Potatoes, 200
  Sautéed Skillet Potatoes, 200
  Seitan "Meat and Potatoes" Stew, 56–57
  Skillet Black Beans with Potatoes and
    Tortillas, 186–87
  Tofu and Potato Hash Browns, 142
  Two-Potato Bread Pudding, 176
  ways to serve, 200–201
Puddings
  made from Chocolate Tofu Banana
    "Cream" Pie recipe, 308
  Pineapple Rice Pudding, 271
  Two-Potato Bread Pudding, 176
  Vegetable Bread Pudding, 174–75
Pumpkin, stuffed, 196
Pumpkin butter, 264
Pumpkin Pie, Not-Just-for-Thanksgiving
  Squash or, 306–7

Q
Quesadillas, 3, 242
Quiche, Eggless Tofu, 136–37
Quinoa
  about, 235

pasta, 102
Simple Quinoa and Wild Rice Pilaf, 232

R
Raisins
  about, 278
  Cabbage, Apple, and Raisin Slaw, 69
  Cinnamon-Raisin Toast, 256
  Curried Potatoes with Peas, Raisins, and
    Cashews, 180
  Oatmeal-Raisin Cookies with Carrots or
    Apple, 299
  Pear and Golden Raisin or Dried Apricot
    Muffins, 289
  Quick Cinnamon-Raisin Bread, 282
  Raisin or Raisin-Nut Muffins, 289
  Zucchini-Raisin Muffins, 287
Ramen Noodle Soup, Simple, 34–35
Ramen noodles, 101
Ranch Dressing, 93
Ravioli with Broccoli, Tortellini or, 119
Red Beans and Rice, Quick Jamaican, 190
Relish, Tomato and Corn, 78
Rennet, xxiii
Rice
  Baked Risotto, 178–79
  in Lentil Barley Soup, 42
  Mexican Green Rice, 230
  Pineapple Rice Pudding, 271
  Pineapple Rice Salad, 85
  Quick Jamaican Red Beans and Rice,
    190
  Southwestern Baked Rice Casserole,
    169
  Southwestern Rice and Black Bean
    Salad, 86–87
  Stir-Fried Rice with Baby Corn and Peas,
    231
  in Vegetable Sushi, 193–95
  vs. other grains, 234
Rice cheese, xxiii, 5, 19, 59, 323
Rice milk, xxiii, 18, 266, 323
Rice noodles, 101
Rice vermicelli, 101
Risotto, Baked, 178–79, 201
Roll-ups, 3
Rolled grains, 17

Rolled oats, 14–16, 279
Rutabagas, roasted, 202

S
Safflower oil, xxvi, 279
Salad dressings, 13, 77, 91–97
  Asian Sesame Salad Dressing, 96
  Basic Vinaigrette, 92
  French Dressing, 95
  Ranch Dressing, 93
  Taco Salad Dressing, 77
  Tangy Tahini Dressing, 97
  Thousand Island Dressing, 94
Salads, 60–97. See also Pasta salads; Slaws
  cold vegetable platters as, 61, 84
  Composed Couscous and Corn Salad,
    88–89
  cottage cheese, 4
  dressings for (See Salad dressings)
  in edible containers, 62
  fattouche, 82
  fruit, 4, 269, 273
  Green Salad with Avocado, Apples, and
    Baked Tofu, 75
  Hearty Seitan Salad, 83
  Italian Bread-and-Tomato Salad, 80
  Mediterranean Salad-Stuffed Bread, 249
  Middle Eastern Pita Bread Salad, 82
  Mixed Greens with Green Beans, Beets,
    and Feta or Goat Cheese, 81
  Pineapple Rice Salad, 85
  potato (See Potato salads)
  Southwestern Rice and Black Bean
    Salad, 86–87
  Spring Barley Salad, 90
  Taco Salad, 76
  tomatoes as, 78–79
Salt, 28
Salt-free seasoning, xxvi
Sandwiches/wraps, 236–53. See also Pita
    bread
  Avocado Reuben, 248
  for breakfast, 5
  celery in, 243
  "chicken" or "tuna" style, 243
  Grilled Cheese Strips, 59
  leftovers used in, 241

Mediterranean Salad-Stuffed Bread, 249
Pita Cheese Calzones, 246–47
roasted vegetables for, 201
super, 238–39
"TLT" sandwich, 238
Veggi Deli Heroes with Herb
    Mayonnaise, 244
Veggie Cheese Toasts, 245
Sauces
  Basic Chinese Sauce, 152
  Cilantro Sauce, 67
  Enlightened Alfredo Sauce, 124–25
  fruit, 8
  Lentil and Spinach Sauce, 127
  Parsley Sauce, 67
  Quick Tartar Sauce, 145
  Secret Silken Tofu Sauce, 110
  Sneaky Marinara Sauce, 120–21
  Yogurt-Mustard Dressing, 192
Scallions, leeks vs., 221
Seasoning, xxvi, 28. See also Spices
Seed butters, 264
Seed oils, xxiv
Seeds
  about, 263–64
  for cereal, 18
  protein in, 321
Seitan, xxvi
  about, 133, 153
  with barbecue sauce, 155
  Basic Chinese Sauce for, 152
  Hearty Seitan "Buddhist's Delight,"
    160–61
  Hearty Seitan Salad, 83
  Homemade Seitan, 154
  Seitan and Broccoli Stir-Fry, 161
  Seitan "Meat and Potatoes" Stew, 56–57
  Simple Sautéed Seitan, 155
  Sizzling Seitan or Tofu Fajitas, 156–57
  Sweet-and-Sour Seitan and Vegetables,
    158–59
  Triple Jade Stir-Fry with Tofu or Seitan,
    150–51
Sesame
  Asian Sesame Salad Dressing, 96
  paste of, 264
  Sesame Stir-Fried Green Beans, 212

Wilted Sesame Spinach or Swiss Chard,
    213
Shepherd's Pie, 172–73
Side dishes, 198–235
  Asian Succotash, 219
  Baby Carrot and Baby Corn Stir-Fry, 208
  Batter-Dipped Vegetable Fritters,
    224–25
  Bulgur with Fine Noodles, 229
  dried fruit in, 273
  Fruited Couscous, 227
  Mashed Sweet Potatoes with Leeks,
    Peas, and Walnuts, 223
  Mexican Green Rice, 230
  Orange and Maple-Glazed Beets, 216
  Quick Couscous and Black Bean Pilaf,
    233
  Roasted Root Vegetable Medley, 205
  Roasted Sweet Potatoes and Apples, 203
  Sautéed Broccoli, Baby Carrots, and
    Yellow Squash, 210
  Scalloped Cauliflower or Broccoli, 206
  Scalloped Corn, 207
  Seashells in the Sand, 228
  Sesame Stir-Fried Green Beans, 212
  Simple Glazed Butternut Squash, 215
  Simple Quinoa and Wild Rice Pilaf, 232
  Southwestern Summer Succotash, 218
  Stir-Fried Broccoli, 209
  Stir-Fried Rice with Baby Corn and Peas,
    231
  Sweet Cinnamon-Maple Glazed Baby
    Carrots, 214
  Wilted Sesame Spinach or Swiss Chard,
    213
Skewered Fruit, 268
Skillet dishes
  Creamy Tofu and Broccoli Skillet, 143
  Skillet Baked Beans, 189
  Skillet Black Beans with Potatoes and
    Tortillas, 186–87
  Stewed Tofu with Corn and Tomatoes,
    139
Slaws, 68–71
  Asian-Flavored Coleslaw, 70
  Cabbage, Apple, and Raisin Slaw, 69
  Tri-Color Coleslaw, 71

Smoothies, 20–25
  Banana-Blueberry Smoothie, 23
  Carrot-Orange Mango Smoothie, 22
  Cinnamon Apple or Pear Smoothie, 24
  Nutty Chocolate-Banana Smoothie, 25
  Sunshine Smoothie, 21
Snacks and treats, 254–75
  All-Organic Fruity Yogurt, 268
  Almond-Maple Popcorn, 263
  Banana-Yogurt Ambrosia, 270
  Chili-Spiced Popcorn, 263
  Chocolate-Peanut Butter Truffles, 257
  Cinnamon-Chili Hot Cocoa, 266
  Cinnamon-Raisin Toast, 256
  cream cheese variations for, 256
  Cucumber, Tomato, and Cream Cheese
    Spirals, 257
  dips (See Dips)
  Fruit and Yogurt Parfaits, 268–69
  fruity, 267–75 (See also Fruit)
  Homemade Bagel Crisps, 262
  Homemade Nut Butter, 265
  homemade versions of store-bought,
    262–64
  hot cocoa variations, 266
  ideas for, 256–57
  Minty Hot Cocoa, 266
  Nondairy Hot Cocoa, 266
  nut butters for, 264, 265
  nuts for, 263–64
  Paper Bag Popcorn, 262
  Parmesan Pita Chips, 262
  PB&J Pizza, 256
  Pineapple Rice Pudding, 271
  Popcorn Parmesan, 263
  popcorn variations, 262, 263
  Savory Baked Cereal Mix, 259
  seeds for, 263–64
  Silken Peanut Spread for, 256
  Sweet Baked Cereal Mix, 258
  Trail Mix, 262, 272
  Vegetable Pickles, 261
  White Bean Hummus, 260
Soba, 101, 104, 107
  Cold Soba and Cucumber Salad, 66
  Soba with Tofu, Tomatoes, and Basil,
    108

Sofrito, Black Bean, 188
Somen, 102
Soups, 26–59
  accompaniments to, 59
  Alphabet Vegetable Soup, 30
  Basic Lentil Soup with Tasty Variations,
    42–43
  bouillon cubes for, 28
  Cheesy Sweet and White Potato Soup, 38
  Chinese Vegetable and Tofu Soup, 33
  Classic Vegetarian Chili, 52
  Cream of Baby Carrot Soup, 32
  Cream of Broccoli Soup, 29
  Creamy Butternut Squash and Apple
    Soup, 46–47
  Creamy Corn Chowder, 31
  Crispy Croutons with, 59
  Dilled Vegetable-Barley Soup, 50
  Garden Vegetable Soup with Tiny Pasta,
    48
  Grilled Cheese Strips with, 59
  Lentil "Frankfurter" Soup, 42
  Little Garlic Toasts with, 59
  Miso Noodle Soup with Crisp Vegetables,
    45
  Mock Chicken Noodle Soup, 36–37
  Navy Bean Soup with Corn and Red
    Peppers, 49
  Quick Black Bean and Sweet Potato
    Chili, 53
  seasoning for, 28
  Simple Miso Tofu Soup, 44
  Simple Ramen Noodle Soup, 34–35
  Streamlined Minestrone, 40
  Sweet Potato and Silken Tofu Bisque, 39
  Tomato-Tortellini Soup, 41
  Tortilla Soup, 51
  wine as seaoning for, 28
Sour cream substitute, 13, 128
Southwestern/Mexican dishes
  Black Bean and Zucchini Chilaquiles,
    168
  burritos, 3, 141
  Creamy Enchilada Casserole, 170–71
  Mexican Green Rice, 230
  Pasta Salad with Southwestern Flavors,
    63

  quesadillas, 3, 242
  Skillet Black Beans with Potatoes and
    Tortillas, 186–87
  soft tacos, 242
  Southwestern Baked Rice Casserole, 169
  Southwestern Rice and Black Bean
    Salad, 86–87
  Southwestern Summer Succotash, 218
  Taco Salad, 76
  Taco Salad Dressing, 77
Soy Canadian bacon, 5
Soy cheese, 59
Soy cream cheese, 323
Soy hot dogs, 42
Soy mayonnaise, xxv, 240, 243, 244
Soy milk, xxv, 18, 266, 323
Soy nut butter, 5, 264
Soy pasta, 102
Soy products, xxiii, 323
  allergy to, xxiii
  protein in, 321
Soy yogurt, 6, 268, 279
Spelt, 103, 279
Spices, 19, 278
Spinach or Swiss Chard, Wilted Sesame
  Spinach or, 213
Spinach Sauce, Pasta with Hearty Lentil
  and, 127
Spoonbread, 284
Squash
  Creamy Butternut Squash and Apple
    Soup, 46–47
  Not-Just-for-Thanksgiving Squash or
    Pumpkin Pie, 306–7
  roasted, 202
  Sautéed Broccoli, Baby Carrots and
    Yellow Squash, 210
  Simple Glazed Butternut Squash, 215
  spaghetti, 222
  stuffed, 196–97
  zucchini (See Zucchini)
Stews, 54–59
  Coconut Curried Vegetable Stew, 58
  Seitan "Meat and Potatoes" Stew, 56–57
  Stewed Tofu with Corn and Tomatoes,
    139
  West African Peanut Stew, 54–55

Stir-fries. *See also* Asian-style recipes
  Baby Carrot and Baby Corn Stir-Fry, 208
  Basic Chinese Sauce for, 152
  Hearty Seitan "Buddhist's Delight,"
    160–61
  Orange-Glazed Tofu and Broccoli, 146
  Seitan and Broccoli Stir-Fry, 161
  seitan in, 133
  Sesame Stir-Fried Green Beans, 212
  Simple Sautéed Seitan, 155
  Stir-Fried Rice with Baby Corn and Peas,
    231
  Sweet-and-Sour Seitan and Vegetables,
    158–59
  Tofu and Mixed Veggie Stir-Fry, 149
  Triple Jade Stir-Fry with Tofu or Seitan,
    150–51
Strawberries, 8, 289
Stroganoff, Mixed Mushrooms, 128–29
Stuffing, 176
Succotash, Asian, 219
Succotash, Southwestern Summer, 218
Sugar, xxvi, 278, 283
"Sunchokes," 221
Sunflower butter, 264
Sushi, Vegetable, 193–94
Sweet potatoes
  about, 204
  Black Bean and Sweet Potato Chili, 53
  Cheesy Sweet and White Potato Soup, 38
  with macaroni and cheese, 112
  Mashed Sweet Potatoes with Leeks,
    Peas, and Walnuts, 223
  roasted, 202
  Roasted Sweet Potatoes and Apples, 203
  Sweet Potato and Silken Tofu Bisque, 39
Sweeteners, 18, 283, 314–15
Swiss Chard, Wilted Sesame Spinach or,
  213

T
Taco Salad, 76
Taco Salad Dressing, 77
Tacos, soft, 242
Tahini, 264
Tahini Dressing, Tangy, 97
Tartar Sauce, Quick, 145

Tempeh, xxvi
  about, 240
  Potato and Tempeh Hash, 181
  in sandwiches, 240, 243
Teriyaki Tofu Triangles, 148
Thousand Island Dressing, 94
Tofu, xxvi
  -based mayonnaise, xxv
  about, 133, 134
  baked, 75, 134, 144, 147, 243
  Baked Tofu Nuggets, 144
  with barbecue sauce, 138
  Basic Chinese Sauce for, 152
  Chinese Vegetable and Tofu Soup, 33
  Chocolate Tofu Banana "Cream" Pie,
    308
  in cold vegetable platters, 84
  Creamy Tofu and Broccoli Skillet, 143
  Eggless Tofu Quiche, 136–37
  extra-firm, 134, 147
  as "fake meat," 138
  firm, 134
  Green Salad with Avocado, Apples, and
    Baked Tofu, 75
  Marinated Potato-Tofu Salad, 74
  Mock Chicken Noodle Soup, 36–37
  Mom's "Tuna"-Noodle Casserole, 114–15
  Orange-Glazed Tofu and Broccoli, 146
  Quick Tartar Sauce, 145
  in sandwiches, 243
  Savory Tofu Burgers, 135
  silken, 110, 134, 308
  Simple Miso Tofu Soup, 44
  Sizzling Seitan or Tofu Fajitas, 156–57
  in smoothies, 26
  Soba with Tofu, Tomatoes, and Basil,
    108
  soft, 134, 140, 243
  Stewed Tofu with Corn and Tomatoes,
    139
  Sweet Potato and Silken Tofu Bisque, 39
  Teriyaki Tofu Triangles, 148
  Tofu and Mixed Veggie Stir-Fry, 149
  Tofu and Potato Hash Browns, 142
  Tofu Scrambles Galore, 3, 140–41
  Triple Jade Stir-Fry with Tofu or Seitan,
    150–51

Two Kinds of Tofu in a Sweet and Savory
    Sauté, 147
Tomatoes
  about, 78
  in cold vegetable platters, 84
  Cucumber, Tomato, and Cream Cheese
    Spirals, 257
  easy ways to serve, 78–79
  Italian Bread-and-Tomato Salad, 80
  Lentil Tomato Soup, 42
  Soba with Tofu, Tomatoes, and Basil,
    108
  Stewed Tofu with Corn and Tomatoes,
    139
  stuffed, 197
  Tofu Scrambles Galore, 141
  Tomato-Tortellini Soup, 41
  Tomatoes and Corn Relish, 78
  Tomatoes and Cucumbers in Yogurt, 78
  Tomatoes with Black Beans or
    Chickpeas, 79
  Tomatoes with Goat Cheese or Feta
    Cheese and Black Olives, 78
  Tomatoes with Olive Oil and Fresh
    Herbs, 78
Tools/supplies, xxvi–xxvii, 278
Tortellini or Ravioli with Broccoli, 119
Tortellini Soup, Tomato-, 41
Tortillas
  Black Bean and Zucchini Cilaquiles,
    168
  Creamy Enchilada Casserole, 170–71
  for quesadillas, 242
  Skillet Black Beans with Potatoes and
    Tortillas, 186–87
  for soft tacos, 242
  in Taco Salad, 76
  Tortilla Soup, 51
Trail mix, 262, 272
  in cookies, 297
Truffles, Chocolate-Peanut Butter, 257
Turnips
  in cold vegetable platters, 84
  roasted, 202

U
Udon, 102, 104

V
Vegans, xiii–xiv, xxiii, xxv, 322–23
  books for, 322, 323
  casein and, xxiv
  children as, xiii–xiv, 322
  flax for, 290
  nutritional information for, 316–28
  source of fat for, xxv
  Web sites for, 324–27
Vegetable oils, xxiv–xxv
Vegetable pasta, 103
Vegetable rennet, xxiii
Vegetables
  Alphabet Vegetable Soup, 30
  Batter-Dipped Vegetable Fritters,
    224–25
  Chinese Vegetable and Tofu Soup, 33
  Coconut Curried Vegetable Stew, 58
  cold, platters of, 84
  Dilled Vegetable-Barley Soup, 50
  dried fruit with, 273
  Garden Vegetable Soup with Tiny Pasta,
    48
  Macaroni Salad with Vegetable Confetti,
    64
  Miso Noodle Soup with Crisp Vegetables,
    34
  offbeat, 220–22
  organic, xviii–xxii
  protein in, 321
  raw, as salad, 84
  roasted, 201–2
  Roasted Root Vegetable Medley, 205
  stuffed, 196–97
  Sweet-and-Sour Seitan and Vegetables,
    158–59
  Tofu Scrambles Galore, 141
  Vegetable Bread Pudding, 174–75

Vegetable Chow Mein, 105
Vegetable Lo Mein, 104
Vegetable Pickles, 261
Vegetable Sushi, 193–94
Vegetable Upside-Down Casserole,
  165–66
in vegetarian diet, 199
Veggi Deli Heroes with Herb
  Mayonnaise, 244
Veggie Cheese Toasts, 245
Veggie Pot Pie, 177
Vegetarians, xiii–xiv
  books for, 323
  children as, xiii–xiv, 133, 199, 294, 323
  flax for, 290
  lacto, xxiv
  nutritional information for, 316–28
  reasons for being, xvii–xviii, 328
  source of fat for, xxv
  and tips for busy cooks, xv–xvii
  Web sites for, 324–27
Vinaigrette, Basic, 92

W
Waffles, 8
Walnuts, Mashed Sweet Potatoes with
  Leeks, Peas, and, 223
Welsh rabbit/rarebit, version of, 245
West African Peanut Stew, 54–55
Wheat-free noodles, 101
Wheat germ, 19
Whole grains
  about, 199, 234
  baking with, 278–79 (See also Baked
    goods)
  for cereal, 17
  pasta/noodles of, 99, 100, 101, 102–3
  protein in, 321

types of flour, 279
various, 234–35
vs. enriched products, 317
Whole-wheat pastry flour, xxviii, 279, 281
Wild rice
  about, 235
  Simple Quinoa and Wild Rice Pilaf, 232
Wilted Sesame Spinach or Swiss Chard, 213
Wine, as soup seasoning, 28
Wraps. See Sandwiches/wraps

Y
Yams, vs. sweet potatoes, 204
Yogurt (dairy and nondairy)
  about, 13
  All-Organic Fruity Yogurt, 268
  Banana-Yogurt Ambrosia, 270
  Fruit and Yogurt Parfaits, 268–69
  fruit sauces for, 8
  protein in, 321
  in smoothies, 20
  soy, 268
  Tomatoes and Cucumbers in Yogurt, 78
  in whole-grain baking, 279
  Yogurt Biscuits, 12
  Yogurt-Mustard Dressing, 192

Z
Zinc, 100, 317, 319
Zucchini
  Angel Hair with Zucchini and Bread
    Crumbs, 122–23
  Black Bean and Zucchini Chilaquiles,
    168
  in cold vegetable platters, 84
  roasted, 202
  stuffed, 197
  Zucchini-Raisin Muffins, 287

About the Author

NAVA ATLAS is the author and illustrator of several popular vegetarian cookbooks, including *The Vegetarian 5-Ingredient Gourmet*, *Vegetariana*, *Vegetarian Express*, and *Vegetarian Soups for All Seasons*. She has also written dozens of columns and articles on food and health-related topics for publications such as *Vegetarian Times*, *Veggie Life*, and *GreatLife*. Her Web site, *In a Vegetarian Kitchen* (www.vegkitchen.com), is one of the most widely visited vegetarian sites on the Internet. Nava has written about and illustrated other subjects as well and is an active fine artist. She lives in the Hudson Valley region of New York State with her husband and two sons.

© AL NOWAK